Leaping Past Zinnias

Elizabeth Tingley

Leaping Past Zinnias: Madness, Murder, Marriage and Me

International Psychoanalytic Books (IPBooks)
New York • http://www.IPBooks.net

Leaping Past Zinnias: Madness, Murder, Marriage and Me

Published by IPBooks, Queens, NY
Online at: www.IPBooks.net

Copyright © 2024 Elizabeth Tingley

ISBN: 978-1-956864-70-0

To the memory of Caroline Costello
You should still be around.

And

In honor of my father, scholar and historian
who taught me the past matters

Table of Contents

Chapter 1

We should not have gone to the cemetery

The late June rain slowed to a drizzle as we reached Newton Cemetery. Our car was near the end of the short funeral procession and was filled with Richard's family, minus his brother Michael, in jail, and family friend Tomas. At the gate, cops directing traffic admitted only those with funeral placards, no press. In the front seat, my future mother-in-law Ruth let out, "Oh, thank god." She didn't want her picture in the tabloids again.

Richard, sitting next to me in the backseat, squeezed my hand hard and muttered, "That's not the tragedy, mom."

"What did you say, Richard?" his mother asked tersely.

"Shut up, Richard," said his middle brother Danny who was driving Ruth's Buick.

I stared across the graveyard; the leaves and grass were summer green, darkened by the overcast sky. The procession wound past well-tended graves, until the hearse pulled off the gravel path.

As we parked, I let out a sigh and took in a labored breath. The horror of the last two days, the wake and funeral for Carrie, my future sister-in-law, was about to end. Seeing the coffin lowered into the grave was going to be tough, a finality. I leaned against Richard and he kissed the top of my head. When Danny turned off the ignition, no one moved for a minute as a kind of paralysis set in. Then, we walked the few yards ahead for the graveside service. This gathering was tiny compared to the funeral turnout. I shivered, realizing we would be awkwardly close to Carrie's family. If it were up to me, I would have turned and left, so as not to intrude. Instead, I followed Richard's family on ahead.

Graveside, the Catholic priest from the funeral and a female celebrant prepared for the committal service. Carrie's parents, her sister, nephew, aunts, uncles, and cousins circled around the grave. For the first time that weekend, the Costello family kept their backs to us. The invitation to join them, proffered for the wake and funeral, was silently rescinded. We were a raw reminder of Michael's psychotic violence. I tried to stand back, but Richard seized my hand, needing me right by his side at the grave.

Carrie's family had more rights to grieve than we did, though Carrie felt a part of our family, too.

With the small casket perched above the freshly dug grave, the priest read the short Catholic service over the coffin. Carrie's mother wept, while her father appeared numb and stoic. The celebrant finished the official service by asking us to recite the Lord's Prayer. Carrie's family was Catholic, Michael's Jewish, a source of tension. Raised as a mainstream Midwestern Protestant, I recited the prayer along with the Catholic attendees. This seemed to startle the priest who would ask after the service how I knew the words.

As the casket was lowered, funeral attendants piled the many flower arrangements on top, until the coffin was barely visible. The bright colors transfixed me and slightly mitigated, as flowers are meant to do, this sorrowful and bizarre occasion.

This was a goodbye to someone I didn't know well, though I had hoped to share so much with Carrie—holidays, gifts, inside jokes, our children's birthday parties, beach vacations, all the regular family joys and stresses, forever. The life I imagined alongside her had evaporated, gone overnight, just a few days before, when Michael killed Carrie in their apartment, believing she was an alien.

There and not there, a silent howl burst inside of me.

How the hell did I end up here, in Newton, Massachusetts, at the grave of a woman I longed to know, murdered, by someone Richard and I loved?

After the service, we returned to our own car at the hotel. Richard drove the two of us back to New York in complete silence. Even Richard, who once said he only felt real when speaking, had nothing left to say. From the passenger seat, my gaze fixated on the path of headlights in front of us. I tried not to think about anything but that trail of red circles along the black highway. I was grateful Richard drove all the way home to New York.

Annie my dog, greeted us at our Riverdale apartment door, jumping up to lick my face and racing through the living room and back. I was enlivened by her energy. I took Annie out for the last walk of the night. By the time I got back upstairs, Richard had shed his clothes and was in bed. Strangely, the omnipresent television was off. He lay staring at the ceiling. I slid in next to him and clutched him to me, feeling his skin fully against mine. There was no relief in it but it felt better to be close than apart. We stayed bodies molded, synched, for a long time, until Richard began to snore. Sleep didn't easily come for me but when it did, I found some release from the dislocating horror of the last two days.

Chapter 2

Meeting Richard

The beginning had been so easy. I met Richard a little more than two years before, in January of 1996, and it changed what it meant to be me. I had felt utterly alone for most of my life, though anyone looking in wouldn't have known that I saw myself like Pigpen, the character from Charles Schultz's *Peanuts*, followed by a cloud of dirt billowing behind me shouting "alone, alone, alone!" Meeting Richard at age forty chased the lonely cloud away forever and brought me to the other side of the glass wall inside, separating me from the world.

How could I describe Richard? Tall, dark, teddy-bearishly chubby, so smart, very funny, sweet, and kind. He was also utterly nerdy and incompetent at anything requiring manual dexterity, sustained attention, nuanced indirect communication, or common sense. He had his ghosts, but so did I. With Richard, it didn't matter that we didn't fit in. We fit together.

We had so much in common: lefty politics, folk music, struggles with depression. (I had spent ten days in a locked ward in 1984; he had spent ten months in one just two years before we met.) Complicated yet common experiences defined both our families. Although from such different backgrounds—Midwestern pioneer stock versus East Coast Jewish folk—our fathers were both professors and our mothers, each difficult in their own ways, were stay-at-home 1950s and 60s housewives. Our only early conflict seemed to be dog versus cat; we called détente on that. Richard and I talked for hours, laughed, cried, held each other, allowed the past pain to exist between us, neither needing to change it or fear it. I loved to cook; he loved to eat. I held him at every breakfast with muffins and cappuccino and with leg of lamb, red and yellow pepper soup, crème brulé at other meals. We were passionately sexual; Richard told me he loved me the first time we made love. We feasted, together, in every way.

Watching Richard fall hard for me was so charming. He was forgetting to eat, driving through stoplights, not remembering where he was going, because he was thinking of me. He wondered if he was going mad, but no, his psychiatrist had to tell him: he was just in love.

One night, after we had known each other less than a month, Richard came to meet me in his Albany, New York apartment; I already had a key. He rushed in from his attorney job at a small law firm, took off his custom-tailored suit, and held me tight. We didn't go out again that night. While naked together, Richard wanted only to look at me; he gently pulled me open and watched, with patience, as I became aroused, before his eyes. His face filled with passion and contentment, seeing me get turned on, just by his gaze. I found him moved by the beauty in my body. We both cried.

When we left in the morning to get breakfast, Richard's car was double parked, almost in the middle of the street, with a dead battery. He had left the blinkers on, intending to come and get me, so we could go out to dinner. We laughed and laughed until I couldn't breathe.

Chapter 3

Getting to the Guy

Before Richard, In the early 1990s, I lived in Dallas, a place I did not belong. After college I spent two years in New York and ten in Boston and felt more at home there, than I had anywhere before. When I finished my first Ph.D. in psychology, I took an academic job at the University of Texas at Dallas. Even in 1990, when you could get a tenure track job, you had to go wherever the job search took you.

Dallas was a very strange place to me. I did not have big hair, aspire to drive a big American car, or dream of meeting a good ol' boy. I was not in the oil "bidniss." I was not born again, did not even go to church, and I was not a Republican. The state of male-female relations at the college was Stone Age. Once, when I was appointed to act as the cross-departmental referee for a dissertation defense in physics, all the other professors and the candidate were male. They were discussing baseball. The Texas Rangers had just acquired Jose Canseco, who was beefcake á la mode. The physics guys were pointedly leaving me out of the conversation, until one of them turned to me with a sickly smile and said, "With Canseco, we might even get the ladies interested in baseball."

I smiled back and turned to the one guy who, like me, had been at the game the night before, where my beloved Red Sox had trounced the Rangers. I said, "Did you see that sequence of pitches Clemens threw in the 6th to Canseco? Strikes on every corner of the plate!" This ended all talk of baseball.

I needed to get out of Texas and started applying to jobs back East. I had a long-distance boyfriend, Hank, twelve years my senior, in New York. We met up nearly every month. We had some good sex, played fiercely competitive tennis, and took fine vacations—Telluride, Maine, Nova Scotia—but there were issues. He had OCD, the real thing. He counted his money every night over and over before he could put his wallet down. When he brought groceries home, he had to swing the bags onto the counter in a certain arc. He got angry when I held the elevator door for him and demanded I press the "open door" button instead. The second he stepped into the elevator there could be no bounces or squeaks. I knew the suffering was mostly his, but the OCD controlled us both.

Meanwhile, my biological clock was going tick-tock at an alarming rate. I thought we should take the next step and Hank reluctantly agreed. When I found a job at Bennington College, in Vermont, we negotiated a deal where he would get an apartment and job in upstate New York (he was a social worker and thus his career was more portable), halfway between Bennington and NYC, so he could still see his psychoanalyst of thirty years, and I could get a room on campus for part of the week. He called the night before I was supposed to accept the job. He didn't want to break up; he just wouldn't make any changes. I dumped him.

When I arrived in Vermont in the fall of 1994, I made friends, mostly with three young couples who were also new to the college, a poet and two historians and their partners and dogs and children. We had a dinner party almost every Saturday night, indulging our foodie tendencies. I also answered some personal ads on AOL, long before it was common to use the Internet to meet people. Over that first year I had dates with several losers: a fifty-year-old who wanted to "Party! Party!" A short guy in the military with two sons who wanted never to live anywhere for more than a year and was excessively nonverbal. A guy with six kids who worked on the assembly line in Burlington making computer chips and bragged about how he made his daughter bring him beer by snapping his fingers.

By late 1995, I was nearing the end of my interest in Internet dating, deciding it was better to be alone than be with someone who wasn't right. I only wanted a man I could marry, make babies with, and grow old. This seemed unlikely given the current, pre-9/11 news stories that forty-year-old women had a better chance of getting killed by a terrorist than getting married. I grappled with the ever-present sense that I was a pathetic lonely loser; my self-hatred and disgust were powerful. I would not have any children of my own, the only thing I ever really wanted. Strangely though, this was progress—accepting who and what I was, a single woman, on my own, even though it hurt like hell.

In late December, I still had a few personal ads from AOL printed out, so I took the top one, and announced out loud, "This one is my swan song," and threw the rest in the trash. The ad I answered was Richard's.

Albany SWJM PROF 38 Seeks SWJF 35-45 (more or less) suffering from "Aging hippie" syndrome. Symptoms include love of folk music and classic rock, leftish politics, increasing religiosity (within reason), tolerance for Incomprehensible Martian male propensities like "space" and sharing devotion to work. All foregoing desirable, none required. Smoking, dogs Tolerated but discouraged. Children OK. Cats preferred. drugs verboten. If you won't scold and dominate us we will never give you cause to hate us.

Albany was only about 40 miles from Bennington, so I wrote a rather lengthy reply.

I live outside Albany, east, in the country but I come to Albany often to hit bookstores and the movies. I am 40, also suffering, although mostly recovered from aging hippie syndrome. I like folk music, definitely lefty politics. By trade I profess. I do have one dog, small but not yappy. I'm really sort of independent, so that "space" thing is not a big issue. I mean jumping way ahead into the substance of long-term relationships, I truly understand the wish to go right to sleep after making love. I only hope that my wish to be held and talked to is honored sometimes too. Not Jewish by birth, but I went with a college friend to visit her Jewish grandma in the nursing home. They were discussing shiksas and my friend asked me if I knew the word. I said, "yeah me." Her Grandma retorted "no, not you. You're Jewish." So, I am honorarily at least part Jewish.

Here are some questions for you: what was the last pair of shoes you bought? Do you have a best friend and what is s/he like? What's your favorite book? Movie? What's the last amazing place you experienced? Is there any food you won't eat?

Richard was impressed and replied by saying, first, "um, could we have coffee before we pick out the silver?" He also asked if I had gotten the cultural reference to Mary Poppins, which I had not. (Hmmm. Did he need a nanny or a partner?) He also cutely answered:

As to your interrogation:
Shoes—Rockport rubber soled dress shoes
Food—I don't refuse any. Not kosher if that's what you meant.
Best Friend—Photographer for a major newspaper (I used to be a reporter.) Looks a lot like me but is less neurotic, enjoys life more.

Favorite Book—*The Power Broker* by Robert Caro
Favorite Place—I dunno. I never go anywhere. Schenectady?

He expressed concern over my lack of feelings for cats and asked that I answer the same questions he had:

Shoes—a pair of sensible black oxfords nice enough to wear with a skirt, at least at Bennington
Food—I refuse to eat dill and canned tuna—the smell makes me nauseous.
Best Friend—I have at least three best friends, one is the old college roommate with the Grandma who pronounced me Jewish, one is a psychoanalyst in New York who is currently gestating and so nauseous she can barely get around and the third lives in Cambridge and I know from my first career as a day care teacher. She teaches sex ed at a private school and is a writer.
Favorite Books—*To the Lighthouse* and *Harriet the Spy*
Favorite Movies—too many to choose from, maybe *Out of Africa* or *The Producers*
Favorite Place—not Schenectady. Maybe my yard after Thursday's snowstorm, or the coast of Wales last summer.

After these exchanges in mid-January 1996, we began to talk on the phone. I found Richard's voice soothing, and he was always witty, making me laugh a lot. Richard told me my voice was sexy and that he couldn't wait to meet. He tried to talk me into phone sex.

"Lizzie, you are turning me on. Come on! Let's do something over the phone."

I refused, feeling slightly weird at this idea but quickly put this discomfort out of my mind. Surely this phone sex request was nothing more than a sign of growing, healthy attraction.

"No, my friend, I'm holding out for true love."

"Oh, I can't keep my lap under the desk," he joked.

"Keep that up," I said. "But really, I want to know you first," I continued more softly.

"Yeah, I know. I never put out on the first date, either" he answered, his voice suffused with gentleness.

He asked me out to a concert in late February, six weeks away, to hear an obscure folksinger, Patty Larkin. Richard was surprised that I was a big Patty Larkin fan from my Cambridge days, where I'd seen her often in the 1980s, at the Idler, a club in Harvard Square where a friend waitressed.

Richard and I discovered we knew people in common. He had done political work in high school with Stuart, a gay boy I had a crush on in college. I called up the one friend I knew who was still in touch with Stuart. Emily reported that Stuart described Richard this way: "Nice Jewish Boy. Very Funny. Fat." Knowing Stuart's body perfect, I doubted this description. Besides, maybe Richard wouldn't insist on a social Xray girlfriend. I found Richard's address in the Albany phone book, and my friend Diane, an Albany native, said it was a good sign, a trendy Albany neighborhood. Richard also knew my former OCD boyfriend's sister. As we talked more, almost every night for a couple of hours, everything felt more and more strangely, perfectly, simpatico.

That concert was still nearly a month away, too long to wait. So, Richard agreed to meet me in Bennington, at the Blue Ben, a funky, real dining car diner painted cerulean blue, for brunch one Sunday morning in late January. He would know me by my violet felt hat, and I would recognize him by his flannel shirt.

Chapter 4

Endless Blind Date

As I pulled into the Blue Ben Diner parking lot, I noticed a chubby, tall, dark guy with a beard getting out of a dumpy, maroon-colored car. He was wearing jeans, a buffalo plaid lumberman's jacket, and wire-rimmed aviator glasses, slightly askew across his weirdly handsome face. As I approached, he smiled, looking nervous.

"Liz?"

"Yeah, hi. Richard?" I hugged him sideways. He patted my back. Then he looked me over. "You don't look like what I expected."

Uh oh, he thinks I'm ugly.

"You're really pretty. You said 'zaftig.'"

This was direct. I could handle this, although it was not typical first-date, coy behavior. I wasn't immediately sure that I was going to be attracted to this guy.

"Zaftig doesn't mean fat; it means curvaceous or pleasingly plump."

"Yeah, but most women only say that about themselves if they are very heavy. You should have seen my last girlfriend." He paused. "By the way—zaftig is spelled with an a. You spelled it with an o in your email."

"Well, Yiddish is not my first language," I teased him.

"Yeah, you're only honorarily Jewish," he said. "That's okay. Some of my best friends are self-hating WASPS."

"I hope you can tolerate the little waspy-ness I have. I only let it out on alternate Sundays, and I am a good speller in my native tongue."

Richard laughed. "Me too. And I care about spelling."

As we headed towards the restaurant, I noticed that Richard had a peculiar gait, almost a limp.

We joined the line at the door of the diner. The Blue Ben was a popular brunch spot with maybe fifteen booths and a counter serving a fusion cuisine, Vermont hippie crunchy-granola and traditional diner. The morning was clear, not bitterly cold with only a little snow on the ground. After three minutes of mildly awkward conversation, Richard peeked at the line behind us. He whipped back around.

"Unbelievable. One of my oldest friends and his wife from New Rochelle are in the line behind us."

A plump, older Irish-looking guy yelled through the crowd, "Is that Richie Laudor? Richie Laudor!"

Richard grinned as the man strode up. "Billy Mullin! What are you doing here?" They sort of embraced in that guy way, shaking each other's forearms vigorously.

Billy said, "You remember Jane, my wife? And who is this lovely lady?"

"This is Liz. We're on our first date."

"No, really?" Billy laughed. He stuck out his hand and we shook. "I'm Bill. This is my wife, Jane." He gestured at Richard. "I've known this good guy since he was a kid. What are you doing up here?"

"I'm working for a small law firm in Albany. Live there too. Liz is teaching at Bennington and lives just over the state line in Hoosick."

Now that we had all located ourselves geographically, Richard and Bill, launched into a discussion of hometown Democratic politics. Bill was a working-class, union guy with left-wing views, derived from his coming of age during the Vietnam War. I chatted with Jane, a pretty, freckle-faced woman. By the time we reached the diner door, it was settled that we would all have brunch together.

The menu at the Blue Ben was extensive, with many kinds of pancakes, burritos, and salads, burgers, and other home cooking. Richard appeared to read every line but finally we all ordered.

The conversation flowed between the two men as they caught up, but Jane and I had a hard time contributing much. I so wanted to impress Richard, to be interesting and attractive, to bring out what I knew were my two best features: my storytelling and my smile. But these other people were in my way. The smile only worked if I offered it with full-on eye contact. Over the course of the meal, I managed two or three. Richard seemed to notice the smile by getting this little shy, sweet look on his face, but it was Billy who commented at the end of brunch, "You have a really great smile."

I got a chance to break out my storytelling when it emerged that Richard had met Billy during the 1972 George McGovern campaign; Billy was the youth coordinator for the Westchester Country organization and Richard was a kid volunteer as I had been out in the cornfields.

"Yeah, Dad knew George when he was still a college professor before he was in politics. They met up every year at a convention on American history. One year, sometime in the 1950s, George told Dad he wanted out of South Dakota. My father learned of a job at the University of Illinois in George's field. He sent off a letter alerting George to apply. Dad didn't hear back and thought it strange. Then, one early Saturday morning, the phone rang in our house in Illinois—George, apologizing to Dad for not responding. He had been out of town, he said, when the letter came, and his wife had put it on top of the piano. They were doing some early morning spring-cleaning, moved the piano, finding it just then. But McGovern said he had decided to leave academia, in the meantime, and go into politics."

"So," I concluded, "if he had gotten that letter in time, he might never have become a politician." I could see from Bill's and Richard's faces that this was an impressive-enough story.

"Interesting," said Richard.

"You never know," said Bill. "You never know."

I smiled at them both.

When brunch broke up, it didn't seem right to say goodbye to Richard. We hadn't been alone together, and my curiosity about him was piqued. After another awkward pause, I decided to be bold.

"Want to see the college and my office? It's pretty."

"Sure. I don't want to leave you yet, but we can't just stand around here with the parked cars," he said. I laughed as I had all morning.

We drove in my car towards the college, me playing tour guide. Richard asked lots of questions about roads and intersections. He was less interested in the natural beauty, remarking that the place was "in the middle of nowhere."

I waved at the security guard as we drove past. I described the Barn, to our right, now the main administration, faculty offices, and class-room building in the Humanities. I pointed to the student houses as we came around the bend behind. There was a gorgeous view of the Green Mountains, a spot the students called "the end of the world." I told him the infamous college story about Groucho Marx's daughter who attended Bennington in its early, free-form years. Local lore maintained that she had lived in one of the white-shingled, green-shuttered student houses and kept her horse in the room next to hers. Now, animals were not allowed on campus, and I got regularly busted for bringing my dog to my office, I told Richard, who laughed at my story. There was something miraculous and soothing in the way the conversation flowed.

I parked right by the Science building, a new roughhewn yet modern space, which contained my office, the conversational patter continuing.

We had now covered many a topic touched on in our emails, including the controversial Red Sox versus Yankees and dog versus cat themes. Richard held the door for me. Gendered, yet mannered, I thought. I unlocked the office door and said, "This is it." My office had a great view of a snow-covered, pine-tree-forested hill. Richard glanced outward, then stepped toward me.

"Are you having as much trouble holding back as I am?" he said, moving in to kiss me.

I stiffened slightly, less sure of the attraction than of the bigger feeling of ease, of somehow belonging together. Just as Richard put his arms around me, my colleague from the next office, Robby, barged in.

"Oh, hello," he said, grinning, taking in the situation. "Who are you?" he asked Richard.

I made introductions, Richard stuck out his hand and they shook. I explained that we were on our first date. Robby continued to smile, asking questions about who Richard was, where he lived, what he did for a living. Robby, maybe ten years older than I, was being fatherly. Finally, he left.

There was a ratty old couch along one wall of my office, and I led Richard over there. We sat next to each other, shoulders touching.

"I guess we are not meant to be alone today."

We held hands quietly for a minute. Richard again leaned in to kiss me, and that felt good too. When the kiss was over, I touched his cheek, and said, "I really like you so far. But I've got to go a little bit slow." This felt fine to say.

Richard chuckled. We were quiet, just sitting, gently touching knees and shoulders.

"Let's do something else," I said. It felt wrong to not be with him for more time. "How about a movie? That's something people do on a date."

"But what is playing around here?" he asked.

"I think *Mighty Aphrodite*, the Woody Allen movie, is at the little independent theatre in Williamstown."

"How far is that? Do you know how to get there?"

"Not too far, under half an hour. And that's a nice little town too. It has my favorite dress shop anywhere close around."

Richard looked pained. "I would go for the Woody Allen movie. I don't know about shopping. "

"That's okay. I won't make you wait or carry packages." I grinned.

Richard laughed. "My old girlfriend, that was all she wanted me to do, sit around, watch her try on stuff that didn't look good on her and say it did anyway. I started telling her that in my life there is just one four-letter word: S-H-O-P."

"Well, don't worry. Compared to most girls, I am not much of a shopper. And I'm strong. Enough to carry my own packages." I flexed my bicep. Richard beamed appreciatively.

Then I pulled him up. "Let's go to the movies."

Heading back to the car, Richard quizzed me about the route to Williamstown.

"It's a straight shot down Route 7. I go twice a week to see my shrink," I told him.

"Twice a week. That's impressive."

"Any good psychodynamic therapist will tell you twice a week is the most effective—clear off the daily stuff in the first session, then you can go deeper in the second session."

"I went twice a week when I was a kid. To Mrs. Grobe."

"You got to go to therapy when you were a kid?" I asked. "I have always thought I wouldn't have any problems if I could have gone then."

"I never trusted her. I thought she worked for them—my parents," he replied, some bitterness in his voice.

"That bad, those parents of yours?"

"My mother and I don't get along. My dad, well, he changed when he got older. And he told me he knew it had been hard when I was a kid. At least he acknowledged it. My mother never will." Richard was quiet for a moment. "I told you my father died right?"

"Yeah. How long ago?"

"November of '95."

"Just three months ago?"

"Is that right? It must be longer ago than that. But no, that's it." Richard seemed a little shaky and disoriented.

"That's got to be so hard. I'm sorry." I patted his knee, next to the gearshift in my little blue Toyota.

"Yeah. Not a good topic for a first date. Sorry."

"No need to apologize. It's what's real for you."

This made me like Richard more: his real, feeling talk. Even though he seemed to me very guy-like in most ways, there was something very different, vulnerable about him. Maybe something odd too, I thought, remembering his obsessive road and route comments, maybe something more than just nerdy, something Asperger-like. I told my psychologist brain to shut up.

We both got popcorn at the movies, Richard got a large soda too and settled in just in time at the small art house theatre. We both laughed at the same moments in the film and Richard held my hand throughout, his big paw covering all my smaller digits. Walking out, Richard put his arm around me, and we said the things everyone said about Woody Allen movies in the late 1990s—how much better the early funny ones were, how his personal life affected our views, how this film held our attention.

Then Richard said, "You look like Diane Keaton, did you know that?" This was foolishness to me. Now he was trying too hard somehow, a truly false note.

19

"You are out of your mind, unless you think all WASPS look alike. Good film though, *Annie Hall.*"

Richard took a strand of my wavy, light brown hair in his hand. "Yeah, all girls with straight blond hair look alike." We both laughed, but I wondered if he really thought my brown wavy hair qualified as straight and blond. "Now what?" he asked.

"How about dinner? That is something people do on dates, too, although not usually the same date as having brunch."

"I don't want you to go yet, so yes to dinner," Richard said, ever so gently.

"Deal."

I found Richard's eyes and he looked back at me, and our eyes widened, sparked in unison. After a few moments of this powerful, mutual gaze, Richard's eyes broke away. I could tell it was a lot of emotion, maybe too much for him.

He took my hand again. "Where to?"

I led him down the street to a restaurant I had been to before, on another blind date, with a guy who turned out to be married. That will make a good story, I thought.

The restaurant was dark and the tables small, giving an extra edge of intimacy to our conversation. We talked on, through four courses, about ourselves, our work, our families, our friends, our therapists, our struggles. We talked and talked and talked. Richard asked good questions; he seemed to get so much about me, and I about him. This had never ever happened to me before, ever. Some new wave of feeling, a feeling I didn't recognize, crept over me. At last, we paid the bill and drove through the hills back to Bennington. We finally ran out of things to say. Richard fiddled with the radio, finding some 60s Rock and Roll. He sang along as we made our way through the star-filled winter sky.

As I pulled up beside his car, I was ready to leave him, to figure out what this meant. We sat in the car, silent for a moment.

Then as if he were about to reveal a deep, dark secret, Richard said earnestly, "I need tell you about Michael, my brother."

"What about him?"

"He's schizophrenic."

"Wow. That must be tough."

"Michael has always been my best friend besides being my brother. We were on the same side in the family, and he always helped me know what to say to girls and what to wear. When he got sick, I was determined to be there for him. He was hospitalized for almost a year, and I went every week. I just treated him like a person. He called me his rock." Richard chuckled. "He escaped once from the locked ward."

"How did he get out?"

"Because he had on a button-down shirt and khakis, he looked more like one of the medical residents than a patient, and he just walked out behind some staff. But a few hours later he went back on his own. Even sick, he's no dummy. And he's still the golden boy of the family. He went to Yale and finished in three years. Then he got sick and the mental health people told him to get a job at Macy's. Instead, he went to Yale Law School and was on Law Review. Now he is working on projects related to ethics and mental illness and trying to craft his memoir. He was just featured in the *New York Times* as a role model for the mentally ill."

Something about this story triggered déjà vu. It dawned on me: I had taught that *Times* article, about Michael, a few months before to my Bennington class on abnormal psychology.

"I read that story," I told Richard.

"So, you know," he said. "And you are not freaked out?"

"No, of course not," I answered, indignant that he might think so.

That secret out, we made plans to meet again in three days, in Albany. He kissed me soulfully good night, and I wasn't sure, but it looked like he might cry. A strong warm feeling spread over me, a new deep kind of pleasure, that was not, strictly speaking, sexual, but came from how intensely connected I felt to Richard. I was satiated, filled up, and somehow whole. The lifelong, haunting loneliness was vanquished just by this, our first date, now.

Chapter 5

His Brother

In one sense, because I read the *Times* article a few months before meeting Richard, I had already "met" his brother, Michael. That semester, I was teaching a Bennington class called "Myths and Madness: A look at 'Abnormal' Psychology." The course aimed to get students to consider the concept of "normal/abnormal." The main text was a recently published book called *Madness and Modernism: Insanity in the light of Modern Art, Literature and Thought*. It asked if schizophrenia was a cultural construction. We covered much of the material in a regular-abnormal psychology class, but through a lens appealing to my bohemian, artsy Bennington students.

The class met in a tiny classroom in the Barn, filled with dilapidated tables and chairs under low-hanging eaves with small windows along one side of the room. Like many places at Bennington, it felt like we were in a time warp from the 1950s, when the college was in its artistic heyday. Although the room had been slap-dashedly painted pure white many times, the furniture, dusty and stained, probably dated from the first moment the building turned from literal barn to offices and classrooms. This class had my usual assortment of students, the ones with a serious interest in psychology and willing to do a lot of reading and writing: Ray, the gay son of a lobster fisherman from New Hampshire; Ryan, a tall, broad, half–Native American young man from Maine; Lyz, a bright, inspiring, red-headed student government activist; Genevieve, the future social worker, composed and purposeful. Jessica was the one who brought in the clipping. She was blond, usually very quiet and seemingly far too normal to belong to the free-spirited Bennington student body. As the students gathered, the scent of Vermont winter— wet wool—permeated the room.

I remember fingering the soft grey of the newspaper as I tried to read it quickly before starting class. The photo of the man in the article was intriguing. He looked robust, preppy, dressed in khakis and a blazer, shown in a half-shadow against a tall stone wall. The image implied something hidden about this man. The text outlined how brilliant Michael was, finishing Yale College in three years, working for Bain Capital (which years later, we'd recognize as Mitt Romney's firm) in Boston before his first psychotic break at twenty-four. After that Michael was hospitalized for eight months at Columbia Presbyterian in New York and diagnosed with schizoaffective disorder, a combination of psychosis and mood disorder. The article also told of the stigma Michael faced as a mentally ill person, partly from within the mental health system, where Michael reported that he was seen as "a high-functioning schizophrenic, not a high-functioning person."

The mental health workers at his residential treatment program thought at most he could work at Macy's. The article recounted how Michael's father, Chuck, had taken him to Macy's to apply for a job, seen the grinding reality of retail work and predicted it would send Michael quickly back to the hospital. His father counseled Michael to go to Yale Law School, where he had been accepted during his breakdown. In fact, Michael did attend Yale Law School, where he had been brilliant as usual, and served as a senior editor on Law Review. In part, the *Times* piece was Michael's coming-out story, as he was unable to find the job he wanted as a law-school professor because the usual things a brilliant new lawyer should have done—clerk for a judge, work long hours for a prestigious firm—Michael's illness prevented him from doing. He had to do things in his own time and way, as he managed his psychosis.

This was a perfect story for the class, and I thanked Jessica for bringing in it and passed it around. The article, and Michael's situation, sparked a lively discussion with most members of the class seeing Michael's story as validation of the ideas we discussed surrounding abnormal psychology and the serious medical and socio-cultural failure to do right by the mentally ill.

At that stage in my career, I had not yet worked with seriously mentally ill people. I was a researcher and academic psychologist. Folks with mental illness were for the most part an abstraction, folks I had read and theorized about. The only person with schizophrenia I actually knew was the somewhat older son of friends of my parents, who lived at home and worked in his father's restaurant. He seemed harmless, not very verbal, perhaps over medicated, and functioned by adhering to a strict routine—if he was cooking a hamburger for a customer and by his schedule it was time to take out the garbage, he took out the garbage. The burger burned. I did not imagine Richard's brother like that—the Michael I encountered in the *Times* article sounded too smart, too functional, and certainly not so limited. In fact, that Michael was someone I would like to know. Michael's story didn't scare me off at all, and I found Richard's heartfelt support for his brother very, very appealing. Brothers were so important to me.

Chapter 6

My Brother

I had my own brother trouble in an otherwise white picket fence childhood and it started early.

I grew up in a small central Illinois college town called Charleston, the house and backyard fence painted white, a well-tended lawn, beds of forsythia and rose bushes and bold zinnias in the dead of summer. The backyard was filled by a swing set, a sand pile in an old tractor tire, the clothesline where every Monday my mother hung endless loads of laundry, and the dog and doghouse.

This was a façade, behind which lurked heartache and grief, some of it about brothers,

My only sibling Jim died, aged four and three-quarters, in 1958; I wasn't quite three. Jim's presence and absence were haunting and elemental in making me, me. Always drawn to small children, sorting out the preverbal mind powered my career. This focus followed me through my work, first as an empathic infant-toddler teacher, then an academic researcher/professor on early development, and finally as clinical psychologist and child therapist. My career, though useful in and of itself, also served to keep my brother and my relationship with him alive.

When I was small, I struggled to hold onto the memories I did have. Otherwise, I might have gone crazy. The voice in my head back then went something like this:

Jim was here. I didn't make that up, despite you people pretending he was never here and never mattered.

My parents rarely spoke about him; after he died, Jim's toy train, stuffed animals, books and clothes were packed up and hidden away. His dog went to live with my grandparents. I was told—"He had leukemia and died." I had no idea what this meant. He was gone.

I retained a few images, sense impressions, of Jim. These are body and sensory-affective memories. Writing about these memories renders them into language and organizes them by my adult brain. The images began to morph into "stories" when I turned twenty-nine and called my parents from an inpatient psychiatric hospital. I was in there because I was suicidal. My parents were surprised; they didn't know that I had "any problems." They agreed to help however they could, and sent letters about Jim and his death, the wellspring of my depression, I believed. These letters gave context and detail to what I could remember and how it might have affected me.

I have very few images of Jim that are not about him being sick or dying but there are a few, likely from when I was about two-and-a-half and Jim, aged-four-and-a-half was in remission after his first round of chemotherapy.

Standing with my tall, thin mother, in her Sunday best, we wait for Jim in the church basement. We're a few minutes early, before the children are released from Sunday School. When I turn three, I will go to Sunday School too. The door opens and first out is Jim, who runs to Mom with a big smile, his whole face alive, so excited to see her after the separation of only an hour or so. Jim has dark crew-cut hair and brown eyes, and is wearing grey pants, a white shirt covered by a fuzzy blue sweater vest. He has on polished black shoes, with laces. As Jim runs towards us, he's holding out a paper with both hands, something he's drawn or colored. He yells with so much joy, extending the paper with both arms.

"*Mommy, Mommy, look!*" *He thrusts the paper into her hands, so proud, happy, and ready to be admired.*

It's only a short video clip, with no clue what happened before or after this moment.

My brother, my father, and I are goofing around in my parents' bedroom. My father, as usual, is teaching us something. This time, it's about middle names. He tells Jim, who is shirtless and bouncing on the bed, "Your middle name is William."

Jim says, "No, my name is Jim, Jim."

Dad reaches out to grab him, roughhousing. "No, it's William. I think I'll call you Willy from now on." They both giggle as Dad catches and lifts my brother high and lets him go, so that Jim bounces down on the bed again. "Willy. Willy," Dad calls him.

"No. No. No. I'm Jim," he roars as he bounces away.

I want in on the action. "Me," I say, as I present myself to my father.

"Your middle name is Catherine. We'll call you Katie," Dad bellows as he hoists me up on the bed.

"No. Jim and Libbits. Jim and Libbits," my brother gurgles as he bounds off and runs into our bedroom. I follow him with glee.

That gorgeous fun big brother was at the center of my universe.

Summer, late afternoon, and Jim sits in a small chair next to his favorite thing, the record player. Wearing a striped t-shirt, loose shorts, and tennis shoes, he is focused, not laughing, or talking to me. On the little aqua record player, which has a rose red disk to play 45s, a shiny dark vinyl record rotates, playing "Peter and the Wolf." The tempo increases as the wolf appears, Jim's body notes the change, swaying just a bit faster, as he concentrates hard on the wolf's advance. I am puzzled, as the music makes no sense to me.

In one of his letters, my father told me that Jim had been "quite musical."

My father, his best friend Lavern Hamand, and Jim drive up to Decatur in the Hamands' station wagon to get our first television. When they return, Jim is in the back, all excited and clapping.

"We're gonna see it. Libbets, we are." Jim's dark brown hair and brown eyes glisten next to the brown TV cabinet and the brown side panels on the station wagon. They match, in glorious commune.

As Mr. Hamand and Dad carry the TV into the house, Jim runs around them, and calls for the TV to come on. We are going to watch Captain Kangaroo *and* Leave it to Beaver; *the two kids' shows we will get on our one channel.*

Then he was also sick.

The very first thing I can remember about his illness could have been in May,1956, when I was just a bit over a year old. My parents had taken Jim to St. Louis, to the Children's Hospital, to find out why he was so tired and why he bruised so easily. Or, it could have been anytime we had to leave him at St Louis Children's.

With Mom and Dad next to me, I toddle down a long, dark hallway. Jim is not with us. The grey hallway shadows go on as far as I could see. Dimly lit in the middle, along the sides where there are open doors, the light fluorescent and blue-edged. It is deathly quiet right around us but, again, in those pockets of blunt light, there is a roar of high-paced action, beeping, jangling, and voices. Other people walk down the hallway borders, but not directly towards or with us. A smell hurts my nose.

No one holds my hand. Usually, Mom or Jim holds my hand.

My parents walk fast, as if they really want to get out of there. Yet everything also happens in slow motion. Dad raises his hand; his skin is darker than my mother's. His head glistens with sweat. He moves his hand towards Mom's head, and pulls her to him, her light brown hair contrasting with his tweed jacket and his black hair. He pulls her head onto his shoulder so that her face is on his neck, skin to skin, the other arm around her back. She is crying, silently. They keep walking faster even though she is bent over. I try to keep up, reaching for the pleats in the back of my mother's skirt. What? What? I try to say but I don't know how to talk yet.

Like all small children, when feeling so bad, I expected and needed my mother. There was an invisible rubber band that kept us together. When she felt too far away, the band would yank me back and she was always all there and the whole world seemed righted. Going down that dark vast hallway, sensing my mother wholly absorbed in something I couldn't understand, that rubber band began to fray.

At that hospital, Jim received the diagnosis of childhood leukemia, always fatal in 1956, and he had to stay for his first chemotherapy. If this is the memory of that first day, I went from there to stay with my aunt and uncle for six weeks, a very long time for a tiny child. I don't remember it at all. John Bowlby, a British psychoanalyst who observed children separated from their parents, said that children first protest, perhaps search for their absent parents, then grieve, despair that they will never come back, and then detach and give up. Adults think the child is fine while in this state of detachment because no distress is visible. I know that rubber band lost a lot of its bounce.

Years later, my parents said that when they came to retrieve me, I didn't recognize my mom. I didn't or relax at all in her lap during the three-hour car ride home with her, Jim, and Dad. The story continued that I only began to seem at home after I inspected the books on the living room shelves, and then sat in my kid-sized maple rocking chair, where I rocked myself, all by myself, for a very long time.

One cold winter morning, Dad is already in the kitchen, putting the coffee on. Mom Jim, and I start downstairs. Jim is having trouble walking and cries as if something hurt. Mom scoops him up and carries him. I sit down and refuse to move. I want to be carried too. I am littler than him.

"Come on down Elizabeth," Mom sighs, her voice weary.

"No. Carry me," I insist.

Mom disappears, carrying my brother to the couch in the study. Dad appears at the bottom of the stairs, and he looks up at me with what seemed like hatred.

"You are being a pill. Come down these stairs."

"No."

My mother returns, walks wordlessly up the stairs, and picks me up. When I am in her arms, it still isn't right.

At the Link Clinic, in Mattoon, the town just west from us, the pediatrician's office is up a flight of stairs. We all go into the examination room where Jim takes his clothes off and puts on a gown. Dr. Thiel comes in and has this round silver thing over his face. He looks in Jim's eyes and ears. He holds his wrist and then Dr. Thiel puts the stethoscope in his ears and listens to Jim's chest. Then he talks to my parents. The nurse comes in with a very big needle. Jim starts to cry hard. They make him turn over so he could have a shot in his bottom. My father holds him down. The paper rustles on the table as Jim cries and gives little weak kicks with his legs. Dr. Thiel gives him a shot in the butt with the hugest needle. The needle looks larger than he is, my big brother.

Jim died in January 1958.

It is early morning, not long before my third birthday. The pale winter sun trickles into the east-facing bedroom window. The room is oddly empty and spookier than usual. Jim is now sleeping downstairs in the study, and not in the bed on the other side of the room. It is only a few nights of this, but I miss him. He always smiles at me and talks to me in the morning even when he is very sick. Before, he gets into my bed to play if our parents aren't up yet. Lately, I go to his bed because it is so hard for him to walk, bringing my musical teddy bear and my blankie to visit his stuffed blue doggie. Now there is just blankie, Teddy, and me. I need my mother, and Jim.

I climb carefully out of bed. It is an old metal twin bed, and the side could scrape my leg if I am not careful. I go into the bathroom and pee. I wipe and pull the red pajama bottoms with feet in them back up. I remember when we got them. Jim's big-boy red pajamas don't have feet.

The door to the stairway is open. I have to go down the stairs by myself. Deep breath and I start. The stairs go around three walls, curving past a little oval window seat and finally met the floor at the bottom. The carved wooden railings are stained an orange-ish, brown. Mom and Dad say the railings are sturdy, but I don't know what that means. I know I could fall right through. I am not allowed to touch the safe wall, because it leaves fingerprints. I have to stay in the middle of each step, without wobbling, Carefully, I climb down one step at a time.

Partway down, I see lots of people below, adults, murmuring and talking. This is not right; people are here at night, not usually in the morning. My feet are cold, even with feet-in pajamas. The minister and his wife are there; Dr. Thiel is here. He smiles at me.

"Don," he calls to my father in the living room. "Here's Elizabeth."

I stand still and look around a little. The urge to be with my mother wells up, stronger than upstairs. After several seconds, my father comes to pick me up, hugs me, weirdly tight, and then puts me down without a word.

Dad usually talks to me. As he leaves to talk to another adult I don't know, I hear him whisper under his breath, "Thank God we have Elizabeth."

Dr. Thiel remains nearby. I am deeply suspicious of him, recalling the shot, but I also urgently need to see my mother, that rubber band tugs me to her. "Jim?" I ask.

"He died last night. That means he is not going to ever come back."

What did that mean? Jim isn't here, now? Where is my mom?

Mrs. Kaley, a neighbor, rushes over and speaks, standing way above my head, without looking into my eyes, "Jimmy left for heaven. He went to see Jesus and is happy."

My father wrote in one of those letters after my breakdown that having someone say this to me upset him, but he didn't come over to me to say anything different.

Then Mrs. Kaley asks if I want some cereal for breakfast. I nod, yes, with great solemnity.

Is mom in heaven with Jim?

I trot off, needing Mom to explain. I run through the dining room. With its long shadows, I go as fast I can into the kitchen. I go into the kitchen where Mrs. Kaley is looking through the cabinets for the cereal. My mother is not there. Maybe, these other people don't know, and Mom and Jim are in the study. I run as fast as I can; the study is where I will find them.

No Jim. But there is Mom, sitting on an upholstered armchair, next to the bed they had rigged up for Jim. Jim is not there, a pile of sheets on the floor shows he had slept here. Mom is utterly still and silent. Her eyes are closed. She looks like someone has beaten her on one side, so that her body is lopsided, folded into itself. People sit close to her but are silent. She is wearing her usual black and white housecoat. At that moment, the coat, and her eyes match, dark, and darker, black.

I start to go towards her; I want to touch her, to feel the softness of her body against my face. I feel a force pulling; the rubber band is working, propelling me towards her; the top half of my body goes in her direction, but my feet don't move. I stop. I resist. There is a counterforce. I withstand the pull; now open, those black eyes attack me. Somehow, I know I am supposed to leave her alone. I don't go to her. The rubber band, already frayed and limp, snaps.

Mrs. Kaley comes to say my breakfast is on the kitchen table. My mother looks up and says, "I don't know what to do with Elizabeth."

Mrs. Kaley answers, "I will keep her for you."

This sends a wave of another feeling, an overwhelming one: would I ever come back and who would be there if I did? Didn't "keep" mean not having to share, to not give back? With these questions, after the cereal, I went to the Kaley house for a few days, until after Jim's funeral.

When I did come back, Jim and almost all traces of him were gone for good. The only proof that Jim had been real and had lived in our house was four photographs my parents hung over their bed, 8 X 10 photographs taken by the Olan Mills studio. On the top row, there was a baby picture of Jim and a baby picture of me. On the bottom row, two photos of Jim and me together, taken about a year apart, sitting for the camera in our Sunday best.

When I came back, I carefully watched, and waited to know what to do. From my parents' faces, I quickly learned to leave them alone as much as possible. And, most especially, most critically, don't ever, ever mention Jim where my mother could hear. I was on my own to remember my brother, and it was hard to remember very much.

Right then, I started standing on my own two feet. I stayed that way, upright and solo. This was the harshest and longest-lasting death—the death of knowing how to go to someone, to declare what I felt and needed.

Chapter 7

Meeting the Family, In Person

I was going to meet Richard's whole family at Passover, including Michael, just two and a half months after our endless first date. We spent every second we could together, weekends at my house in Hoosick and as many weekday nights at Richard's Albany apartment as was manageable. If we were separated in the evening, we talked for hours on the phone. We met each other's local friends, academic dinner parties in Bennington on my side and the synagogue and Capital District restaurants with Richard's friends. By April, it was onto family, and the chance to meet the characters Richard told me so much about. I was nervous, as I so wanted to make a good impression. I was often shy and stuck to an observing role in new situations, but I would be with Richard, and it would be all right.

With two weeks to go before the Seder, one Sunday in the middle of the day, when Richard and I were lounging in my dining room over omelets and homemade bread, the phone rang. It was Richard's mother, Ruth, calling to speak to me for the first time.

With only a minimum of pleasantries, she said, "Dear, do you think you could get Richard to wear a clean shirt to Seder?" I detected no love in her tone.

"What kind of shirt should it be?" I replied, thinking this was a bit intrusive.

She said, "How about a white shirt?"

Keeping it light, I agreed to help, though this demand made me wary. When I told Richard, he was annoyed. I tried to laugh it off, to appreciate Ruth's bluntness—no one in my family ever said anything so directly.

After the two-hour drive south to New Rochelle two weeks later, Ruth greeted us warmly, hugging me and kissing her son on the cheek. She turned quickly back to meal preparations. She appeared cheerful, though a little hyper and a bit distracted. She was about to entertain a houseful. I observed her carefully, wanting to take in her presence. Could I detect the difficult, critical person Richard described to me and I glimpsed in the phone call?

Ruth was a tall, long-legged woman in her early sixties, her short, grey, sensible hair parted on one side. Ruth's eyes, behind thick glasses, seemed far away. Her cheeks were extra rosy, perhaps from the exertion required to stage the Seder. She clearly had a lot of energy, as she flitted, not ungracefully, from kitchen to table and back. Richard had told me she'd been a dancer when she was young,

Not wanting to get his shirt and suit pants wrinkled during the drive, Richard needed to change before the other guests arrived. I asked Ruth how I could help. She asked that I put a piece of gefilte fish on each of the little salad plates, which were difficult to fit on the little kitchen table she pointed to. Then, as an afterthought when this job was done, she told me to put them out around the table set for 18 in the dining area, where it would have been so much easier to complete the task.

Lost in the weeds, not a big picture thinker, insensitive, or rigid?

In just a little while, Richard came downstairs, wearing a white shirt, and little else, most particularly no trousers.

Ruth looked at him, burbled and had trouble laughing. "Rich," she said, accusation in her tone. She looked at me, out of the corner of her eye, her face filling with disgust.

"What?" Richard replied. "You told me to wear a white shirt. You didn't ask for anything else."

Ruth glared at me, rage contorting her face. Clearly, I failed her first test of family membership. Richard was acting outrageously, even though I had been enlisted by Ruth to get him to act appropriately. Was this the main purpose she saw for me? I remained very quiet.

Just then, the first guests rang the doorbell, and though Ruth told Richard to go add to his outfit, he lingered.

The first in the door were Richard's Uncle Lewis, Ruth's brother, and his wife Judy. Lew was a tall, slender man with a kind smile and a ready wit. Judy (not "Aunt" Judy, as she was the second, younger wife) was a very thin, pretty woman, dressed in well-cut black slacks and jacket and tasteful jewelry. She did smile broadly at seeing Richard and he kissed her. Lewis looked down at Richard's bare legs and back at his thirty-nine-year-old nephew's face.

"Where's the pants, Rich?"

"Mom told Liz I should wear a white shirt. She didn't say anything about pants."

Lewis looked both amused and pained. "Cute," he said and turned to me. "And you like this clown?"

I burst into a really big smile and said simply, "Yes, I do," and took hold of Richard's hand. Then I whispered in his ear, "Please go and put on your pants so I get off your mother's shit list." He grinned, but complied, lumbering off in his peculiar gait.

The house began to fill with people. When Richard reappeared fully clothed, he led me to the living room couch. We sat, holding hands, legs touching, watching as every new relative entered, including his middle brother Danny, the one Richard didn't get along with. Danny was thinner, shorter by a bit, the dark-haired brother in his middle thirties. He pointedly ignored his eldest brother and new girlfriend while schmoozing with everyone else.

Next, Michael came in the front door, with Carrie, his long-term girlfriend. He looked bigger in person than in the *Times* photo, well over six feet, with an athletic build. His hair was a sandy reddish, he had a curly beard, and wore round wire-rim glasses. In spite of his size, he had a gentle, slightly remote aura. As in the *Times* photo, he was dressed preppy, khaki pants, white button-down shirt, blue blazer. Carrie, a petite woman with round eyes in her thin face, was at least a foot shorter than her boyfriend. Dressed conservatively in a skirt and blouse, with perfect makeup and simple silver earrings, she hurried in alongside Michael and greeted family members all around with a big smile. She took the dish of charoset she'd made, the apple walnut and wine dish, which was part of the ceremonial meal, into the kitchen where she remained, talking with Ruth and whoever else wandered into the kitchen. She and Ruth were pals; they went to yoga together once a week.

Richard stayed seated, holding my hand. "Michael," he called enthusiastically across the room. Michael came straight over, and hugged Richard bearishly, each brother grinning and taking pleasure in each other's company. Richard had made plain to me before this meeting that Michael was the only living member of his family he loved without ambivalence. They were allies, in what Richard had described as a complicated family.

Even if I hadn't known, it was obvious these two were brothers, though Richard was maybe an inch shorter and rounder than Michael, and Michael was more classically handsome. Both were bearded, both had the same sweet brown eyes behind their glasses. They also had at least one mannerism in common: a tipping of the head to the side when being sincere.

"Michael. This is Liz." Michael stretched out his hand and I rose to shake it.

"I've heard about you," he said and laughed, a kind of short, double laugh, nose crinkling, eyes squinting, looking toward me without eye contact. This expression was labored and the feeling in it seemed false: put on, perhaps to mask a different inner state.

"Likewise," I replied.

Carrie came out from the kitchen, and we too were introduced. Then Michael and Carrie turned their attention to the other guests, an assembling group of cousins and family friends. Richard and I kept our spot on the couch. We were still in that glued-together phase of first love, and it was a good vantage point for me to take in the view of the room and study Richard's family for the first time.

This house, a classic suburban Tudor, on a quiet street in New Rochelle, was stucco tan with a fake half-timbered exterior. The living room ran the full length of one side of the house with a baby grand piano in the middle, and at the back a Danish modern wall unit, with books , a bar with liquor, and family photos. I would look carefully at the photos after the meal. One of a very young set of three naked little boys lined up in the bathtub, Richard called the "sodomy" photo to annoy his mother. The dining table, set for at least 18, ran into the middle of the living room. Low bookshelves, painted white, lined the far side of the living-room wall. It would have been a tasteful room, except for the bizarre, 1970s loud blue shag carpet, from entryway up the center hall stairs through the living room into the dining area. It was garish, outdated, and didn't fit. Richard later told me his mother chose the carpet herself, overruling the decorator and the rest of the family.

Lewis suavely played bartender, brought me a glass of wine and stayed to chat. He asked questions, where was I from, what did I teach. I felt shy, though I warmed to his charm and wit. A few moments later, an older woman sat down in the armchair to our left. Michael and Carrie talked with her, and the circle opened so that we were all talking. Jane Ferber was the mother of a high-school friend of Michael's, a psychiatrist who had once helped get Michael access to high quality mental health care, and a former colleague of Murray Shane, Michael's "wonder psychiatrist." She inquired about him, and Michael dipped his head. "Good," he replied, a little coy smile crossing his face, saying nothing more.

Richard turned to me to explain. "Jane used to have this amazing house with a turret, overlooking Long Island Sound, where Michael lived and tried to write." Richard had told me about this time in Michael's life, between his initial paranoid symptoms when he left Bain Capital and before his complete breakdown into florid psychosis.

"I loved that view," Michael said, "such a great place to work, high above the ocean." But I knew he had not really been able to write there, that the demons had grown bigger and bigger during those days in the turret. "But Jane sold the house."

"Are you still doing the ethics work at Columbia Presbyterian?" Jane asked.

Michael seemed agitated, his eyes blinking rapidly and his voice straining. "No, I quit. They wanted my advice on how to ethically obtain informed consent from mentally ill patients for research projects, but they only proposed ideas that were not ethical. I think I was only window dressing so they could say, 'See, we asked a schizophrenic himself how to do this properly.'"

We were interrupted by Ruth calling us to the table. Richard knew that despite my once having been labeled an honorary Jew, I had never actually participated in a Seder. I knew it commemorated the liberation of the Jews from slavery in Egypt. As we approached the table, a squabble arose; the seating plan had not been thought out for the first Passover without Richard's father. Chuck Laudor always sat at the head of the table and presided over the ceremonial meal. Who would take his place? A lengthy and somewhat uncomfortable discussion ensued. Richard, as the eldest son, felt he should, but Uncle Lewis held that Richard would be longwinded and tangential if he led the Seder. Michael was the most adept at Hebrew and most religious, but he might get too involved in Talmudic-style commentary and keep the meal from progressing. Danny, the middle brother, wanted no part of it as he opted out of most family religious practices, but asked that they make up their minds. Uncle Lewis won out and sat at the head. There was some heat in their discussion. Though not comfortable with so much quarreling, I was intrigued and grateful at the same time—so different from my quiet, controlled family. This was lively.

The meal began with the familiar blessing over the candles, Ruth standing in the center of the table, match in hand, as she and Richard and Michael began to sing, with feeling. I could see that the three of them were invested in the religious part, unlike the others, not the third brother Danny, nor Uncle Lew, nor the cousins and friends, who did not seem to share this fervor. When this blessing was done, Michael closed his eyes and took a deep breath, seeming to center himself in a spiritual mode.

"Mom, what are these?" Richard asked gruffly as he held up a thick pamphlet that advertised Folgers's Coffee on the back.

"The Haggadah," she said, the text that accompanies the seder, narrating the Exodus from Egypt. "I got them at the synagogue."

"But where are there real ones? The ones we wrote with Grandpa Jim when we were kids?" Richard said, this time angrier.

"Oh, I couldn't find them." Ruth looked about to cry.

Danny joined the fray. "Mom, did you even look for the Grandpa Jim one?"

"These are *fine*," she answered weakly, perhaps trying to enlist sympathy.

"Did you even look?" Richard retorted.

"I didn't see you offering to help," she replied.

"Okay. Okay." Michael was thumbing through the new Haggadah. He grinned. "You are really going to like this Haggadah, Lew. It's much longer and more complete than the ones we made."

"We won't eat 'til midnight," said Danny.

"So just start," Lewis said.

I learned that that night was different from all other nights, that the holiday meal and the readings and songs accompanying it, could be matters of controversy and creativity. Michael and Richard argued a few times over what to include and what to leave out, for ideological, religious, and nostalgic reasons, in the face of cries around the table to move along. At one point, the whole family all burst into singing "Tura Lura Li," something that had been in the Grandpa Jim version, from his Boston roots, an Irish song somehow relevant to spring, which we were celebrating along with liberation.

Once, I noticed Michael and Carrie talking to Seth, a cousin on the Laudor side of the family, and his boyfriend. Seth was clearly a cool guy, into theatre, blond, lithe, and young. He was suggesting to Carrie that they have lunch in Manhattan one day. Richard tried to join the discussion of where to eat in midtown, something he'd done often when he'd worked as a Wall Street lawyer. Seth and Carrie turned their heads towards him with looks of forbearance, then turned back to each other, broadcasting that they knew better how to choose somewhere chic to dine. It took a moment, but I suddenly realized that Richard was not respected much, in his own family. By association, I thought, I'm not going to be cool or respected either.

After the long meal, as folks were leaving, I remarked to Richard that he and Michael liked to argue. He started laughing, hard. "Michael," he called. "Lizzie says we like to argue."

"No, it isn't," said Michael in a high-pitched English accent.

"Yes, it is," replied Richard also with an accent and several octaves above his regular voice.

"You didn't."

"I did!"

"You didn't!"

"I'm telling you I did!"

"You did not!"

"Oh, I'm sorry, just one moment. Is this a five-minute argument or the full half hour?"

"Oh, just the five minutes."

"Ah, thank you. Anyway, I did."

"You most certainly did not."

"Look, let's get this thing clear; I quite definitely told you."

"No, you did not." By now, both brothers were laughing so hard they doubled over.

I was confused. "What the hell?" I asked Danny.

"It's a Monty Python routine, the 'Argument Clinic,'" he said. "They can do the whole thing."

"Oh, Monty Python was hot during the years I had no TV," I said to cover my cluelessness.

After everyone had left, we were helping wash dishes when Richard and Ruth started fighting. She was still upset about the shirt-only episode. I tried to smooth things over, explaining that Richard was joking, got them to hug and make up, and this pleased Ruth. When she went to the living room to put some dishes away, I wrote her a thank-you note, for including me in the Seder and saying how much I enjoyed meeting everyone. I ended, "Thank you for making Richard in the first place."

We were spending the night at Leslie's, a friend of Richard's; she was away so we had her small Manhattan apartment to ourselves. We were exhausted from the family and fell right to sleep, cuddling close. When we woke, we made love, tenderly. Everything felt magical that morning, the early light coming in the window, the bed piled with sweet-looking quilts, and we very in love. I was content just to be with him and no one else.

After, Richard lay there looking at the ceiling, in contemplation. Then, all of a sudden, he said, "Will you marry me?"

I was stunned. "Do you mean that, really?" We had known each other for just about ten weeks.

Richard gazed at me soberly, his brown eyes blazing. He answered passionately, "Yes." He also looked scared.

More practical than he, I answered, "Yes," and paused. "If."

"What's the 'if'?"

"*If* we move in together and it seems like we can live together. If that goes okay, then yes. I love you so much." I turned and molded my whole body to his, and in that moment, felt more alive and more connected to Richard and to love than I ever had. And for all its faults, he had a real live family, brothers, while mine was so diminished, with my dead brother, and my parents so far away. This might be a life.

Chapter 8

Corn or Peas

My family was opinionated too, but not like the Laudors. We argued with and about Republicans, our passions directed towards the John Birchers, Richard Nixon, the war in Vietnam, corporations, the KKK and all racists, polluters, and fat cats with rightwing views. Conflict with each other was avoided at all costs, never heat or criticism amongst us. My father, a tall, somewhat overweight man with shoulder length thick black hair, was an American historian and a liberal Democrat in a conservative, Republican town. This made him an occasional crank as Dad was never loath to speak up or write a controversial letter. Once when there was a proposed nuke dump, he wrote a letter to the editor indicating that if this were to come to pass, the town would need a new industry, sperm banks, as the nuke dump might make all the men sterile. My mother avoided the grocery store for a couple of weeks after that one, but she did not raise her voice with her husband.

Dad grew up on a small family farm during the depression, never hungry, but poor. He served in the Navy in World War II and the GI bill allowed him upward mobility. Dad returned to the small state college where he spent his undergraduate years to teach history, after he earned his Ph.D., at the U of I, the best state school in Illinois. Dad collected campaign buttons and other political items and these, along with floor-to-ceiling books, littered the walls in his study.

My mother grew up in another small town across the state, more middle class, but in reduced circumstances when my grandfather lost his car dealership in the Depression. Although Mom never failed to put on lipstick and comb her hair when she went to the grocery store, she did wear jeans out and about, which many of the other kids' mothers would never do. After all, she was a part-time gym teacher, prone to the practical, and preferred comfort when doing chores. She did the Royal Canadian Airforce exercises daily for years.

My parents were unique, yet not too odd or truly outside the norm.

Intermittently, though, my parents were quite strange. Mostly they were kind, loving, and generous, but I could never predict when they would do something peculiar or something that seemed cold or harsh. The strangeness was never named; often it stemmed from what my mother called "your father's bad mood."

Dad's moods came from nowhere and went nowhere but when they flared, Mom and I were handcuffed, as he glared silently and stomped around. It was better not to make any sound—no playing, joking, or talking. If anything disturbed him, Dad became extremely irritated. Once Dad spanked me because I stuck out my tongue at him. Most days he would have just joked with me, but he was in a bad mood. His moods could last a few hours or a few days, before leaving as mysteriously as they arrived.

My mother tried to pretend these moods didn't affect her. When they occurred, she would walk around even more stiffly than usual, purse her lips, and withdraw. Then, she'd become silently critical of me, cold and unresponsive. Why was she turning on me rather than my father? He was the source of the trouble. She wanted, I think, not to indulge him, but this conveyed to me that there was nothing to be done about these moods but endure them.

One late-spring afternoon, I was sitting with my parents at the kitchen table, covered in its usual, blue-checked oilcloth, between two south-facing windows, opening to the backyard, with its flower gardens and white picket fence. The sun shone in; the kitchen was the brightest room in the house.

My mother, thin, blue-eyed, masculine looking, was fiddling with her wallet, trying to reorganize something. She had already begun supper preparations; the fried chicken sizzling on the stove, filling the room with a luscious scent. Dad stared out the window with a wild, sad look in his brown eyes. No one spoke. I was thirteen, by now enraged at being held hostage, over and over again, by Dad's moods. The look he could give you if you bothered him in that mood was withering. I tried to stay away.

But there I was at the table. I too looked silently out the window, watching my dog, Lady Valentine IV, a purebred basset hound, chase a squirrel up a tree.

Dad slowly turned his head back towards us. "I can't see any reason to go on living," he said, aiming his gaze at the silver and black saltshaker in the center of the table. All was quiet for maybe half a minute.

Mom, not looking up from her wallet, replied, "Do you want corn or peas for supper?" There was another long pause, while Dad continued to stare at the saltshaker. I studied my feet.

Then my father turned to me and made lingering eye contact with those bad mood eyes, as if to say, "You, see?" and perhaps enlist my sympathy. What he said was, "Corn. I guess." He got up, slowly turned, and went out onto the back porch where he lit a cigarette.

A month later, on the May afternoon, the last day of seventh grade, a plumber came to do some work in our basement. To get there, he had to go through the backyard, where Lady lived. She was never allowed in the house. In winter, if the temperature fell below zero, Mom let her sleep in the basement. I adored Lady's short, sad-faced self. I was imagining having the whole summer to play with her, take her on walks and give her baths, lathering with soap those long, soft, always dirty basset-hound ears. On warm summer nights, I planned to cajole Dad into taking Lady and me out to Lake Charleston for a swim. Lady liked to swim, her little legs going a million miles an hour to keep her afloat. When I got home from school, I called for her at the white picket gate, to begin our summer of fun, but she never came.

Someone realized that the plumber had left the backyard gate open. After some searching, my mother called the dogcatcher's office.

"Lady was killed by a car," was all she said when she got off the phone. She was so calm. Later, I'd learn that she'd been told Lady's corpse had been found down the street and taken away by the county. Having heard Mom's words from the other room, my father came into the kitchen and looked at me with some concern.

I started crying hysterically. I could not stop. I had not cried in front of my parents since I was very small. My parents both said they were sorry, my father patting my arm.

Alone in my room, I continued crying, my whole-body heaving and writhing, moaning and shrieking. I knew I should stop, but I couldn't. My father came up once, patted me on the arm again and said once more he was sorry. Then he left. I had done the most crying of my young life at Girl Scout camp when I was nine and homesick, missing the dog, not my parents. I had learned the lesson of Midwestern stoicism well. Emotion was a private matter. Besides, a main goal in my young life was not to admit if I needed something, not to allow my vulnerability ever to show to Mom and Dad.

My parents were having a party that evening, and I was supposed to spend the night at my friend Wendy's house. A party meant the downstairs would be filled with grown-ups, and I couldn't watch TV, better to go elsewhere.

Half an hour before I was supposed to leave for Wendy's, my mother came upstairs, looking fierce and irritated.

"You have to stop crying," she said. "If you want to go to Wendy's, you cannot cry over there. If you can't get yourself under control, you will have to stay up here, by yourself."

I sobbed on. "I do want to go," I managed. "I promise I will stop."

More sternly, she said, "In fact, if you go over there, you have to promise that you will not even tell them that Lady died. No one cares about this but you. No one."

With shock, I pulled in a deep breath and made the tears stop. "Okay," I said, in my smallest voice, feeling weak all over.

Dad dropped me at Wendy's and once inside, Wendy's father, my father's best friend, took one look at me and asked, "What's wrong, sugar?"

I started to tear up. "I'm not supposed to tell you."

Mr. Hamand smiled. "You can tell us. It's okay."

"Lady got hit by a car and killed today."

He put his arm around me and pulled me to him, then called Wendy and her little brother over. "Kids, you be especially nice to Liz tonight. Her dog got killed today and she's really sad."

Wendy and Jeff regarded me kindly. I sniffled a little, but then I was okay, the relief from Mr. Hamand's warmth taking some of the sting away.

Chapter 9

Block Island Crazy

I owned my house and Richard rented, so he really needed to be the one to move. He would have an hour commute each way, through the foothills of the Green Mountains, into Albany for work, a bit tricky in the winter. Richard said he was game, though he was not a country guy and Hoosick was really in the middle of nowhere. He wanted to be with me, he said. By the end of June, however, he hadn't made concrete plans.

One morning, over breakfast on the July 4th weekend, I had to ask if he was backing out. I was scared.

"What's going on with your moving in, Richard?"

He paused and looked worried, started to speak, then stopped. This was unusual. Richard was a chatty guy, usually not at a loss for words. He looked out over the yard, and then turned back to me and touched my head.

"I am not good at anything practical. I told you that. So, I don't know how really to move. It feels like more than I can handle."

As someone who had moved a lot, around the Boston area about ten times in the 1980s and to Dallas and back in the 90s, I was good at moving. "It's just the practical part? I am good at that if you need help to, actually, literally, move," I said.

"It's mostly that." He paused again. "Well, when I moved from Allen Street in Albany to the State Street apartment two years ago, it was right before my nervous breakdown. I got really, really depressed at the time of the move. I don't know if moving had anything to do with it. But I don't know that it didn't." He was quiet for a few seconds. "After I got better, I realized that I would never be scared of anything again, except maybe getting sick. And I am not scared of this. Being with you, I feel different, changed, like I never felt before." Richard got a little teary. "I don't want to mess this up."

I took his hand across the table. "You won't. I won't let you," I said. We both laughed. "Seriously, do you just need help with boxes and deciding what to bring and getting the U-Haul?" I asked.

He nodded.

"Done."

And over the next month, feeling a bit like his mother, I threw out some of his most nerdy items of clothing, packed the rest in cardboard boxes, arranged for disposal of much of his ratty furniture, rented a van, and got him moved into my house, just in time to go to the beach with his family.

Through much of Richard's childhood, his parents rented a place on Block Island, off the coast of Rhode Island, to spend two weeks alone, away from their rowdy, uncontrollable sons who were left with an assortment of babysitters and grandparents. Michael was the first of the boys to make his way to his parents' hideaway as a young adult. One summer he had stayed at Yale to take organic chemistry to apply to medical school (but gave up on both). He left New Haven and called his parents from the Block Island Ferry to say he was on his way. They didn't make him turn back and Michael had been a frequent visitor to the island since. The previous summer, when Richard's father Chuck had been terminally ill with prostate cancer, Ruth went to Block Island anyway, leaving him in hospice. She invited Michael and Carrie and Danny and his then-girlfriend to come. Now, Chuck was not dead a year, and, as a widow, Ruth invited her eldest son and me to join her with Michael and Carrie. Danny couldn't make it.

I was so looking forward to the vacation, and my first trip to the coast with Richard. Always calmed by the sea, I wanted to play in the waves with Richard and kiss him, hold his hand, looking out at the water crashing against the sand at the gorgeous Block Island beach. I hoped the romance of it would soften the hard parts of being with his family, and I did want to get to know Michael and Carrie. Richard kept telling me they were the good parts of his family.

Michael met us at the ferry, and we followed him around the Island, past the dramatic red clay cliffs and the many grey-shingled cottages, to the house the elder Laudors had rented for years. As we turned down onto a bumpy dirt road to the interior of the island, it was past dusk and a line of dark blue air hovered above the horizon, broken only by a few small house lights dotted nearby. I breathed it all in, so happy to be there.

The five of us sat in the living room chatting, with soft drinks for some and wine for others, and snacks opened from the provisions we had brought. Michael and Richard, always competitive and boyish together, began telling penis jokes. Ruth looked confused.

Michael said to his big brother, "She doesn't get it."

Richard answered, "After all these years and three sons, you think she would understand boys and their dicks."

"You two are terrible," Carrie interjected. "You shouldn't tell jokes like that in front of your mother."

I too would never be so crude in front of any mother, but I was not male. I smiled quietly, trying to stay out of it. Ruth stood abruptly and went to get another soda from the fridge. After she filled her glass, she turned back to us, looking primarily at Richard and declared, "I want to make sure you all look after yourselves. Just take and get what you need. No meals provided. Don't expect me to cook for anyone. You all can do your own thing." Her tone was unwelcoming.

Michael and Carrie, who had been there for few days already, exchanged looks but said nothing. Neither did Richard.

As no one was speaking up, I answered. "Of course, Ruth. We can take care of ourselves and will be sure to wash up after ourselves and won't be a bother."

"I sleep in in the morning. That's my vacation," she carped. "So, I hope you can respect that with some quiet."

"Of course. Richard and I sleep late too, but we will be very quiet in the morning," I continued, trying to appease her.

Richard grimaced and then snarled. "Don't worry, Mom. We'll stay out of your way." I eyed him, trying to signal not to add to the bad feelings. He stopped. The silence was uncomfortably awkward.

This was Ruth's first time on Block Island as a widow and I reckoned that was hard for her. I wanted to give her the benefit of the doubt.

She wants us here, but she really doesn't. She really wishes Chuck were here but doesn't know what to do with that. Of course, she could have been nicer to me, welcoming me more clearly as a newcomer to this family vacation, but she was grief stricken. I wanted to be understanding, though ill at ease.

Another woman, as a new widow, might have picked a different vacation spot, so as to not be confronted so directly with what was missing. Ruth, though, craved sameness, doing things the same way repeatedly, holding onto routines even when everything really had changed dramatically. This was the first time she'd invited 39-year-old Richard to Block Island, probably because she could invite me too. From her first contact with me, asking me to get Richard into a white shirt for Seder, I felt, she tried to make me an ally in her subtle, constant disdain for eldest son. I refused to play; she had already asked Richard why I didn't like her.

Michael took Carrie's hand, and they walked out onto the deck to gaze at the stars. Ruth busied herself in the kitchen. I moved closer to Richard on the couch, and he put his big arm around me and pulled me to him. As always, I felt safe in his bear hug embrace. We sat quietly for nearly half an hour, and the tension in my body started to ebb away. I was on vacation.

Carrie and Michael came back in. "You two look comfy," Carrie said, smiling.

"Yeah, I can tell they know how to relax," Michael said. "Remember Danny and Lynn last summer?" Carrie laughed.

I was curious about Danny, the middle brother, whom Richard had described as his childhood enemy. "What were they like?" I asked.

"They broke up and you could see why. He wasn't very nice to Lynn last summer," Carrie said.

Michael laughed. "Yeah, Lynn wanted to take a nap and Danny didn't so he said, 'You're so fat, who would want to sleep with you?'"

"He said that? In front of people?" I asked.

"He did. Can you believe that?" Carrie said, looking directly at me, girl bonding.

"Was she heavy?" I asked.

"Not at all," Michael answered.

"Amazing," I said, trusting Richard for the first time that his middle brother was not a nice guy.

"That's Danny," Richard said.

"What about Danny?" Ruth asked, coming back into the room. "It's really too bad he couldn't come." Danny was her favorite son.

Just then, Michael seemed exhausted, his face going slack. "Want to go downstairs to bed, Boo?"

Carrie, tiny next to Michael's six-foot frame, stood on her tippy toes to kiss him, concern in her eyes. They left for their room on the bottom floor.

"I'm tired, too," I said. "I think I'll get ready for bed. Goodnight, Ruth."

"Goodnight, dear," Ruth replied.

"I'm right behind you," Richard added. He wasn't going to spend a minute alone in his mother's company.

The next afternoon we all left together for the beach. "We're headed to the parking lot just past the volleyball net. Nearly to the end of Town Beach," Michael said as he drove along Corn Neck Road, on the tip of Block Island. He was at the wheel of his mother's huge Buick sedan, Ruth next to him in front, Carrie, Richard, and me in the backseat.

"That far? I'll have to walk back down the beach to find my Scrabble-playing friends," Ruth complained.

"It's less crowded down there, Mom."

"Maybe you could park here, and you could walk down the beach," Ruth whined in a little girl voice. She waved at an opening in the line of cars parked along the shore road.

"Mom," Michael said firmly. "It's better at the end."

He had given me the destination as the far end of the beach before we left the house, so I could tell some friends from Cambridge, also on the island, where to meet us. Richard, squished against me, squeezed my hand, and smirked at Michael's management of their mother. I sensed that if Richard and Ruth were having this discussion, it would escalate into a fight. Ruth always seemed scornful of anything Richard said. In turn, Richard reacted angrily. Michael had more charm, and without giving an inch, did better with his mother.

I was just so happy to be by the ocean, the dunes to our right, green tufts of beach grass and the pink of beach roses rising above the cream-colored sand. The salt air scent was sharp and clear. I wasn't going to let petty family tensions get to me.

Michael found a spot in the farthest parking area big enough for the Buick. I gathered the beach towels and my book and handed Richard the cooler of ice water. Michael and Carrie, both very fit, took off quickly down the path through the dunes. Ruth too went ahead. Richard was taking off his shoes to leave in the car and, as always, was slow. Though I was impatient to get to the water, I stayed with him. Richard eyed the path. He had never been to this beach and couldn't know how far it was to the water. With his weird gait, Richard had trouble walking even on level ground. I stayed by his side, slogging slowly through the hot sand as he labored and stopped frequently to swig from the water jug. Finally, we got to the top of the dunes and could see the small waves breaking on the shore. Richard smiled and said, "Da Ocean."

"Yeah," I answered and left him there to run down the dunes to Michael and Carrie on the beach blanket. "Where's Ruth?" I breathed.

"Oh, she doesn't want to sit with us. She went to find her friends," Michael snorted. "I'm going to join in the volleyball. Carrie, want to play?"

"No, I'll sit here and read," she said. Michael jogged off and for a couple of minutes before Richard staggered over, Carrie and I were alone. I tried to think of something to say. The vibe I got from her from was one of intelligence and, funnily, conventionality. She was a Yalie, after all, like Michael.

"You have to go back tomorrow for work?" I asked.

"Yeah, this is a hard time to take time off from my job, the end of the summer, because we're helping get our schools ready to open." Carrie worked for the Edison Project, a group that claimed to be able to operate public schools for less money than regular school districts, a brainchild of some vaguely rightwing types I despised, but I wanted to be polite.

"What do you do there?"

"Technology of all kinds, and pitch in with whatever else is needed. I travel a lot to get computer networks up and running in different school districts."

"How long have you known Michael?" I asked.

"We met a couple of times in college, like 13 years ago. He went out for a bit with my roommate, and I thought he was cute but he didn't really notice me then, even though I tried to get his attention. We met again in 1990 when he was in law school, and I was working in New Haven for IBM. We've been together since." She laughed. "With a few ups and downs."

I knew from Richard that the two of them had lived together for quite a while in the tiny family studio apartment in Riverdale, in the Bronx, purchased when Richard was in law school at Columbia as a cheaper alternative to dorm fees. Carrie had moved out of the studio quite recently, finding the quarters were too close, and I heard, the two of them could really fight. Richard claimed that Carrie had once bitten Michael during a fight.

"I told Michael we could only live together again when we can afford to have two bathrooms."

"Richard and I have been officially living together for about nine days," I said. "But it's in a three-bedroom house and we do have a bathroom and a half."-

I liked Carrie. She seemed sort of staid, but she was smart, kind, even if not a kindred spirit able to fully embrace the absurdities in life, my test for friendship. She loved Michael. I was curious to know her better.

Richard joined us, puffing. I patted the beach towel next to me and he sat.

"Want to go in soon?" I asked.

Richard shook his head. "I gotta catch my breath."

Carrie said, "The water is too cold for me. I only go in with a wet suit."

"Okay. Got it," I said, thinking they were both sticks in the mud. Then from behind me, I could hear children screaming loudly, and I turned to find my Cambridge friends and their kids, Jake, and Owen, aged six and nine, and their cousin Mollie, my goddaughter, aged thirteen. They raced across the dunes onto the beach to get into the sea. Right behind came the boys' mother Connie, one of my dearest friends, running glee-fully after her sons. Some paces back came their father Jeff, slower but laughing heartily at the children's zest. As they ran past, I yelled hello, the smaller boy yelled "Lizzie" and he and Mollie ran to me. I hugged Mollie tight and then got up and ran after Jake, with Owen and Mollie following, Connie close behind. We all crashed into the water and swam and played for a long time. The boys wanted to be on our shoulders and fight each other, trying to push each other into the water. Then I put thirteen-year-old Mollie up on my back to let her try to dethrone her skinny, intensely competitive cousin Jake. At last, even the boys were ready to get out and we flopped down on beach towels.

Michael was back from volleyball and I did introductions. Owen, though he was getting to be a bigger boy, sat in his mother's lap and sucked his thumb, oozing his usual sweet soulfulness. Jake continued to roll in the sand, never one to sit still. Mollie started reading. Then Owen grabbed his shovel and moved closer to the water to dig.

Michael went to swim and when he came out, he sat by Owen, their mutual sweetness resonating. Michael gently and patiently helped clear sand from Owen's hole with his hands. They dug together, wordlessly, for a long time.

We made plans for the evening, mindful of Ruth's dictum that we shouldn't expect meals from her. Richard and I decided to eat dinner in town. The Cambridge folks asked us to come by after dinner to play some party games.

When Richard and I returned to the house after our evening out, everyone else was down for the night. The next morning, we slept a bit late, but I could hear Carrie bustling about getting ready to go back to the mainland. I made Richard roll out of bed so that we could say goodbye. Ruth was up too, looking puffy-eyed and tired. She took her coffee out to the deck. After we hugged Carrie goodbye, Richard and I joined her there, and we talked about little things, how it looked like it was going to be a hot day.

When Michael returned from dropping Carrie at the ferry, we discussed plans for the day. I was going with my friends to the step beach in the afternoon. Michael decided to join us, but Richard felt he wasn't up to the challenge of walking down the steep steps abutting the red clay cliffs on the south side of the island. He would hang out in town.

Ruth suddenly demanded, "Michael, now that Carrie is gone, I want you to move into the bedroom upstairs. Richard, you and Liz can move to the basement." Her tone was imperious and spiteful.

Richard, not the most flexible of human beings, shrieked, "I am not moving, Mom. I just got used to the bed up here."

"Mom, I want to stay downstairs anyway," Michael was firm.

"No, Michael," Ruth objected, her voice rising to a hysterical pitch. "I want Richard gone, down there, and you up here with me."

"Forget it, Mom," Richard yelled. "I am staying put. You can't make me move."

I didn't know what to do. This was crazy. I sat stunned and speechless.

Michael's face went white. "Stop it, Mom," he declared, some anger entering his tone too. "You can't have it the way you want it."

"Besides," Ruth wailed. "You all just keep disappearing. I mean, I thought we would have dinner together every night. You are my guests. You should be here for dinner. I mean you should cook dinner. I am not cooking but I expect to have it with you."

I was confused. Who was she talking to? And wasn't this a complete about-face? I decided to try to help, even though my gut impulse was to get in the car and go home.

"Okay Ruth," I said. "What do you want for dinner tonight? I will be happy to cook." Everyone was quiet.

"That's nice, dear," Ruth said, abruptly cheerful. "There are kosher hot dogs in the fridge."

When Richard and I got in the car an hour later for him to drop me at the step beach, I begged him to leave the next day.

He said, "Oh, no. She is not getting her way. We are staying and having a good time. Forget her." He laughed. "After Dad died, she tried to get Michael to sleep in the bed with her. I forced Michael not to. I knew it would really mess with his head to sleep with Mom. I am not leaving Michael here alone with her."

This was so weird, and more than I could take in.

We stayed, as planned, for four more days and it was awful. My instinct always was, when you are not wanted, get-the-fuck-out. There was something different in this family, something I couldn't have imagined. They were mean, unreasonable, and unreasonably mean. Though my parents could be cold or distant, they were never mean on purpose or hostile and aggressive.

Though I did know something, from a very long time ago, about mean and hideous behavior.

Chapter 10

The Raincoat

That summer Mom bought me a new, robin's egg blue raincoat, all rubbery, with silver buckles, just like on a fireman's coat and new white rain boots to wear when kindergarten started.. Late August had been sunny and hot, for too many days. I wanted rain so I could wear them, and kept venturing into the hall closet, to finger the coat and practice the buckles—such a fine raincoat, that I was willing to risk the hall closet, even though witches lived at the back of it. I believed that if I flung the closet door open wide enough, they wouldn't come out. I loved to touch and feel this best-blue raincoat, and all that summer, if I wasn't in that closet, waiting for rain, I played in a big cardboard box in the garage. My mother had gotten a new washing machine, and that box was big enough for a friend to fit in there with me, even though I almost always had to play alone.

Finally, while driving two hours home from Sunday dinner at my grandmother's, an afternoon rain began, a sudden midwestern thunderstorm sweeping across the cornfields outside the car windows, blackening the sky. When lightning struck, it tinged the firmament deep violet followed by the thunder's sudden, breaking crack and then boom. My father had the windshield wipers on high. I wanted to keep the window rolled down, part way, to feel the rain and the air getting cooler. Mom wouldn't let me. She didn't want to car seat to get wet. I sat very still, watching the storm. When we turned onto Harrison Avenue, where we lived, the car wheels started to rumble, because it was still paved with bricks. I liked that, a bookend to this two-hour journey, because the street where my grandmother lived was also paved in brick.

The rain was letting up as we pulled into the driveway.

"Mom, can I please wear my raincoat now?" I asked carefully. Down to just a drizzle, the clouds were lifting, and it looked like the sun might peak out.

Mom wasn't always stern. She smiled at me with affection. "Sure, why not?"

I ran inside, straight to the closet, forgetting to open the door very wide and fretted for a second about the witches. I struggled to unbuckle the coat and pull it down off the hanger. The boots were on the stairs to the basement. I knew I could never get them on over my shoes, so I undid the shoelaces on my red tennis shoes and pulled the boots over my socks. I had to get outside fast as I could. Mom probably wouldn't approve of this short cut, but she was busy putting leftovers from Grandmother's house in the refrigerator. My father was outside the back door, smoking a cigarette, inspecting his flower garden. I passed him on my way.

"You are ready for a monsoon, Libs."

"Okay, Daddy."

I had no idea what a monsoon was, but I knew if I asked, we might have to go look at the dictionary. The sun was peeking out and I started to sweat a little in my rubberized coat. I made my way to the alley just past the garage, where there were these deep, gorgeous brown mud puddles. I spent quite a while stomping in them, and making waves, swirls, kicking in rocks. I studied the water and my feet, in my white boots in the water, quite intently. When I looked up, Dad had disappeared into the house. I was alone with the mud and my best blue raincoat.

After some time, Donny Wright, the fat kid from up the alley, also aged five, came walking toward me.

"Hi, Elizabeth."

"Hi, Donny. These are great puddles," I said as I splashed particularly effectively, making the puddle overrun its banks and swirl around some bigger pieces of gravel.

"Yeah, I don't have boots."

"Just take off your shoes and socks. You can go barefoot." I had gone barefoot in the alley puddles before and remembered the luscious feel of slick mud on my toes.

"I don't know how to tie, so I don't think I could get them back on. My mother might get mad."

"I can tie. I'll tie them when you're done."

"Nah." Donny was never very adventurous. He watched me puddle jump for a little while more. "Wanna do something else?"

"Sure," I said, grateful to have someone to play with. Whatever we did, it had to be outside, as my mother didn't allow the neighborhood children to come in and play. Though it was never said directly, I believe this was because our neighbors were working class, and perhaps she saw them as slightly beneath us, while children of the professional friends of my parents or that I knew from four-year-old kindergarten at the college lab school, were allowed in.

Then I realized that Donny had not seen the washing machine box in the garage, detached from the house, right next to the alley.

"I know. Let's go play in the garage. There's a big box there and we can get in and pretend. Maybe space." I knew that Donny, as a boy, probably wouldn't want to play "house," but he might like to fly to the moon.

"Yeah, great," he said. "I get to be the pilot."

"Sure," I said to the pilot request, wanting to be sure that he would stay and play. I made a few more big splashes before we walked to the garage.

Before I got in the box, I took off those white boots so the box bottom wouldn't get all soggy. There was just enough room for us to sit across from each other, legs stretched out. Donny and I weren't usually this close to each other. We pretended to blast off, and then fly around the world. Then Donny stopped.

He said, "I have another idea." I was little surprised. Donny, although so much better than having no one around, was not the most brilliant playmate. What did he want to do?

He whispered, "I'll show you my butt if you show me yours."

This was a surprise. I thought about it for a good fifteen seconds, staring at him.

Slowly, though suspecting this was starkly forbidden, I said, "Okay. You go first."

He started to whine a little, but I kept staring and he backed down. He turned around and pulled down his pants. His butt was fat, soft, and very round. There were little fat pockets, dimples. I stared at it the way I had been staring at his face. I kept thinking that there was something more interesting to see in the front of him, but I knew, somehow, this was all I got. Suddenly he pulled up his pants.

"Now I want to see yours," he commanded.

I turned, gulped, and pulled down my pants. "Here."

"No, I can't see," he said, loudly.

What did he mean? I had pulled my pants down; I could feel the air on the bare cheeks of my bottom. I inched a little closer to him in the box.

"No fair. I showed you. No fair." His voice escalated, whiney and menacing. I panicked, didn't want to disappoint him, which might make him leave. I tried to raise my butt higher in the air. Donny kicked at me, catching the edge of my raincoat. Then I got it. The beautiful blue rain-coat was hanging down, covering up my butt. I reached back and lifted my coat up and Donny got to see my naked butt. When I turned around to see his face as he looked at me, he appeared really excited, transformed into something—cruel. Donny leaned forward, as if to spank me on the butt. I pulled my pants up, quickly.

Three weeks later, Donny came back to play, bringing his friends, Mark and Jeff, other neighborhood boys. I saw them walking down the alley to my yard. Mark was laughing and holding his crotch through his jeans. He was always a weird kid and I never played with him much, although he lived just across the street. He looked like he never washed and when I did go to his yard to play, Mark's little brother Eric was even weirder; he regularly defecated in their backyard or garage. I never went inside their house, but you could see the kitchen from a window in the driveway, with stacks and stacks of unwashed dishes littering every surface. Mrs. Jennings worked nights as a nurse and always seemed utterly exhausted. She never came out when we played or called her children in for supper. Sometimes you could see Mr. Jennings, Mark's father, chasing one of his sons around the front yard with a belt in his hand.

I didn't know Jeff well. Cuter and smarter than the other two, he lived across Division Street, down several blocks. His father was a local doctor, a GP my father called "a quack." Many years later, there would be a suspicion, never proven, that Jeff's much older brother Eddie, also a doctor, killed his first wife by pushing her down a flight of stairs (instead of the official version that she fell). As they approached my garage, Jeff stared at me; it felt peculiar.

"Hi," I said with discomfort.

"Hi," the three boys said back in unison.

Then Jeff said, "Liz, do you want to come down and play in Donny's yard?"

I never liked playing alone and as always, unconsciously, wished for a boy/brother to play with. So even though I kept my eye on Mark's hand on his crotch, I called out to my mother hanging up the laundry in the back yard.

"I'm going down the alley to play, Mom."

She smiled and waved at us.

As we walked along the alley, the three boys surrounded me, hemming me between them. I was simultaneously suffocated and thrilled, in some uncharted way. I hoped this meant that they really wanted to play with me, that we could have fun, the four of us. The ring around me loosened, and Mark scuffed his feet through the gravel in the alley. I playfully slid down into the two big potholes in that section and made dramatic, pirouetting leaps up out of the indentation. Donny and Jeff laughed. Going this way, we passed the neighborhood garbage cans, all a dulled metal and smelly. Tall weeds grew up along the alley too, although the Edman house had a nice back garden, filled with white daisies. I tried to run ahead but Mark chased me and caught me and squealed as he jumped in front of me, still holding himself. I wondered if he really needed to pee.

As we turned into Donny's driveway, Jeff suggested that we play hide and seek. He said I had to be *It*. I really wanted to hide, but agreed, to be sure they would keep playing with me. As they ran off, I hid my eyes in the crook of my arm, counted to thirty, then yelled, "Ready or not, here I come." I listened for any nearby rustling but heard nothing. I walked along the side of Donny's house to the front but didn't find anyone. Then I stood still, listening, but no giggling or sounds of boys' shoving gave anything away. I looked into the double garage. One side was empty, where Mr. Wright parked his truck, but on the other sat Mrs. Wright's big car. I ventured into the cool, dark garage, hoping to find someone. As I rounded the car, all three boys jumped out at me and screamed. I stopped dead in my tracks, alarmed. As they had in the alley, the three boys surrounded me and then pushed me up against the car.

Donny spoke haltingly, almost as if the other two were forcing him to speak. "They want to see your butt."

I wanted to cry. Why had Donny told them? Also, I kept thinking that I wanted to see the part of them that was in front, not their butts, but my butt was what they wanted to see. Mark started jumping up and down, squealing in this very odd, frightening way.

Jeff, like the other two was my age, five, but smoother. He pleaded, "Yeah, show us, Liz. Show us. We just want to see." Mark jumped at me and tried to pull my pants down. I grabbed at them.

Then Donny said the magic words, the words that held me hostage that day and for months, years to come: "We won't play with you anymore if you don't show us."

Mark grabbed at me again, but I pushed him away. "Okay," I spit out and pulled my pants down quickly. I felt so scared, in the middle of those three boys. They took turns walking around me, looking. Mark put his hands down his pants and seemed transformed by my butt. I tried to pull my pants up.

"Not yet," Jeff commanded.

I froze. He came closer and rubbed his hands along both of my butt cheeks. I shivered. He backed away. I was so exposed, three boys looking at me. Then Jeff took out his pink dangling part and came back to me. He spread my butt cheeks this time and put it in. He was too small and too limp to penetrate, but he kept the pink part between the cheeks. It felt moist, hot, like a fat, muddy, wriggling earthworm.

Could that pinky earthworm go up inside of me and gobble up my insides?

I held my breath, waiting for Jeff to back away. Watching, again Mark squealed, louder and then laughed hysterically.

They're laughing at me.

71

Donny just kept staring at my backside, which was now squished up against Jeff. I could feel Jeff's sweaty head and humid breath next to my neck. I wanted to jump out of my skin. After a few minutes, Jeff stepped away. I nearly cried but fought off the tears. I pulled my pants up, turned, and ran home as fast as I could. My whole body felt different, soiled and alien. I was now a very, very bad girl.

Mark ran past me, on his way to his house, calling in high-pitched sweetness and light, "Let's play again tomorrow."

As I walked in the back door of my house, all was quiet and still. Where was my mother? Was she in the basement or the yard, still working on the laundry? Would she figure out the very bad thing I had done with those boys? As I thought this, a kind of terror entered. What would happen to me if my parents found out that I was a wicked, dirty girl? Maybe they would send me away. Maybe they would never speak to me or spank me, hard. Would they hate me because I was bad? Maybe they would just be cold and far away, all the time, like they were sometimes when they were just a little mad at me for when I had done something a little bad. Maybe my badness would hurt them, damage them too and that was even worse. I so felt the weight of their love and need for me, since Jim died, their need for me to be perfect and alive.

Just then the door to the stairs to the basement opened and Mom popped up. I jumped, startled, and asked urgently, "What's the matter?"

My mother seemed puzzled. "Nothing, sweetie," she said. "What did you do at the Wrights?"

Lying was a new skill; lying by leaving something out was especially new. "We played hide and seek."

"That's nice. Do you want something to eat?" It was mid-afternoon now and time for a snack. I asked for something I knew was allowed.

"Some cheese, please, Mommy."

"Okay. I'll cut you a piece of Colby. Do you want salt on it?" Suddenly, I was nauseous and there was an intense pressure to get away from her.

"No." I shook a little. "No thank you, I mean. I'm going upstairs and play with Tiny Tears." Tiny Tears was my favorite doll. I had to get away from Mom before she could smell my badness.

Mom closed the refrigerator door and asked, "Are you sure you're not hungry?" probably with no tone of criticism.

"What's the matter?" I asked her again, desperately, sure she could see or tell or know that something was now completely different in me.

"Not a thing," she said absent-mindedly, opening her recipe box. "If you change your mind, come back to the kitchen."

I ran upstairs into my bedroom, grabbed my doll, and slid under the bed. I tried to talk to Tiny, but she didn't seem real, though she usually did. Hiding might be a little dangerous; if someone saw they might ask why I was doing this, so I slid out from under the bed. I was a little dusty and the room seemed unusually big and open. The bottom half of me was numb so I went to pee. As I sat on the toilet, I shivered, remembering Jeff's penis sort of inside me. I couldn't relax enough to pee. Nothing came out. I carefully took the three sheets of toilet paper my mother taught me to use, folded them as instructed into a flat square and wiped furiously, all around down there. I wanted to take a bath, but it was not bath day.

Back in my room, I took down from the toy shelf the plastic bag containing a set of small plastic shapes, rectangles of all lengths and widths, a few squares, and triangles, which came in primary colors and white and black and fit into a particleboard pegboard. I poured out the whole bag on the floor and slotted in a bottom row of all white pieces, across the whole row on the pegboard. I was absorbed by the pattern I was creating, an organization of shape and color. After the white row, a yellow row, then a red row followed by blue. I wanted a black row next, but there were not enough black pieces. I was engrossed by what to put next and returned to the bottom row. I took out every fifth white one and replaced it with a black piece. I kept at it, divining patterns, and places to put things so there was order, fixated by color, shape, and pattern. When I did look up, into the room, I saw patterns, the geometry around me. Instead of windows, I recognized clear rectangles, and the perfect spheres of the wooden knobs of my rocking chair. The carving in the bedposts of lines and circles also enfolded me.

I had almost filled the whole board when my father, home from the college, came upstairs and startled me. I jumped up, spilling the pieces in my lap.

"Whatsa matter, Daddy?" I asked sharply. I would keep asking my parents this for several years, whenever I inferred that they might be the slightest bit upset.

"Nothing, Liz. What are you working on? Your mother says you have been up here for hours. It's just about supper time and she wants you to set the table."

"Okay." I wanted to run down the stairs fast so that I would be doing my job like a good girl. But then I wanted Daddy to see what I was doing. He always liked my patterns. "Look." I held out the covered pegboard.

"Wow. Nice work."

I started to explain the patterns, of colors, black and white, and the whole lines, then patterns of four, then down to three, then two of each and how the top row would have black and white again.

"How old are you again? I swear you have a mathematical mind." Dad smiled at me. I looked down, proud but also embarrassed.

"I'm five, Daddy," I said.

He laughed. "I know how old you are. You are getting so big now."

"I better go down."

"Tell your mother I will be down as soon as I change."

"Okay, Daddy."

I jumped down the stairs, and then slowed, as I remembered that I was not supposed to jump up and down too much. Plaster ceilings could crack and crumble, they told me. There was so much to remember about being good. As I pushed this thought out of my mind, I started to see the geometry around me again, the lines of the stairs, the circle of the window by the window seat, the rectangle of the rug, covering the lined, wooden floor of the rectangle room. The shapes seemed pure and took me away.

"Ready to set the table?" Mom asked.

I nodded but I really hated setting the table. The sounds of the silverware rubbing against itself was so irritating, like fingernails on a chalk board. I usually tried to get my mother to get the forks and spoons out of the drawer. This time, instead, I went straight to the silverware, resigning myself to the teeth-on-edge experience of manipulating the metal, round spoons, pronged rectangle, saw-toothed lined knives. I was going to be as good a girl as I could. After I put the silverware around, Mom handed me three dark charcoal grey melamine plates to put on the place mats. Circles on rectangles, and then the squares below on the checkered tablecloth, yet another shape popping up, to complicate the order. These squares let me imagine a square, 3-dimensional, jack-in-the-box. I could feel the moment where the evil clown bursts up, to leer at me. I shuddered.

"I'll hand you the water glasses," my mother said. "What color do you want?" These were hard plastic tumblers, in an assortment of colors, garnered free from the grocery store, with each twenty dollars spent.

"Could I have the tangerine one?"

More circles, circles, circles.

Mom handed me the glasses and I put them around, then got the water jug and poured for all three of us. My mother went back to the stove and turned the pork chops.

"Call your father. I think this is all ready."

I went to the bottom of the stairs, pondering the relationship between squares and rectangles. "Supper!" I yelled. This jarred me out of my shape world and back to the real one. I sat at my seat, next to Mom, across from Dad, took a sip from the tangerine glass. I wanted to run away but I had to stay there, no matter how strange and dirty I felt, and pretend to be just so fine. Before I just had to remember not to go to them with strong feelings or needs. Now it was all different. Now I had to hide what I was, shroud every part of my body, my wicked soul, from the eyes of my parents and even from myself.

I would keep asking, for years to come, "Whatsa matter?"

Chapter 11

Delightful Compromises

Richard moving in took some getting used to. At middle age, me forty-one, Richard thirty-nine, we had both lived alone for a long time. We were both a little set in our ways and both stubborn, to boot. Richard made it clear he was not going to do any housework, calling our shared space, "your house" but happily paid for a cleaning woman twice weekly. I hoped he would occasionally make the coffee in the morning, but he couldn't master my espresso machine, though he hardly tried. Richard did not make any efforts at coming home in time for dinner, or even letting me know when he would arrive. I protested this unreliability to no avail. He also banished my little beagle-something dog Annie from our bed, believing he was making a significant compromise to live with the dog at all.

Richard had additional specific requests that required other changes to my lifestyle—cable television on a big screen, and air conditioning, both entirely unnecessary in my view, and his own phone by the bed. He had handled living alone by talking on the phone late into the night and wasn't ready to give up this lifeline so I got a second phone line installed with Richard's old Albany number. He talked on the phone a lot, often as we relaxed in the king-sized bed he had brought from his apartment to our newly joint household. I insisted he toss all of his polyester sheets and that we get high thread-count cotton sheets and real down pillows.

Richard had objected to the expense but acknowledged the bed was more comfortable.

As he chatted, I loved to look out the three windows in the front of our upstairs bedroom at the star-filled night sky always visible in Hoosick, soothed by the sound of Richard's voice and his living, breathing presence. Sometimes I felt like a voyeur, listening in on these calls. I was uncertain what privacy meant—where the lines were—when you lived with someone, but Richard wanted me near. He relayed my nonverbal reactions to what I was hearing to his listener or asked me what I thought about whatever the topic was. Certainly, I learned a lot about the most important relationships and events in Richard's life by participating in his telephone talk.

Ruth was a frequent caller. Richard hung up on her in rage about half the time. Michael also called often. After a couple of months of our living together, if he didn't get Richard, who often stayed late at work in Albany, he would hang up and call my line. We were getting to be friends. Michael told me he was glad Richard had met me: it proved that there is someone for everyone. Besides, I was smart, and he had a hard time finding people smart enough to talk to, Michael said. This seemed incredibly arrogant on his part, but I took the compliment, glad to be welcomed by someone into the family. I knew Michael's opinion mattered to Richard.

During one of those phone calls Michael described how he experienced his illness. "Staying in touch with reality is hard. Even talking to you now is a challenge," he said.

"Like how?"

"The voices, the images can be overwhelming. It's like sitting in front of two TVs. Reality is on one screen and the psychosis on the other. On a good day the psychosis is on a really small screen and reality on a big screen. It depends."

"Is it okay to ask what is on the psychosis screen?"

"You don't really want to know. Fires. Nazis."

"It's amazing that you have distance from it and can talk about it like this."

"Not easy. My intelligence helps." Michael paused. "When I first got sick, it was all real." He was quiet. I stayed quiet with him. Then he continued.

"Dad was there for me then. Once, I remember being in the studio in Riverdale and thinking that I was about to burn up when he called. I answered and told him about the flames. And he talked me through it."

"How?"

"He said, 'Put your hand out, Mike. Reach out into the flames. I promise you your hand won't get burned. You'll see. The flames are just in your mind.' I was terrified but I listened. I put my hand out and nothing happened. I didn't burn up."

"I really regret that I never got to meet your father."

"It's not the same without him." Michael paused. "But he was ready to die by the end. He had been in so much pain."

"It was about a year ago now, right?"

"Yeah." Michael was quiet for a long time.

I decided to change the subject. "Richard will be home soon, I think. Do you want him to call?"

"Yeah," Michael said slowly.

A few days later, Michael called again. We knew he had completed a ninety-page synopsis of a memoir, essentially a father-son story that climaxed with his graduation from Yale Law School, a kind of triumph over his schizophrenia. Michael's agent, an old friend from Yale, had submitted it to publishers. That night, Michael had news.

"Wow," said Richard into the phone. "Lizzie, you are not going to believe this."

"What?"

"Michael, you tell her," he said, handing me the phone.

"Hey, Mike," I said as I adjusted the pillow behind my head. "What's up?"

"Hollywood is potentially interested in my book project as a screen-play."

"Are you kidding me? How did that happen?"

"Apparently, my agent tells me, someone at Scribner's knew that Ron Howard was on the lookout for an inspirational story about mental illness and pirated a copy of my book proposal and sent it out there. He's interested."

"Oh, my god. That's amazing."

"It could be big. I could make some money. I need money. But there is a lot to negotiate. It's just interest at this point."

"How wonderful. You so deserve a break, my friend. Do you have someone good to help with the negotiations?"

"My agent is going to help find someone who knows Hollywood."

"Mazel tov," I said and laughed. Michael laughed too.

"What did the Rabbi say? —you have a Jewish soul," he said.

"How are you doing otherwise?" I asked, as I was learning to monitor Michael's mental health along with the rest of the family. Michael took a breath in and then began to speak, haltingly.

"Some bad days." He took a long pause. "And they are going to have to change my meds. Always difficult."

"How come?"

"I've been on this old-time antipsychotic forever. It was what got me through law school, but the side effects are starting to pile up. I could go blind."

"You trust your doctor on this?"

Michael chuckled. "Does a paranoid trust anyone?"

"Point taken. Keep us posted on how all of this goes and I'm looking forward to seeing you at Thanksgiving." I handed the phone back to Richard.

After Richard hung up, I said, "Unbelievable. That could be amazing if they make a movie about Michael."

"If it isn't a delusion of grandeur," Richard said.

"Do you think he could be hallucinating this whole movie thing?"

"Probably not. But you never know. I mean, the woman he supposedly chased all over Europe when his breakdown began. I was never convinced she was real. I wonder if Mom knows about this."

"If it were only in his mind, I think it would be more of a done deal. I don't think he would be worried about 'the negotiations,' if it were a delusion."

"Except negotiating a big deal would be something that would make Michael feel important, like a real lawyer, not just a law school graduate."

"It sounded pretty real to me," I said.

"You're probably right. But is it too late to call Mom or Danny?" he asked, looking at the clock, which read 1:00 a.m.

"Yes, even your night owl mother is not up this late. Tomorrow is soon enough to check up on your baby brother," I rolled over into his arms and kissed him. Richard kissed me back.

Over Thanksgiving, we spent time with Richard's family and friends, and the big news around the holiday table was that Michael had not in fact, hallucinated this good news. In a few weeks, he was going to meet Ron Howard at the Plaza Hotel.

Before we drove back upstate on Saturday, Richard and I took Michael out for breakfast at the Riverdale Diner. Michael looked tired and pale as we sat down together in a red vinyl booth by the window. He wasn't making eye contact and kind of smiled into his juice, in a very peculiar way. Richard and I looked at each other. This was not a good day for Michael, but Richard wanted the details of how the deal was going.

"Nothing is set in stone yet. The numbers they are throwing around are over a million," Michael said, eyes still down.

"Good. You'll need that money. It might have to last the rest of your life," Richard replied.

"I'm scared. I don't know what they will do to the story. I don't want a cynical or overly Hollywood-ized version of me out there."

"Mike, for that money, they are probably going to take liberties with the story, and you might have to live with that," I answered.

"Yeah," Michael said, distress in his voice. "I'm trying to retain some control. Like Ron Howard might direct himself, depending on how the script comes out. But I am negotiating for the right to approve another director if it's not him."

"That's good," Richard replied. "Who should play Michael?"

I jumped in, "I think it should be Leonardo DiCaprio. He was great in *This Boy's Life* a couple of years back and was just terrific as Romeo."

"No, he's too white boy." Michael managed a grin.

Richard answered, "There aren't too many great young Jewish actors. There's Michael Douglas but he's too old. So is Dustin Hoffman."

Michael snorted.

"What else are you negotiating?" I asked.

"Another great thing from all of this is the book deal. Scribner's is also now seeing the memoir as a hot project and are ready to snap it up. They are also talking about at least half a million for an advance." Michael paused. "But now there is a lot of pressure to write the entire book." His hand shook as he held his water glass.

Our food came then, and we changed the subject, so that Michael was not center stage. He seemed to calm down as he ate. He and Richard talked about the possibility of the Yankees repeating their World Series win next season and we all approved of the recent political news. Bill Clinton had been re-elected President.

Later, as we drove, Richard and I talked about how sick Michael appeared, even though the potential movie and book deals seemed like such good news.

"He always tells me that the key to staying somewhat sane is to avoid stress. This seems pretty stressful," Richard said.

"But if he can make all this happen, think of how much financial and future life stress he could avoid."

"Yeah. If he gets there," Richard answered.

"Carrie seemed psyched about the movie and book news at Thanksgiving," I said. "I think she has been worried she might have to support him financially if they commit. If he gets this money, they could move back in together to a place with two bathrooms, which is what she said she needs."

Richard nodded. "I hope it works out. She's really good for him, but Michael cannot wrap his head around the fact that she's not Jewish and so far, she has not agreed to convert."

"I haven't agreed for sure to convert either. I'm thinking about it."

"I know. It's okay." Richard's voice was sweet and soft. "We'll take that as it comes."

Chapter 12

The Confession

The boys found a way to keep me "playing" with them until I was eight; it happened every few weeks when the weather allowed us to play outside. The games often started with us pretending something, like we were playing baseball and they made me hit a ball through the window of the White House (a big white house visible from my back yard). The punishment was our naked games. They would always giggle hysterically, plead with me to do more, poke at my butt with long black sticks. The worst was always when one of them put their penis in my butt-crack. In addition to just how creepy and uncomfortable it felt, I always worried that they would pee inside of me.

They had their hold on me. I needed playmates, because otherwise I felt so lonely. I must have let it slip how terrified I was that my parents would find out because the boys would threaten to "tell" on me. I never considered, if they told, they too might be in trouble. Eventually, I decided that playing alone would always be better than this. I wanted it to stop. I began a nightly campaign to find the courage to "tell" on myself and be free of the obligation to bare myself to their wishes.

Late one Saturday night in October of 1963, I was crying alone in bed. It was darker than usual and the state of my soul ever more desolate. I was racked with guilt and terror, at what my telling might bring, but I was determined to tell my mother how bad it was so it could end. My parents were out at a party, and the babysitter was far away, downstairs somewhere, unaware of my crying. The tears flowed hard down my face, the mucus leaking onto the pillow. I worried that when Mom changed the sheets, she would see the stain and know how dirty I was. The waiting felt eternal, although they were home before midnight.

Always attentive to the noises of the house, I heard the back door open and my parents come in, chatting with the babysitter and then Dad leaving to drive her home. My mother's heels clopped on each step as she made her way up the stairs. When the door at the top of the stairs opened, I inhaled sharply. I forced myself to call out to my mother. Her fluttery cocktail dress whispered as she came in. Mom asked, kindly, how come I was still up? I couldn't stifle the crying, and she sat on the bed with me. She seemed surprised by my tears.

Mom said, with a trace of gentleness in her voice, "What's your problem, Liz?" This made me sob more loudly. She helplessly patted my back.

My pain and fear intensified but the need to tell, so I wouldn't be told on, remained. I couldn't stop the tears. Eventually I got out something like, "I did something so wrong."

"What?" Mom asked, again, kindly.

"So, so bad I can't say." I broke down again, heaving, snotty crying.

She waited a minute, seeming puzzled. "Sweetie, you can tell me."

"No, no it was so wrong. So wrong."

"Hmm." Being a practical sort, my mother kept asking questions to get to the bottom of whatever it was that I was now trying but failing to tell her.

"When did you do something so bad?"

"For a long, long time." I slowed a little, sensing that maybe she would figure it out.

"Where was this?"

"Outside. Outside here. In the yard and other yards."

"Oh," said my mother, now seeming to know something. "Whom did you do this bad thing with?"

"Boys."

"Which boys?"

Crying now in some relief I said, "Donny, Jeff, and Mark."

Mom nodded her head with some certainty. "Only those three?"

"Yes," I said, which was kind of a lie, because occasionally there had been one other boy but when he was there it was different; it felt okay with him, not torture. Why tell on him, too?

"Did you show them your uterus?" My mother never learned the word vagina or couldn't bring herself to say it; only in sex ed in junior high school did I learn the word and location of this body part; she had taught me the word uterus to refer to all of my private parts.

"How did you know? How did you know?" I sobbed.

"Well first of all, little boys and girls want to know how each other are made," she paused. "But you mustn't do it again. Right." Until now she had not been stern, but then she was, and continued, "And I knew. Well, do you remember the summer we travelled and some people with a little girl stayed in our house?" This was the summer two years before.

I nodded.

"Well, the boys tried to get her to do it too. They said, 'The little girl that lives here does this all the time with us.' She told her mother, and her mother told me."

This was strange and unsettling information. I had so lived in fear that she would find out, but she knew? I felt stunned, dislocated from what I thought I understood about the world and about my mother.

More importantly, I was free. I never had to play with those boys again.

"You are not going to do this anymore. You may not," my mother said.

"Don't worry Mommy. I won't. I won't even go out to play."

"Good girl." She patted my arm again before she went to change for bed.

We never discussed it again. I was an adult before I realized that my mother could have ended the abuse years before.

Chapter 13

First Flight and Da Fuzz

Richard and I were going to visit my parents for the first time for Christmas. His nervousness was apparent even before leaving for the Albany airport. Clutching the map tightly, he checked the road signs at each intersection, though he knew better than I where the airport was. He had been on planes before, though not often. Richard liked to stay in one place and avoided novelty if possible. Now, beyond his usual nerves at being anywhere that wasn't under the bedcovers, he had worries about meeting my parents, at Christmas. I always felt a strain, too, going to Illinois, with so much left out of the conversation.

I made sure we had plenty of time to get to the airport, and although Richard was not a careful packer, we got our luggage checked, travelled through (pre-9/11) security and arrived at our gate on time. Richard had a wild-eyed look and was sweating.

We sat on the runway awhile before take-off, triggering my own anxiety about making the connection downstate from Chicago. The way the terminals were arranged at O'Hare, it was a good twenty-minute walk between the big and little planes. And that was if we walked at my pace; Richard moved like a tortoise.

Richard perused the inflight magazine and studied all the buttons overhead to know what they meant. He then remembered to flag down the flight attendant for a seat belt extender, which embarrassed him, but he still tried to chat the woman up. She was all business.

Richard asked me again, "So what all are we going to do in Charleston?"

"It will be very slow moving," I said. "We are going to do the Cookie Bake at Wendy's on Thursday. Christmas is Friday, and then we may go to the big Tingley family party down in Marshall on Sunday."

Richard nodded, seeming to take that all in. "When you say Christmas is Friday, what does that mean? Do we go to church?" As he asked, I realized that in his family, many religious holidays involved going to synagogue.

"No, no, no. No one in my family goes to church anymore, thank god." I laughed. "I bet my mother would kind of like to, though." Since I petitioned to quit Sunday school when I was thirteen, I had no knowledge of either of my parents going to church, though I was sure they were still nominal, dues-paying Methodists. "But I don't think, unless Christmas is on Sunday, there even is a church service. Maybe on Christmas Eve."

"I would like to go," he said. This was shocking, given his religious anti-Christmas views. He continued, "I have been to a lot of midnight masses on Christmas Eve—my friend Pam often plays the flute. I like the music."

"We could ask my mother about it." I hesitated. "Mostly Christmas means food, eating a really sweet coffee cake for breakfast, lighting a fire in the fireplace, and opening presents before lunch, which is kind of a repeat of Thanksgiving: turkey, stuffing, you know. And always an oyster stew on Christmas Eve."

Richard nodded, an uneasy look on his face.

Our flight took off about a half-hour late and was uneventful but arriving at O'Hare with only ten minutes to get to the commuter flight. We practically ran through the airport, sweating. Richard lost sight of me at one point and began screaming, "Lizzie, Lizzie, where are you?" I was just three steps to his left. We arrived finally at the little gate to find the commuter flight was also running behind. I gasped, catching my breath at the check-in desk, in front of a very harassed looking American Eagle Airlines customer service agent. Trying to make a joke, I said, "Couldn't you arrange the airport a little better, so we didn't have to run a mile to get here?"

The agent took this as a nasty customer complaint and raised her voice, letting me know this was not her problem. I sensed her attitude was fat shaming. She seemed to be implying that we were barely ambulatory, fat, and ought to arrange our travel plans accordingly. Richard looked as if he might yell at the women for being rude to his girlfriend.

"Sorry, sorry," I said, putting my hand on Richard's arm, catching his eye as if to say, *Can you believe this asshole?* As we stepped back from the counter, the agent announced that boarding would begin in fifteen minutes.

I told Richard that I had to go to the restroom and would be right back.

"Can't you just wait until we are on the plane?" he pleaded frantically.

"No," I snapped and reversed course to the restroom. I called over my shoulder, "She's not boarding the plane for fifteen minutes."

I took my time in the restroom, needing a minute away from Richard's frazzle. Seeing my parents was not stress-free for me, either. Besides, never a morning person, I had gotten up ridiculously early and was already worn out. Back to the gate, boarding had begun, Richard standing in line with all of our carry-on luggage and both our coats.

He yelled, "I thought I was going to have to hijack the plane for you. What took so long?"

The same service agent looked incredulously at Richard and said, "I heard that. I can't believe I heard that." It appeared she might stop us from boarding, but instead left the ticket-taking line and returned to the customer service desk.

We settled into our seats on the tiny commuter plane, then waited a long time, with no announcements. The holiday spirit was upon most passengers and there was a buzz in the air. I started to relax. Then, I heard distant sirens, odd at an airport. The sirens grew closer. Glancing out the tiny plane window, I saw three Chicago police cruisers surrounding the plane.

My stomach lurched. The door to the cabin burst open and in came four cops and the agent. "That's him," she cried out, pointing at Richard. One cop approached and asked Richard to come with him.

Richard turned to me and said, "Go ahead. I'll figure this out."

The cop turned to me. "Are you with him?" I had to say yes, and after asking if we had checked luggage and giving over our tickets with the luggage tags, we were both escorted off.

Surrounded by four cops, with the airline agent in the lead, lugging coats and carry-on luggage, which included shopping bags loaded with wrapped Christmas presents, we headed into the bowels of O'Hare International Airport, trekking for about fifteen minutes before coming to a door labeled "Airport Security."

I was scared. What would happen to Richard? Threatening to hijack a plane, even in jest, was potentially a federal offense. And how were my parents going to react to this large and impressive snafu? My views of the Chicago police were formed during the 1968 Democratic convention, when they beat up protesters. *Pigs*, I was used to calling them. I would have to try hard to keep that vibe out of whatever came next.

We were taken inside a warren of small, glass-enclosed offices and cubicles, to a windowless room with a small conference table. We could see cops and what appeared to be supervisory personnel and the service agent conferring. Richard face was grim, but he was quiet, as if composing himself.

I said, "Jesus. Fuck." He smiled.

I had no idea how he was going to behave next. One of the apparent supervisors and two cops entered, the beefy one taking the lead.

"You want to tell me what happened?" he asked Richard. I could see something shift in Richard's body, and he made direct eye contact with the officer.

"Yes, Officer. I am sorry about this. I think there is a misunderstanding." Richard paused. "Some of the problem is that very excitable clerk. My fiancée was taking too long in the restroom, and I got concerned that she was going to miss the flight. When she returned, I tried to make a joke with my fiancée, saying in a low voice that I thought I 'might have to hijack the plane.' Let me be clear. I did not say that I *planned* to hijack the plane. And, I did not say it to any airline personnel. I believe the clerk was eavesdropping on a private conversation."

Richard paused and smiled at the officer. "You know how it is with women. They can be so slow."

I got it. He was going man-to-man with the cop.

"Yeah, okay. Anything else you want to add?"

Here I had to interject. "That lady had an attitude towards us from the minute we arrived at the gate. She was rude to begin with and I think she had it in for us. I tried to joke with her, and she got really upset. I'd question her about that."

Richard waved at me to shut up. He thought he had this. He started to speak again, quite deliberately, as if his inner attorney, Columbia Law School graduate was emerging. He was treating this like court. "Look Officer, we are sorry for the misunderstanding here and I do take seriously the error in judgment I made when I made that remark. But I do think, as my fiancée says, that there was an overreaction. Before this unfortunate situation arose, I was thinking of making a complaint to the airline company about the clerk's insults."

I stayed quiet; he was right to shut me up.

"Okay. Be back in a minute."

They all left the room, but this time left the door open. We saw the lead cop get on the phone and could hear part of what he said.

"Yeah. Yeah. Well, the guy's wife was taking too long in the john, and he was worried she would miss the flight and then he said it to her, that he thought he might 'have to,'" the cop made quotations marks with his free hand, "you know 'hijack.'" He continued, "Yeah, I also think there was a situation with the girl at the ticket line." If we looked beyond the cop, we could see the service agent being addressed by the supervisor, perhaps being berated. That looked promising.

After leaving us to cool our heels for quite a while, the beefy cop and an airline guy in a suit returned.

"Just so you know, you could have been facing serious charges, pal," the cop told Richard. "But we are going to let you go."

"Thank you, officer," Richard said. We rose to leave.

"Not so fast," said the airline guy. "As a consequence of your actions, American Airlines is banning you from further flight with us today."

"So how are we going to get downstate, to my aged parents?" I asked.

"That's not our problem. You'd be eligible to fly tomorrow, although getting a reservation may be difficult," he paused. "And costly." They were clearly not going to roll this over as just a missed connection.

Richard stood, offered his hand around to the guys, and said, "We'll manage."

We picked up our stuff and started out, Richard's hand on my back. I appreciated his protective gesture. When we were about 20 yards down the corridor, we both burst out laughing—in our shared 1960s ideals, we had survived an encounter with "the fuzz." For me this was quickly replaced by anxiety about my parents' reactions and what they were being told. How distressed they would be when we did not arrive on our flight. Not to mention the reason.

"How are we going to do this?" Richard asked.

"We could take a train or a bus, but that would involve going into downtown Chicago and that's not close. Maybe we could rent a car," I said. At the first bank of pay phones, I called Hertz and Avis, but no one had cars this close to Christmas. My stress level shot up, and I began to fear my parents' reaction. I had spent my life trying not to upset them and this delay, without a clear end, and the reason for it, was certain to "discommode" them—their term when things didn't go according to plan.

Surprising me, Richard stepped up. With a card from his wallet in hand, he picked up the receiver next to me and dialed customer service at the American Bar Association. He said he needed a car for an emergency trip to visit a client. Hertz had a car just for us. I also reached my parents, who had gone home from the airport, and were waiting to hear from us. They had been informed by the airline of the reason for the delay and were, I could tell, "tense," the only adjective they ever used to describe a negative emotional state. I reassured them we would be there in time for a late-ish dinner.

Dad, dressed in khakis, his button-down Brooks Brothers blue shirt covered by a tan sweater, opened the back door, smiled broadly at me and shook Richard's hand. "Glad to meet you, Richard." I knew his inner mantra at that moment was "Anyone who is okay with Liz is okay with us." Just inside, my mother, in her sensible shoes, dried her hands on her apron and greeted Richard with a friendly smile. We sat right down for a reheated dinner of my favorite foods, steak and parsleyed potatoes, at the ridiculously late hour of 8 p.m. (Mom normally served dinner at 5:30 sharp.)

In their characteristic midwestern stoicism, my parents uttered no words of complaint at our lateness but seemed quite worn out. After dinner Richard even helped do the dishes, clearly trying to impress the folks and make up for his faux pas. Cleanup chores done, Richard whispered asking if he could go out to smoke a cigar, one of his main stress relievers. I motioned him out. After an hour, he was still out in the cold night. I chuckled. Richard must need mega-stress reduction after this day, now at a close at nearly 10:00 PM, when everyone my parents knew, including themselves, were about to go to bed.

In the dark, quiet midwestern night, the phone rang.

"Who on earth could that be at, this hour?" asked my father.

"I'll get it," I said, though adding on pounds as I lived with Richard, I was still faster on my feet than either parent.

"Hello," I spoke into the heavy receiver of their 1940s standard black telephone.

"Yes, this is the Charleston Police. Is this the Tingley residence?"

"Yes," I answered cautiously.

"Yes, ma'am. We got a call about a suspicious person on your block of Harrison Avenue, and we have been talking with this gentleman. He says he is visiting you. Do you have someone visiting you?"

"Yes. Yes, we do. Is he in trouble?"

"No, ma'am, as long he is who he says he is."

"Yes, that is Richard Laudor, my fiancé."

"Okay, ma'am. Thank you for your cooperation."

Hanging up, I started laughing hysterically.

"Who was that, Liz?" Dad inquired.

"Someone in the neighborhood called the cops on Richard," I gurgled out between the laughter. "They thought he was suspicious."

"Really? That's bizarre." Dad seemed incredulous.

The phone rang again. "Hello?"

"Lizzie?" came Richard's plaintive voice. "I got lost trying to come back to you. I had to flag the cops back down to call you."

"Oh, Jesus. Where are you? Should I come outside?"

"Maybe you better." Without putting on shoes or a coat, I dashed out the front door, to see Richard at the end of the block, next to the police car, lights flashing.

I yelled "over here," and Richard started down the block. I ran to him in my stocking feet, grabbed his hand, and made him run back with me. Inside, Mom was on the stairs just past the front door, going up to bed.

"Everything all right?" she asked.

"Yeah, fine, Mom. Just been a long day."

"I put the sheets out for Richard on the bed in the TV room and you are upstairs in your room."

I waved, "Sure, Mom," having known all along that Richard would be sleeping downstairs and me upstairs. I didn't expect, even at age 41, to share a bed in my mother's house, pre-marriage, but we kind of needed each other then. Trips home with other boyfriends had shown that Mom and Dad never came back downstairs, once they were in bed. Richard and I cuddled on the pull-out bed, relaxing into each other. Then Richard pulled back a little, got an impish grin on his face, and began to sing to me, in his usual sweet way.

"Over the river and through the woods to Grandmother's house we go… The horse knows the way…" And at that verse we both started laughing deep belly laughs.

I punched his arm, only sort of gently. "Some horse. You should be glad you are not in the Federal pen right now."

Richard continued laughing before choking out, "I know," and taking me back in his arms. We held each other for a long time before I went up to my childhood bedroom for the last hours of sleep.

In the morning, my parents were up before me, having coffee. When I entered the kitchen, Mom asked, "How did you sleep Liz?" She didn't know I was a lifelong insomniac. "Pretty well, thanks. Have you heard from Richard yet?"

"No," Dad replied. "Hoping he gets a good rest."

We sat quietly, companionable over very weak coffee, theirs always black. Mom had learned to buy half and half for me, so I tolerated it. I had to drink about six cups of their coffee to feel appropriately caffein-ated.

"Do you know what time the cookie bake is?" I asked. Mom looked startled.

"That's up to you and Wendy and I suppose Martha" she said, refer-ring to Wendy's mother.

"Okay, I'll give a call." I returned after phoning Wendy from that same ancient phone in the front hall.

"You need to get a new phone, Mom. I can't even check my voice mail on that phone."

"Oh no. We are not getting a new phone. We wanted to keep renting the phone from the phone company, so they are responsible for fixing it. But they wouldn't let us do that, so they *gave* the phone it us. Now we will have to pay for any repairs," Mom answered with a touch of outrage in her voice.

"Your mother is nothing if not thrifty," Dad said. Mom sniffed.

Just as this conversation ended, Richard appeared. Mom offered him coffee which he thanked her for, and promptly filled with cream as I had. It was nearly noon.

"We are due at the cookie bake at 2."

"Can you give me the full plan for the weekend?"

I reiterated the schedule, with today for baking cookies, tomorrow for Christmas at home, and Sunday for the Tingley family Christmas party. "We can relax tomorrow." Richard nodded.

We spent the afternoon rolling out, cutting, and icing sugar cookies, with a lively crew—Wendy, her brother and sister, our other childhood friend Andrea, and Wendy's mother whose warmth and good humor filled the space. As in any new situation, Richard watched, and appeared frightened to try his hand at cookie decorating. He was quiet, although he made a pun or two, which were immediately groaned at in affectionate ways by the group. Jeff created his annual anatomically correct snowman, which got a laugh as always. Richard asked somewhat incredulously, "Is that allowed?"

Jeff cheerfully replied, "It was only shocking 25 years ago," and we all laughed again. This was comfortable enough.

On Christmas morning, after coffee and coffee cake, Dad lit a fire in the fireplace and we sat around the tree, opening presents. I had done all the buying myself but pretended some of the gifts were from Richard. Later Richard remarked, "That's kind of just like Hannukah when we were kids."

On Sunday as we drove to the extended Tingley family Christmas party, a potluck affair, I was explaining to Richard who we were going to see. "My grandfather had four brothers and they were all orphaned early in the 20th century. This gave them a strong bond, all staying close to family land. The people we are going to see are Dad's first cousins and all of their very large extended families. Most of their children already have children." I paused. "We will get to meet Cousin Howard, who is a little off. Last we met, he asked if I had 'found a man yet.'" Richard laughed.

Dad said, "Yeah I don't know what Howard's problem is." Silently I hoped no one would say anything overtly anti-Semitic." I realized I needed to warn Richard about the food.

"Be ready, Richard. There will be lots of highly starched and salted dishes and desserts with Jell-O and Cool Whip."

Richard laughed. "You know, I love that stuff."

We arrived at Guy and Helen Tingley's farmhouse, set among cornfields, now empty and frozen. Some bundled up little kids were playing in the yard. Dad waved at them, and we trailed after him inside. My mother had never really enjoyed these gatherings. She and Grandma, Dad's mother, had a tortuous relationship—never addressed directly. Those who knew Grandma would always report on her "highs" and "lows." In these mood swings, she could be quite mean and onery, and likely her genetics contributed to the vulnerability to depression, in my father and me. Now with Grandma dead, the tension around Tingley events was less intense.

Mom seemed to enjoy talking to the cousins I grew up with, and the Tingley wives, who were quite chatty. They had to be because Tingley men rarely, if ever, spoke. Occasionally one of them would sidle up to me at these occasions, pat my shoulder and say, "Good you could get home Elizabeth." Then there was Harry Bill, the middle son of Dad's eldest cousin Bill. Harry was gay and had gotten out of town. He had a partner and lived in Chicago, where they both held church music jobs. Harry would go on to study to be a minister in a liberal tradition. Strangely it was Harry who set my nerves afire, about potential antisemitism. His partner Gary, a man with an operatic voice, was teaching at a fancy private Chicago high school. Harry began to discuss how hard it had been for Gary at the holiday season, as he wanted the high school choir to sing all the sacred classics for their holiday concert. There were too many Jews in the school who rebuffed "Christmas music" but this music was the height of beauty. Richard did not remark on this, but later said, "He just doesn't have a clue."

Inside, the place was packed, full of people I didn't even recognize. This was better attended than some of these functions. Dad has two female cousins but only one of them was present. The other escaped, to Utah. Carl, Bill, Guy, Edgar Gene Tingley and families were all present.

We got through the rest of the holiday intact, with no more mishaps and Richard in his own nervous way seemed to enjoy meeting everyone and seeing everything. I was so happy for him to see the little world I came from.

When getting ready to return to New York, my mother found me packing Richard's suitcase. She put her hand on my shoulder and said, in a low, quiet voice, "I believe he depends on you a great deal." Mom was usually concrete, quite un-attuned to the subtleties of interaction or emotion, and rarely spoke to anything directly. This sentence from her was completely uncharacteristic. An ancient rage tried to come into consciousness. *Where did I learn to need to be needed, but from you and Dad?* But then, I moved quickly to another thought. *I'm happy that she could see that Richard and I are so very close.*

Chapter 14

Backwash

After my brother died, and then after those neighborhood boys lost their power over me, nothing bad happened *to me* for a very long time, but there were aftershocks, of seismic proportions. I got quite depressed in eighth grade. The depression dominated and constrained me for a very long time, changing who I was and what I could be.

Until then, I was a smart, funny, lively child, a leader of my peers. In third grade, I had organized a pencil drop, the whole class dropping pencils at the same moment. Our teacher laughed. In junior high, there was the time we ran away from the Girl Scout leaders on a hike. Huffing and puffing as the adults caught up, I led the troop in a chorus of "We Shall Overcome." I was president of the Student Council and the Methodist Youth Fellowship, and editor of the junior high yearbook.

It was as yearbook editor that I found myself slipping down and away. I stopped calling meetings of the yearbook committee, working solo, just to *finish*. I didn't find any fun in it. I put the yearbook to bed, all by myself, without a crew to joke around with or celebrate the accomplishment. I didn't feel like celebrating anything.

As president of Methodist Youth Fellowship, I planned an ice-skating party. Suddenly I loathed ice skating. I had always fallen frequently, though cheerfully, on the ice but now I minded. I didn't want to be cold or look like an unfeminine klutz. As skating ended, I went into the church kitchen and found the refreshment committee goofing off.

They had *not* heated up the cocoa and all the other cold skaters would be in soon. I shooed the other kids away, angrily. Just as I had with the yearbook, I would take care of everything myself.

My main preoccupation, never admitted, was boys. I thought I was ugly, boy-like, and too smart for any boy to like me. I was still a tomboy—working to be something else, though I didn't really understand what that was or how to transform. I still loved beating Larry Paap after school at tetherball in my back yard. But I also wanted Larry to like *like* me, and I could tell he never would. I also worked at being stupid in school, but it was hard to silence my intelligence. I failed daily.

If only a boy would like me as a girl, but I knew I was too damaged and disgusting. Kenny Ramsey confirmed this for me one junior high summer. We went for a walk near dusk, but I explained I had to be home before dark, alluding to my mother's fear of rape. His nasty reply, "Who would want to rape you?" verified, so clearly, what I already knew, and killed any hope otherwise.

By fall 1970 at age fifteen, I experienced a full-blown major depression. I had transferred to the public high school, as the shelter of my progressive university elementary school ended in ninth grade. At the high school, all the tough townie kids didn't know me, weren't friendly, and didn't much like us "university brats" altogether. I was no longer a "big man on campus" and it stung. One of the first days in homeroom, I heard a boy one row over ask a fellow uni-brat who I was. That girl said, "Oh that's Liz. She is a brain. She doesn't like boys." And then, the worst of *those* boys, from the neighborhood, showed up in my math class. He was now very, very fat with long stringy, greasy hair and a nasty, guarded look in his eye. He sometimes stole glances at me across the room. I was sure that he was going to spread rumors, and give me a "bad reputation," for what I had done as a little girl, something that was to be feared more than death.

I fell into a dark hole.

Every day, I wore the same clothes, a dark navy skirt, a blue chambray work shirt, and a navy sweatshirt, so I would be invisible. I couldn't give up my distinctness altogether and wore a blue pin with half a white dove on it, still protesting the Vietnam war, but silently. At school, I did not utter a word all day long. I refused to wear a winter coat. I wanted to be cold; perhaps I could freeze to death. I tried to hide, sitting on the floor in front of my locker grasping my knees to my body, head down.

All the color leached out. Literally, my eyes saw only black, the world inside and out splashed with coal colored India ink. I spent long hours fantasizing about killing myself. I needed pills, I thought of razor blades. I could throw myself in front of a freight train. I could crash the car. I could dive into the quarry and hit my head on a rock. One of the druggie kids I connected with a little said if I was going to do it, take a few hits of acid and jump off Old Main, the tallest building in town.

Surprisingly, I did not ever *try* to kill myself, then or later, though it was a primary preoccupation. I had this tough internal voice that would surface in those moments, asking if there was even an ounce of wanting to be "rescued" and if so, I couldn't follow through. I was tough on myself, and there was my sacred duty. When Jim died, I had to keep my parents alive. They needed me to be okay, and this was constant pressure, a mountainside of rock bearing down on me.

In school, this meant I had to excel, while caring nothing about it. I had to get all A's because that mattered to them. Fortunately, the high school was not rigorous. I did my schoolwork in a haze; it was mostly so easy as to be laughable, but I took no pleasure in succeeding. I forced myself with every ounce of strength. I cheated sometimes by copying others' work. No adult noticed a thing; no one said *we ought to be concerned about this kid. This is not who she is.*

One time, in my house alone, looking at myself in the upstairs bathroom mirror, I imagined slicing my throat open with a razor blade, when my father came home unexpectedly and startled me. I started screaming, wordless uncontrollable terror. His response was to retreat back downstairs and pretend nothing had happened. I pretended too.

In the end, the teenage depression receded, although I didn't ever again feel exactly right—for decades. It left without any psychiatric or psychological attention. I did confide, sort of, in the hip young minister of the youth group. He took pains to look out for me, whenever I showed up at a church event or the coffee house at the campus ministry. He lived with a communal group of seven adults and seven children and I became their babysitter. In a scenario that continued for much of my life, the kids saved me. With them, I was in the moment, playing and caring for them, which sometimes included even chasing them around the block when they refused to take a bath or go to bed. The roughhousing, laughter, affection brought me back to life.

The other thing that saved me was reading *Summerhill* by A.S. Neill, the story of a "free" school in England. Neill had some tie, somehow, to psychoanalysis, and knew that children are inherently sexual beings. In his writing, for the first time, I learned that other children—and not just me—when they are little are interested in each other's bodies and engage in "sex play." Although that wasn't really what happened to me, at the time this knowledge took the tiniest edge off my sense that I was a pervert. Maybe I wasn't just bad, wicked, disgusting, and weird. The dark cavern of my depression finally sprouted a few holes, pinprick-sized only, but some light began to trickle in, penetrating all the way to the bottom, and to me.

That was my first depressive episode. The depression came back often and with more intensity each time. But since I also functioned well, few knew this about me. In college I struggled nearly every day to beat the blues, and managed. I got by. I sought geographical cures by transferring colleges twice. I made a pact with myself, if you don't get a boyfriend by the end of sophomore year, you can kill yourself. I got a boyfriend.

After college, as an English major with still unarticulated writer ambitions, I moved to New York. Instead of writing or a publishing career, I enrolled at Bank Street College in a program called "Infant and Parent Development." I was going to work with very young children—the age I was when Jim was dying and then dead. I was on a mission, to take seriously the experience of young children, even before they could talk. I didn't know that I was still grieving for Jim and that my daily work put me in touch both with both the joy-moments of being fully present that children take you to, and with the dead weight of unmetabolized grief. New York was hell for me; I got beaten up at 88th and Broadway on my first day by a crazy street person. I hated the crowds, the speeded pace, the subway, and the dirt.

I attempted yet another geographical cure, landing a job as a toddler teacher in one of Harvard University's childcare centers and moved to Cambridge. With a master's degree in 1979, I made $5,400. I lived communally, mostly with people I knew through Oberlin, made ends meet, and went to the ocean a lot. I met people who would become some of my very best friends, for decades, during those Cambridge days.

I tried to change into an adult and sought in 1983 to go to grad school in psychology. I was rejected everywhere I applied. I was sucked back down into the darkest river, rapidly headed out to sea. I functioned barely, although I did manage to get a new job, kicked upstairs and out of the classroom, as director of the Harvard Law School Child Care Center.

Before the new job started, I planned to visit Illinois in June of 1983. Just before I left, my father called to tell me that Granddad Tingley had fallen and maybe had a stroke. He was in the hospital in Terre Haute,

Indiana. This dropped me into the glories of my complicated family web, into its taut, tense vibrating mess—a significant part of which was unacknowledged, failed grief, now on the increase. I loved my grandfather. He was a simple, kind, good man, a farmer, who had known sorrow in his life. Orphaned at age five, he and his four brothers were sent to different relatives, some who were not always kind. He made it plain that he thought I, as his only grandchild, was the best. He beamed when I entered a room, always.

Arrangements to visit him in the hospital were not easily negotiated. My father had a thorny relationship with his mother, made more intense by the repressed, yet always present, hatred between her and my mother. Grandma wanted Dad to take her to Terre Haute and back, about a ninety-minute drive each way, every day. My father felt this was too much; my mother certainly did, although she would never say so. After all, Granddad was in a coma; he would not know if anyone was there. Did I want to come on the next visit? My parents asked me this hesitantly, as if sure that I should say no. I went, with Dad and Grandma.

The scene at Granddad's bedside was one of the most enraging experiences of my life, and certainly close to the saddest, none of which had any outlet, or expression, there in the bosom of my family. Grandma held Granddad's hand.

"Squeeze if you can hear me, Fred," she said, loudly.

My father stared up at the ceiling, in angry contempt, at what I think he saw in his conscious mind as uneducated sentimentality, a failure to consider the scientific facts governing a coma. Granddad was unconscious. A tear rolled down Grandma's cheek. Dad escorted her to the waiting room, but I stayed behind. I too held my dying grandfather's hand, and talked to him in the soothing tones I used when I put children down for a nap. I didn't want him to be alone, even though my father was likely right that he had no conscious awareness. I kept talking, soothing, and at times it seemed like Granddad opened his eyes. I felt fine; I would have stayed like that, with him in some sense, all day. But after about fifteen minutes, Dad came charging back into the room.

"What are you doing in here?" he asked, angrily. I was speechless. "You've been in here too long. We are leaving. Grandma can come back in and say some sort of goodbye if she wants."

I felt ripped away, but I stayed true to my family ethos: I said nothing.

I never saw Granddad again. I was so angry, confused and dislocated, and full of sorrow. Why couldn't I stay with him? That dark river, the depression, turned into a tidal wave, an inky black sea rushing over me, swallowing me whole. This depression would take me into uncharted waters.

I fell apart in the spring of 1984. Since the winter I had been utterly faking it. I lay down on the floor of my office and tried to sleep most workdays. Then it came on, at its worst.

I was resolute. I would put a note outside on the door. My cousin, who was staying with me during the week, would find it when he returned: "Don't come in. Call the cops."

I would put the chain on so he couldn't find me himself.

I had the rope and the hook in the ceiling. Really though, I didn't know how to tie the knot. So maybe it was just the idea of a plan, not a real plan.

But I had practiced, placing the rope around my neck and pulling tight. That felt good, feeling the breath get cut off and thinking I would black out. Perfect. I sat quietly. Thinking, feeling nothing. Empty. Strangely fine. This was a better plan than a bottle of good Scotch and all the pills I had in the dunes on Plum Island.

There was nothing around me but black air, in the literal sense: I looked into the open air and saw only that it was black. I thought this was real.

The phone rang. For some reason I answered. It was Gayle, a friend and mother of Mollie, a baby I liked to play with. She knew I was going through hard times and asked how I was. I said something, I don't know what. She said, "We will be right there. Hold on."

I sat in the darkness, not thinking she would really come.

Then, there she was, with her baby Mollie, and Connie, another friend. She had me hold the baby and Mollie's baby's breath let me feel something. I told them about practicing with the rope. Connie told me to call my therapist, Dr. Seidman, who told me that I had to go to the hospital. Gayle was getting directions and she asked for a pen. I couldn't find one. Gayle said, "No wonder you want to kill yourself. You're a writer and you don't have a pen in your house."

I was sent to a hospital in Jamaica Plain, across the city from my place in Cambridge. Gayle drove, Connie in back with Mollie. It was late now, close to midnight.

Something broke in me as we drove, broke in a different way. The entire pretense that I was strong or special or different, that my mission was to keep my parents alive, broke. I thought fleetingly that my breaking down might kill my parents, but realized I had no choice. I let go. Instead of more darkness, instead I suddenly felt human in a new way. I was no better or worse than anyone else. I was simply trying to get through the night. Wasn't everyone?

I spent two weeks on a locked ward of a very bad psychiatric hospital. And there, I continued to find a loosening of every sense of my supposed specialness and an expansion of my average membership in the human race. I did feel a kinship with everyone else who had broken down.

Two weeks in a very bad hospital did not make me better. But finding I belonged there would change me forever.

One image from that time, near the end of my stay, stuck with me. In one way at least, I was different, though not any more special than my fellow depressed patients; I was different because every night I had a parade of friends come to visit. All the workers and other patients sort of wanted to be in my room, too. Though I still felt alone, I seemed different from most other depressed, isolated patients I encountered there. I had friends. One night there was quite a crowd. Connie, Cathy, my cousin Stephen, and others. My friends were just getting to know Stephen, who was living in my apartment while job hunting in Boston. A recent graduate of the Rhode Island School of Design, and a painter, he had to find a way to make a living. He had also known me as a kid.

Connie asked, "What do you remember about Liz when she was little?"

Stephen, a very sweet guy, smiled. "I loved going to visit her in Illinois. She was so fun. I remember her jumping over zinnias in her father's backyard."

I thought to myself *I just leapt past them. I couldn't feel their colors,* but I didn't say this out loud. They were, after all, trying to be here for me, and cheer me up. I was glad that Stephen knew something about me, and that he cared.

When released from the hospital, I saw my therapist twice or three times a week for seven years. Larry Seidman, Ph.D. saved my life.

Chapter 15

Mission, Michael

As 1997 began, Richard and I faced some big decisions. The jobs that had brought us both north to upstate New York and Vermont were ending. I was caught in a nationally publicized crazed faculty-administration war at Bennington and needed out. Richard had been hired to do one big case, and victory was in sight. Where would we live and what would we do? I thought we wanted a future together, but Richard appeared to develop cold feet about getting married. I hesitated over making a geographic move, without some assurance of a commitment. So, as experienced consumers of mental health services, we began couples counseling. After listening carefully to our story, the older woman social worker told Richard in no uncertain terms that I needed a ring on my finger and a wedding date. Without these conventions, she said, he couldn't expect me to move anywhere with him. While I found this sort of hilariously traditional—diamonds were never on my list of needs or wants—Richard took her lecture to heart. Besides, he said, he didn't want to lose me.

We made a big deal of the engagement and summoned my parents from Illinois and his family and friends from New Rochelle for a "surprise announcement" in the late spring. Richard gave me a sapphire ring and I presented him with a watch, our families looking on. What was left, to make a life as a married couple, was to figure out where to live, what we would each do in our careers, and then—plan a wedding.

I had contemplated going back to school so I could add clinical work to my repertoire as a psychologist, and Richard said he hated being a lawyer. So, in our forties, in a highly unpractical approach to our futures, we decided to become full-time students and begin all over again, together. I applied to programs that would allow me to re-specialize in clinical work or programs that would give me a second Ph.D. in clinical psychology, and Richard applied to graduate school in public policy. We would go wherever we both could study, hopefully New York City. I believed that, given how much Richard bitched about living in the middle of nowhere, how much he needed to be close to his brother Michael, to a Jewish community, to his old friends and haunts, and how much he hated change, the only place he could be happy was in or very near New York City.

I had a very ambivalent relationship to the city, where I'd lived in my early twenties in the late 1970s, when it was crime ridden and unsafe—proven by my beating at the hands of a drug-addled half-naked woman. I had made the mistake of making eye contact and thinking in my wondrously open midwestern way, that she needed my help. She ran at me screaming, "I'm going to kill you bitch," and pummeled me down Broadway as I tried to get away. I developed a bit of a post-traumatic stress reaction and had fled to the kinder, gentler city of Boston at the end of my master's program. But I could see that life with Richard, who I was willing to follow to the ends of the earth, might take us there, and I psyched myself up for that possibility.

I was invited for interviews at two graduate programs in New York in the middle of March, and Richard accompanied me for the weekend before the interviews. We had dinner with Michael and Carrie.

"It's really happened," Michael said over Chinese food on the Upper West Side.

"I heard. Tell us," I said.

"I closed both the book and the movie deal." Michael was recently back from a trip to Hollywood, where he now had an agent and had partied with film industry royalty.

"Amazing."

"Yeah." He grinned down into the teacup and then up at Carrie. Her eyes were shining like beacons back at him and she squeezed his hand in a moment of what appeared to be joyful intimacy.

"I wasn't sure I could get him on the plane before he left," Carrie said. "But Murray prescribed some extra Valium so he could cope."

"It was very LA, west coast, driving around to studio offices and restaurants," Michael explained. "Some of the people I met were real cynics and not nice folks. But I trusted Ron Howard. He seemed like a mensch. He told me his father had been really important to him, too, and he promised he would honor that part of my story. I looked him in the eye, and we shook on the deal." Then Michael got that wonderful impish grin again, and it suffused his whole being.

"Before I met with Howard," Michael snorted, "these three blond bimbos took me to the restaurant for the final sit down. As he came through the front door, one of them leaned over to me and whispered, 'Whatever you do, don't call him Opie.'" Michael started laughing hard. We all joined in.

"What was the final price tag, Michael?" Richard asked.

"One point two million for the rights to the screenplay. And the contract with Scribner's to do the book came in at six hundred fifty thousand!"

Carried added, "We found an apartment to move back in together, a garden apartment in Hastings in the apartment complex where Tomas and Amy live." Tomas was Michael's best friend from law school; Michael's father had called Tomas his fourth son. "Now we can afford a place with two bathrooms," Carrie said, looking so happy.

"Yeah," said Michael, tenderly, gazing into Carrie's eyes again.

This was such good news. I glanced up at Richard, beaming over the success of his little brother.

I realized that if one day we settled in New York, we could see Michael and Carrie every weekend, make meals together, maybe raise children together, and be a family. Along with wanting Richard, I wanted, and needed, a family.

My interviews went well, and I was accepted into the CUNY clinical psychology doctoral program. Richard was going to study public policy at NYU. We were moving to New York City.

"Lizzie, do you think you could help Michael out at the end of the month?" Richard asked me.

"What does he need?"

We were lying in bed in a dark basement room in Albany. I had sold my house, and we were buying a small coop in Riverdale, in the north-west Bronx. Richard would be staying on in Albany for a few months to finish the big anti-trust case before joining me in New York full time, renting a room in a friend's basement for the short term. Meanwhile, I was homeless, briefly staying with him in that wretched basement, and with other friends in Cambridge and New York until we closed on the Riverdale apartment.

"He's going to be in the house Mom rents on Block Island, but Carrie has to come back to work for his second week there." I knew Ruth had decided not to go because she'd broken her shoulder, even though she paid the rent on the place. Richard continued, "Michael is thinking it might not be a good idea for him to be alone there."

"Do you think I could bring Annie?" I asked. Finding a place that would house my dog and me together was challenging in this brief period between homes.

"I will ask Mom if the Cushmans allow dogs in their house, but I don't think we would need to tell them."

"You know I love the beach. Of course, I would babysit," I said, thinking that I would never go back there if Ruth were there. I enjoyed Michael's company and was trying hard to be a good helpmeet for Richard.

In spite of Michael's newfound success, he was not doing well. His psychosis was peeking through again, especially because the new medication cocktail was not yet working. Michael reported he was often exhausted by a few hours of lucidity and needed to sleep many hours a day to compensate. He was under a lot of pressure to write the book and was also consulting on the screenplay.

I agreed to go to Block Island to be with Michael after Carrie left; Ruth secured a special dispensation from the owners so I could bring Annie. I was thrilled to embark on this free vacation on a glorious summer morning when I loaded up my little blue Toyota with beach gear, plenty of novels, groceries (I was going to be the cook), dog food, and Annie. I made the ferry in Point Judith by its 2:00 sailing time, and on the top deck, Annie and I drank in the salt air and calming colors of the ocean.

We docked by mid-afternoon, and as I drove off the boat, I saw Michael ahead. He looked pensively up at the crowd; he seemed nervous. I honked and leaned out, waving. He smiled and waved back then turned to say something to a dark-haired woman standing next to him, someone I had never seen before. *Oh, he's made a friend in the crowd.* He motioned me to follow him across the parking lot, so I pulled up behind his car, a big red Lincoln Continental he had purchased used with his newfound riches—he was tall and got back problems when driving a little car. The black-haired woman was still next to him. This was startling. He was supposed to need *me* to keep him company.

117

"Hey Michael," I called out, smiling broadly. He leaned in to kiss my cheek and we exchanged pleasantries. Then he introduced me.

"Liz, this is my friend Elizabeth. She's helping me with the book."

"Hi." I was so confused but said nothing. Elizabeth peered into the back of my car.

"Cute dog," she said. "I brought my dog too. She's bigger than yours but a mutt too."

"Wow. That's great. A dog vacation."

Already I didn't like her. My dog was not cute; she was a tough little thing. Elizabeth and her dog were not in the plan the family had arranged for Michael. I stayed silent. I was still so new to this family. But how bizarre—another Elizabeth with another dog?

I followed Michael to the house, and I felt myself relaxing into vacation mode, waves of tension leaving my body. The previous few weeks had been hard, not having a real home, and I was so looking forward to getting to know Michael better, being of help where I could, and doing all the beach place things I loved. We turned to the inner part of the island and drove down a little dirt road, passing a couple of houses before coming to the funky, octagonal house from the summer before.

Annie leapt out of the car instantly when I opened the door, racing around outside the house, wagging vigorously at the freedom to run. She too had been cooped up since we left Hoosick. This gave me immense joy, to see her free. This sense was short-lived though, when Elizabeth's large black dog came charging over. She chased Annie down, and they began growling at each other. Annie, though small, was quite alpha and didn't take shit from any other dog. I hustled over and collared Annie. Elizabeth called her dog back in. It turned out the dogs would have to be separated for the duration of my stay.

"You're going to stay in the bedroom downstairs," Michael told me, as he hoisted one of my suitcases over his head.

"Great," I said. "These groceries will go up to the kitchen."

Elizabeth reached into the trunk to pick up the plastic supermarket bags.

"We need to put the stuff from the cooler into the fridge right away. I brought everything for veal piccata and roasted vegetables for dinner tonight. Challah too." I saw Michael's quizzical expression. "Don't worry Mike, I got the meat at the kosher butcher." He smiled.

Michael's religiosity, never consistent, increased with when he was more ill. I was sure that the vacation house owners did not keep a kosher kitchen and that meat and dairy had mixed freely on the dishes we would eat from, but Michael managed that, somehow.

Later, we all sat on the deck, Elizabeth and I sipping wine, Michael sticking to soda, as alcohol didn't mix with his meds. I stayed in my observing role, trying to find in the behavior of this new woman who she was and why she was here. She seemed quite taken with Michael's charm. She too was Jewish and religious and they discussed some arcane point of the Talmud for some time. They were planning to go to services that night at the pick-up congregation that met at a local church his parents had frequented in their years on the island. Michael loved seeing people who had loved his father. Chuck Laudor's absence was keenly felt by his son, as the degree to which he had "triumphed" over his illness, Michael felt, was due to his relationship with his dad. Michael was explaining as much to Elizabeth.

"Dad and Richard were the ones that got me through the first part of being sick. Then Dad got sick. He died a about a year and a half ago. I still need him," Michael said, with a deep shaky sadness.

Elizabeth looked intensely at Michael and they shared a moment of sustained eye contact. "You are doing better now? Yes?" she asked.

Michael grimaced. "Those Hollywood bastards are messing with me," he said, with some desperation.

I interjected, "What is going on, Michael, with the movie?" I didn't know if there was something truly afoot or his paranoia was in command.

"I'll know more tomorrow, when I talk to my agent," he said. I didn't pursue it.

The bright summer afternoon light was fading and though it was August, the air took on a bit of an evening chill.

"If you two are going to services, you should get ready. I better start dinner," I said. In the kitchen, I put the lemons, butter and olive oil, flour, wine, and veal out on the counter. Elizabeth studied what I was doing and asked me how I prepared the dish. As I described sautéing the meat in a combination of olive oil and butter, she interrupted in a scolding tone. "No, no butter." I realized she was right. Cooking veal in butter would epitomize the Biblical prohibition of boiling a calf in its mother's milk.

"Oh my god," I said. "Of course. I should have realized. Thank you for catching that. How stupid of me."

I put the butter quickly back in the fridge, ashamed and feeling like a failure already in my effort to take care of Michael. Clearly this other Elizabeth was meant to be there, and I was out of place. I thought back to the arrangements. I had talked directly to Michael once, and he had asked me to come help when Carrie was not there. But most of the discussions about the trip had been with Ruth or Richard. Still, Michael *had* asked me to come.

Even though Richard seemed not to care that I wasn't Jewish, I still seemed to put my foot in it when around the extended family. I had considered converting to Judaism, had gone to the conversion classes Rabbi Jonathan had recommended, but they were on an inconvenient schedule, and I found them intellectually silly. I promised Richard that if we had children, I would follow through—convert and raise them in religious, Jewish tradition. The one moment where I had significantly doubted if I could marry Richard came at a second Seder with family friends who had four sons and a daughter around the ages of Michael, Richard, and Danny; one son was dead from AIDS, but his partner still came along. After the meal, all the young men were singing folk songs, songs of liberation from the civil rights movement, and during a lag, and a request for other ideas for songs, I suggested "Amazing Grace." Silence and an awkward pause followed, and the wife of one of the brothers sniffed haughtily. Another brother suggested we sing a different song, without acknowledging my suggestion. Later I would figure out that "grace" is a particularly Christian concept—but I didn't know that then. I just knew the myth that it was written by a guy who decided to turn a slave ship around—relevant I thought to singing about the Jews liberation from slavery. I left the table abruptly to talk a walk. *I will never fit in here. I can never marry Richard.* Later, Richard was outraged that I had been made to feel uncomfortable. But the memory haunted me, lingered, and I was aware that as a shiksa I had to curb my unconscious Christian cultural ways. Now, on Block Island, I had fallen down on the job by planning to cook veal for Michael in butter.

While they were at services, I prepped the salad, vegetables, and cutlets to sauté. Michael and Elizabeth would not be back for an hour still, so I let Annie out of our assigned basement room and went for a little walk. The sun was setting to the west, the sky mauve and midnight blue. I breathed deeply, feeling more relaxed. Annie sniffed and roamed and she seemed quickened and alive. Returning to the deck, I sat out in the quiet night with the dog at my feet until I could see car lights coming down the little dirt road, then put Annie back downstairs, went to my skillet and started to sauté the meat in olive oil only.

Elizabeth and Michael came in quietly. I asked about the service.

"All of Dad's friends were there," Michael said softly.

I smiled and replied, "That must have felt good to see them."

121

"Yeah," Michael said, making eye contact with me for the first time all day, and did what Richard did when he was saying something most sincere, tilt his head to the right.

"Can I help with dinner?" Elizabeth asked.

"No, it's almost ready but you could put out the challah and the candles," I said, suggesting the Shabbat preparations to this Jewish lady. I turned the veal. When the cutlets browned, I transferred them to a platter and turned to making the sauce. As I added lemon juice to the hot pan, it roiled up and then, with the wine, settled down. I whisked away until achieving the perfect just-thickened consistency and poured the sauce over the meat, all looking and smelling perfect.

At the table, Elizabeth lit the candles and we sang the blessings over the bread and wine. Michael seemed calm and centered for the first time all day. We ate companionably, although I missed having Annie under the table. Elizabeth and Michael washed dishes while I went out to star gaze and let Annie out to pee one more time before we both retreated downstairs to the bedroom; Michael and Elizabeth were in the rooms upstairs.

The next morning was glorious, clear air, a hot sun beaming down. I was enjoying a cup of good coffee on the deck, when Michael emerged from his room, looking overmedicated and sleepy. Elizabeth was not yet up; her dog remained in her room with her and so Annie could be freely with me.

"Coffee, Mike?"

He nodded without speaking. He was wearing blue gym shorts and a tattered t-shirt, shuffled out to the deck, again without speaking and accepted the coffee I put in his hand. He looked out across the dunes toward the salt pond, sitting wordlessly for several minutes. I kept glancing at him, trying to take his mental temperature, which appeared close to feverish. I kept the quiet, aiming just to be gently present if he wanted to talk. About half an hour later, I could hear Elizabeth showering.

"You want some breakfast?" I asked. Michael shook his head. I decided to try to bring him out a little. "What's going on, Michael?"

"I got a call from California yesterday."

"About the movie?"

"Yeah," he said, very slowly.

"What about the movie?" I knew from Richard that Michael had been unhappy about the choice of the scriptwriter, Chris Geralmo, who Michael didn't like and felt might not do justice to his story. He was so paranoid about how he would be portrayed. More silence, Michael seeming to struggle to find the words.

"I think," Michael said, again speaking very slowly, "that they are writing out the Judaism. They are gonna make me a WASP from the Chicago suburbs. All their focus groups say that Middle America is not ready for a sympathetic portrayal of Jews and their families." He paused for several long minutes.

"I shook hands with Ron Howard over this. He seemed like a stand-up guy. He said he would keep the story intact. He told me he would likely be the director. Now my agent says that's not true. He may pass it off to Geralmo, who has never directed before. I met him. He's a cynic. The worst of what I feared from Hollywood. A real cynic who will have a cynical view of me." Now Michael was talking quickly, nearly shouting, staccato words infused with bitterness and fear. I wondered how much of this was real, how much delusional.

"Do you have any say over the script and director?" I asked, trying to be reasonable.

"Yeah, I could veto the director. I could, but I can't really. If that's what Ron Howard wants, that's what he'll get. As always, I lose. I have schizophrenia. I lose." Michael started pacing.

When Elizabeth stepped onto the deck, Michael stopped abruptly and turned to her. Something else switched on. I noticed the smile between them. Suddenly, I knew something else. I was not a babysitter. I was a beard. They were sleeping together. Did Carrie know? What a perfect set up. He would never be lying. He could say, "Oh yeah. Elizabeth and her dog were here." Meaning her or me. Genius. Mad genius.

Much later, one of Michael and Carrie's friends would look at me, witheringly, and say, "Oh, you are Elizabeth. With the dog."

"No, no one calls me Elizabeth. Especially not *that* Elizabeth. I am Liz."

Chapter 16

New Life

At the end of the summer 1997, I was no longer homeless, settling in the coop in Riverdale. Richard's Albany horse racing case wasn't over, so he deferred his entrance into the NYU Wagner School of Public Policy. For a few months, I would only see him on weekends.

We got a deal on the co-op, a sunny, west-facing apartment with one large bedroom where Richard's king size bed fit, and a "maid's room," which I would use as a small study. The kitchen was galley style, but big enough to cook in. The pre-war building was one where lots of little old Jewish ladies lived, including two with Holocaust tattoos, and an assortment of cops, teachers, and postal workers. I enjoyed nesting, finding places for all our stuff. True to form, Richard gave no input on any practical matters, save the TV and air conditioners. We still had no real furniture, befitting our student status.

Annie, who had run free upstate, was now stuck inside all day. I took her to the park every morning for a good workout and hired the super to walk her during the week.

At age 42, I was starting graduate school again. On the day I set out for orientation, I missed Richard. I wished he was there for a goodbye hug, or a pep talk. I was excited, curious and just a little nervous. I wanted to fit in, find comrades, and make a good first impression. If Richard were here, I would feel more centered, but I had to go, without his reassurance. The City University Ph.D. program in clinical psychology was located in Harlem, at City College. Any sane city dweller would have taken the subway, but I hated the subway—one reason I had left town 20 years earlier. I drove, spent twice the time of the 15-minute trip looking for parking, arrived late and sweating in the August heat. I found the building housing the grad psych program, an ugly behemoth concrete structure built in the 1970s, meant to look like a ship. Inside would turn out to be ugly, cold, and inhospitable, always crumbling in one way or another. The story told by generations of City grad students was that it was the last building constructed by the mob and a dead body might fall through the ceiling at any moment. I got lost due to a labyrinth of entrances, escalators, and elevators, and by the time I found the appointed room, I was truly late. I took my seat, chagrinned, failing the first task of graduate school, punctuality.

Dr. Tuber, a slender man with wire-rimmed glasses, was explaining overall requirements for the program, qualifying exams after the first or second year, the dissertation, the yearlong internship. As he laid out this information, boring on its own, it was clear that he was smart, and funny. I liked him. I looked around the room at my classmates, a diverse group; one very blond curly haired woman probably near my age. After introductions, I found there were Asian, Mexican, Puerto Rican, Eastern European, gay folks among us. I wondered who I would get to like. Dr Tuber emphasized what was unique about the City program, a long-standing commitment to diversity, given its location in Harlem. We would learn about working with folks from different cultures, about our own biases and how that might impact our clinical work. Learning *theory*, especially psychoanalytic theory, Dr Tuber emphasized, would be central to our education.

After a lunch in the Faculty Dining Room, where I made some first day friends, we re-assembled in the library, where a couple of professors who would be teaching the first years stopped in. Then the Department secretary arrived with paperwork, including applications for CUNY ID cards. We would need to go to the graduate school at 34th and Fifth, about 100 blocks south, to get photos taken and obtain the IDs. At that time the clinical program, though housed uptown at City College, was under the auspices of the CUNY Graduate School, who had just built a new headquarters on Fifth Avenue at 34th Steet, in the former B. Altman Department Store, a landmarked building. And really, the only sensible way to get there was two subway rides, down and across town.

As the meeting broke up, I walked with my lunch buddies outside into the light of a gorgeous late summer day. The sky was blue and the city summer hubbub of children in wet bathing suits, old people pushing shopping carts, fast walkers of all colors and the buzz of traffic on the avenues surrounded us. I smiled. After my three years in the wilds of Bennington, this city thing had potential. I offered folks a ride downtown, and with some hesitation they agreed. This was a good sign, maybe we had bonded. As I drove in my usual breakneck speed, just like a New Yorker, the car was filled with laughter and a few grabs for the seatbacks when the Westside Highway curved for the first time. I got off at 34th Street and drove across town, this taking longer than the drive downtown, and my passengers grew restless. We really needed to get there before the offices closed, and I worried that driving with me would mess up my colleagues' needs. Finally, at around 4:30, I pulled alongside the Graduate Center and my new friends cheerfully got out while I parked in a very expensive garage, managing to get my own my ID just under the wire. I felt happy, starting a new adventure, in a city that held so much to experience, though none of my classmates wanted a ride uptown.

I was headed uptown to have dinner with one of my best friends, Hattie, a roommate from Oberlin days, and her family. Back in New York, I would get to see her more often. Hattie lived on Riverside Drive, with great views of the Hudson. She had married a finance guy. When I arrived, Hattie was in the kitchen, making salad, the rest of dinner already in the oven. We chatted companionably about the program I was beginning. One of the professors was someone Hattie knew from the institute where she was training as a psychoanalyst.

"No, Steve Ellman was not there today," I said. "I'm sure he is still in Wellfleet with all the other vacationing analysts."

"Have you set a date for the wedding?"

"Yeah, next Labor Day, in a year."

"You have to have a shower. I'll host it here."

"Really? That's so nice. You don't have to," especially because you can't stand Richard, which I did not say. Her reaction to him pained me, as I had worked hard to like and befriend her investment banker husband, David, whose materialism was not my cup of tea.

"I can see it now," Hattie laughed. "Lots of bows." She shared some of my sense that this was a drama meant to be performed to perfection. I assisted her with her wedding some years ago, helping them choose a venue that broke through David's ambivalence—his parents' house.

In a bit, David came in from work at Morgan Stanley, attired in Brooks Brothers suit and tie. He greeted me warmly, changed out of his suit, and opened a bottle of red wine—he was an oenophile and could afford good wine. I sipped appreciatively and remembered to ask Hattie about the New Yorker piece on James Salter, someone we had both read two decades before.

"He's very male," I said. "I hadn't known he had gone into film-making."

"I think he was actually mildly pornographic," said Hattie. She was now a mother, a practicing psychoanalyst, no longer in the just past coed state, where all writing about sex, even sex defined by the male gaze, was compelling. David returned to the kitchen after putting some loud rock and roll on his very fancy stereo system in the living room.

"What about porn?" David asked. We all laughed.

Hattie threw him a slightly stern expression, replying to his music choice. "I was thinking Chopin."

We all chuckled over their ongoing musical marital feud.

"Tell me about this wine, David."

Back home, alone, I took Charley out for his last walk of the day. I so wanted Richard there. I was used to having him in the bed with me. I missed the night of reassuring warm full body contact, something I was surprised to see I now counted on.

✶ ✶ ✶ ✶ ✶

The academic year went well and was almost over by April 1998 when Richard moved to Riverdale full time. I could get a daily dose of my sweet guy. Michael proposed to Carrie and it was official: they were going to get married, too. We would all be family.

After the news of their engagement, I wanted to bond with Carrie and suggested a trip to the Westchester Mall. We could shop a little and browse the modestly upscale home-furnishing stores. I was ready to create our wedding registry, and she could begin to think of what they needed. We could look at dishes together and dish on the family.

On a cool, drizzling Saturday afternoon, Carrie drove the 20-miles in from Hastings, the suburb in Westchester County where she and Michael shared a garden apartment, to pick me up in her little Honda sedan.

"Hey. How are you?" I asked as I clicked in my seatbelt.

"Good." Carrie smiled broadly. She was so petite, dressed in jeans, but with a dainty blue cotton top.

"How's Michael?"

Carrie sighed. "He's still asleep. He is getting worse. I don't think being alone all the time, trying to write, is good for him."

"Writing can be really isolating. Does he have a deadline?"

"I can't really tell. I think he might have missed one already."

"Uh oh. What does Murray say?" I asked, wondering what Michael's psychiatrist's thought.

"He's worried. He says that Michael is very paranoid. Murray thinks Michael could snap. Like if the guy behind the counter at the bagel shop looks at him funny, Michael could hurt him."

"Damn! What about putting him back in the hospital, then?"

"Murray wants to avoid that at all costs. He says Michael was so traumatized by the hospital 10 years ago"

"This must be really hard for you."

Carrie was quiet and stared at the road ahead. After a few seconds she said, "The only thing I care about is that we never go out together as a couple anymore. We used to see friends, have dinners together with other couples. I miss that."

"Yeah," I said trying to be empathic. "You can always hang with us, even if Michael is struggling. Now that Richard is here full time, maybe he can be there more for Michael."

We drove the rest of the way to the mall in silence, and in the parking garage, I glanced up at the Neiman Marcus sign. "Here we are at Needless Mark-up. Ready to be our best bourgeois selves?" Carrie shot me a sideways glance and didn't laugh.

Oops. I forgot that she had little sense of the absurd and was quite conventional. "Bride" was a role I was playing, in the great drama of life and I intended to play it well. I doubted Carrie had that perspective. I stopped my attempts at humor.

"I already did a dry run of some places. Do you want to start at Williams-Sonoma?" I asked.

"That's good. I really like their stuff."

Carrie headed to small appliances while I checked out the china. I hefted several plates, turned them over and scrutinized their form. None of them seemed quite right, either too delicate or too patterned. I was looking for sturdy and white, with clean simple lines. I found Carrie in the pots and pans.

"See anything you like?"

"It's very preliminary," she answered. "You?"

"No, nothing quite right. But it's good to compare. I think I am more of a Crate and Barrel girl. Let's go down there."

We trooped down a level and finally, I found so many things there I could imagine having in our newly married life—painted stemware, white dishes with the right lines, pots, flatware. One good thing about Richard's domestic incompetence was that these were all my decisions. I felt like a kid at Christmas as I filled out the registry forms. Carrie continued to look without choosing anything definitively, but she did linger in several areas, picking things up, turning them, eying them, putting them down.

I showed her the dishes I had chosen. "You and Michael will be the first people we have over for dinner, and we'll eat on these plates."

Carrie smiled. "You bet."

"My feet hurt," I said. "Before we do any clothes shopping let's sit down over here." I pointed to a fountain. We parked ourselves on the low bench surrounding the fountain. I felt cooled and relaxed by the sound of the gentle spray of the water flowing around the three bronze horses, soft classically inspired Muzak in the background.

"It's kind of funny to be thinking of setting up house with Richard, who is so domestically challenged. Does Michael do stuff around the house?" I asked Carrie.

"There are a few chores he will do, but he absolutely refuses most of them."

"Like what?" I asked, curious if there was a family resemblance.

"He'll wash dishes. He'll do laundry. But something like vacuuming? Or cleaning the bathroom? Forget it."

"That is hilarious. Those are exactly what Richard will and won't do, too, although the laundry is sort of questionable." We laughed in a moment of mutual recognition. "Ruth did not train them up right," I continued.

Carrie laughed. "I don't know if Ruth ever did much heavy cleaning herself. I think her mother came over and made sure it was done."

"Really? That's not the version of Grandma Pauline I heard."

"Well, Ruth had three tough boys," Carrie said, now taking what I understood was Ruth's point of view—her three sons had been impossible to raise. My point of view was that Ruth was not cut out to be a mother.

"I wonder if Richard and Michael are alike in other ways too?"

"Like what?" Carrie asked.

I thought for a second. "Well, Richard and I don't really fight. Do you and Michael fight?"

"Oh yeah. We fight. A lot." She hesitated, stiffened, and said ever so softly, "Knives have been drawn." She looked into my eyes fully, and then away.

My eyes popped open. *Did I even really hear that?*

"We don't even argue," I said, ineptly, finding myself unable to react properly to what she'd revealed.

Real knives? Possible violence?

I had to rush past this scary news but I would tell this to Richard later that night. I changed the subject. "Where to for clothes shopping?"

"How about Nordstrom's?" Carrie proposed, though an awkwardness entered her tone.

We walked to the other end of the mall for the second half of what I hoped would be many girls' days out.

Chapter 17

Knives

The day began as a glorious June morning, the air clear and cobalt blue. The hint of a breeze, the early sun not too hot. Richard was taking me out to breakfast before dropping me at LaGuardia where I'd soon be enroute to my parents' house. I was to attend a luncheon in my honor, as the bride-to-be. We drove down the deep green, leafy hill, from our middle-class neighborhood to the Riverdale Diner on Broadway, where the subway tracks were elevated, and the neighborhood noisy and dingier. I was content. The spring was a dazzling, luminous time. At forty-three, I had found THE ONE and we were getting married over Labor Day, in Brooklyn's Prospect Park. I never dared imagine this.

As we approached the diner, Richard begged me to order something besides my usual scrambled eggs and whole-wheat toast. "Come on, Lizzie. They have a ten-page menu. You could try something new."

"I know what I like, and I stick to it," I said, grinning lustfully at him. Richard laughed too and put his bear claw hand at the back of my head as we continued to banter and tease.

Even this joy, like most joys, was wrinkled, but only ever so slightly, by Michael's deterioration. He was increasingly delusional and paranoid and had stopped all his meds. The new pharmaceutical cocktails hadn't worked, and he was convinced they were poison. The night before, Ruth and Carrie, newly and unhappily pregnant, had driven Michael to a crucial therapy appointment with Murray Shane, his psychiatrist.

Murray had been in France for three weeks and Michael had been catatonic most of that time. Michael refused to get out of the car, so Murray came out and spoke with him curbside.

Over breakfast, Richard said, "When I talked to Michael last week, I thought he was going to be okay. He didn't like it that Carrie was going to go through with the abortion, but he was going to hang tough, because that was what she wanted. I told him to act like Humphrey Bogart in Casablanca, where all he really wanted was for Ingrid Bergman to stay, but he urged her to go, saying he didn't care. I thought he was going to take my advice."

Richard continued, "I could tell from his voice that he was hallucinating, but he didn't mention the CIA across the Hudson from their apartment or Nazis at all. He's making Carrie sleep next door, at Tomas's, because he says he can't keep her safe from the spies who are trying to kill him."

I nodded and thought, fleetingly, about the meaning of this. Where was the danger? *Was* there danger? In Michael's head, I concluded, like the flames he once told me his father had helped him understand wouldn't really burn him. I too had talked to Michael the previous week. There were long pauses in our conversation, wherein he clearly was struggling to respond to what was real, as opposed to the internal psychosis, the terrifying voices, and visual images of fires and threat he saw on that other TV screen in his head.

After our talk, I had a strong intuition, a freakish flash that Michael would do something really crazy, violent to Carrie. I had heard from Carrie about knives. I was in a tough spot. As an academic psychologist who had taught abnormal psychology, I had no experience dealing with people with schizophrenia. Besides, as a newcomer to the family, I had no permission to butt in. I had wanted to call Carrie and tell her to move out that evening but doubted she would have received my interference well. She listened to Ruth. I stayed out of it, to my eternal regret.

"It's such a hard decision about the baby," I answered Richard. "But he is so sick right now. I guess it's not the right time for a kid."

"Yeah, no." Richard paused. "I do want to be an uncle. I'll be an uncle like Grandpa Jim was a grandpa." Richard had felt so loved by his grandfather, and not by any of the rest of the family.

"I know." I thought for a minute, sad that we were probably too old to have our own kids. "Maybe later on, they can have a family we can be a part of," I said hopefully.

We were quiet. It was ice cold in the air-conditioned diner. I didn't deviate from my scrambled egg plan. Richard had a bagel deluxe, with several slabs of lox, extra cream cheese and red onion, plus a large Pepsi.

"What does Murray want to do about Michael?" I asked, after the Greek waiter poured my coffee. Over the last month, with Murray away, we had talked about Michael going back in the hospital for a while, but every time Richard brought this up to his mother, she hung up the phone on him. She wouldn't do anything until the psychiatrist was back. This paralyzed Richard. I didn't understand why Ruth had the last word.

"Mom and Carrie are going to try to get him into the hospital today. They are calling the Westchester Crisis Team to bring him to Columbia Presbyterian. I'll check with Mom, but maybe I'll go to Michael's after the airport. Maybe I can convince him the crisis team are not Nazis."

"That's a good idea," I said.

After breakfast, Richard used the payphone in the diner lobby to call his mother. I stood a little distance away, watching his large, lumbering self, gesticulating as he spoke. It did not seem to be going well. After he hung up, I asked, "What's up?"

Richard was clearly angry. "My mother. What else?" Richard especially didn't like the way he felt his mother treated him—like "staff."

"Do you have a plan?"

"I'm not going to let her tell me what to do."

I dropped the subject. We returned to Richard's car and made our way to the airport. Richard asked about the celebratory events in Illinois. I explained that it would be a group of older ladies, mostly friends of my mother's, sitting around a table, with a linen tablecloth and napkins, eating small sandwiches without crusts, chatting about inane topics. But they would all be so very polite and gracious and truly happy for me and my parents. Maybe some one of them would remember a funny story about me as a kid. I hoped for some good cake.

At the airport, Richard began to sing "Leavin' on a Jet Plane," as he always did when I went away, gazing straight into my eyes. I was so in love I didn't even mind how corny it was. I kissed him, tenderly and passionately goodbye. I would be back in four days.

The two flights, one to O'Hare and the puddle jumper downstate, were uneventful and my parents, now both in their late 70s, were so pleased to see me, their eyes gleaming, though words—clear, direct communication of any feeling—were never uttered. We hugged all around. The hour drive from the airport to their house through the deep green, square cornfields, not yet knee high—not yet the Fourth of July—was so familiar and comforting. I carried my own bag in, as Dad's knees were shot. Mom managed another arm squeeze and a bright smile at the back door. For supper, she made a childhood favorite, parsleyed potatoes, and boiled fresh sweet corn they had driven south to find for me. Dad grilled steaks, leaving mine as bloody as I liked, even though it made him gag. By the time food was served, we had run through all the topics we could think of to discuss, including the ongoing Monica Lewinsky scandal, which as ardent liberal Democrats who lived in a rib rock Republican community, my parents saw as a vast rightwing conspiracy, with my mother also critical of what she called a "boy crazy, lovesick" girl. We ate companionably, but silently, as the sun went down.

Later, while unpacking in the room that had been mine since I was a baby, the phone rang. This was long after the time I had told Richard the night owl that he could call so as to not wake my mother who went to bed at precisely 10:25, at the conclusion of the late local weather, the last of many forecasts she watched each day. Dad, still up watching Jay Leno, chatted briefly with Richard, as I came downstairs, and handed me the phone. I began to gently chide Richard for calling so late.

All Richard got out was "Hi, Lizzie" and I knew something was quite wrong. I could hear voices in the background, not the quiet of our Riverdale apartment where he should be, as it was past midnight in New York. Then came the clear voice of Richard's oldest friend Jim saying, "Just tell her."

"Richard! What is up? Where are you?"

"I'm at Mom's. I didn't want to call but Jim said I had to."

"Okay." I waited.

"Carrie is dead and Michael is missing," Richard choked out.

"What the fuck!" I started to yell, but immediately remembered the big ears of my parents, who didn't know that in my regular life I cursed like a sailor. "What happened?" I asked, frantic.

"We're not sure." Richard paused. "Michael is missing. The police are looking for him." He paused again. "The phones might be bugged."

"Ooooohhhh."

What did Richard know but couldn't say? I started to pace around the front hallway with the heavy black receiver up to my ear. I scratched my head, ran my other hand through my hair, rubbed my right eyebrow up and down. My neck and shoulders stiffened. The pain in my chest I spent years of therapy getting rid of, reappeared with sudden, stabbing intensity.

What could have happened?

Maybe Michael overheard them making plans to hospitalize him. He believed, when paranoid, that the hospital was a concentration camp, where Nazis did horrid medical experiments on him, like cutting his body to pieces without anesthetic. *Could he have killed Carrie, thinking she was a Nazi?* Or, if he had focused on the abortion Carrie was planning, it could have wreaked havoc with the crazy religiosity he got when psychotic. *Did he crazily think he needed to cut the baby out of her to save it?*

I had to say it. "I'll be back as soon as I can." Leaving so soon would upset my parents, though they wouldn't say so, or protest my abrupt departure.

"You don't need to come back," Richard said.

Jim, in the background, said, "Oh, yes, she does."

"Jim." Richard sounded so scared and so annoyed all at once.

I repeated, "I'll be back as soon as I can. Let me call the airline."

Carrie was dead? How could I possibly explain this to my parents? I couldn't think of a way to say this indirectly. Could one allude to murder? Never prone to precipitous action of any sort, my parents would have to accept a rapid turnaround. I would rudely miss the next day's bridal luncheon; it would be too late to call it off. The food was surely all prepared and the guests would have laid out their best floral dresses. I knew too that my parents would never clearly explain why I wasn't there—perhaps a vague mention of a death in my fiancé's family?

Then there was the problem of getting back to New York. Now past midnight in Illinois, arrangements would have to wait until morning, I was sure, although morning in the Midwest did start ridiculously early. How to figure this out? In 1998, my parents had no cell phone, no internet access, not even a push button phone that would help with getting through the endless prompts with the airlines. And the expense of booking last minute flights. Perhaps I could say I was bereaved so the airline would extend a cheaper ticket?

With Carrie uncomprehendingly dead, I *was* bereaved. We were still getting to know one another, but I thought we had bonded a bit during our trip to the mall. Yet, thinking about that afternoon, I had to struggle not to puke. I let Carrie's comment, "Knives have been drawn," fully coalesce into consciousness only now. *She was dead? Stabbed, maybe? What had gone down? Damn. Oh damn.*

As my mother observed, Richard always needed me. Now, he needed me as fast as I could get there. I had already accepted that being a wife to Richard meant managing almost everything for him. Although in shock, it did occur to me: how the hell was I going to manage *this* for him? Resolved, loyal, determined, as the fight/flight energy took hold and the nausea receded, I would do whatever it took to get back to him.

When I had the arrangements in hand, I called Richard back. There was news. Michael had been found in Ithaca, about 225 miles north-west in upstate New York. Likely he had gone there to kill himself, like scores of others had done, by jumping into one of the gorges around Cornell University. Instead, he flagged down a campus cop and reported he might have hurt his girlfriend. Someone should check on her, he thought. Michael was all bloody. Carrie *had* been stabbed, more than 10 times, in the back and chest—with two kitchen knives.

I decided to tell my father; he was more approachable than mom. "Dad, I have some bad news. Richard's brother Michael snapped and killed his girlfriend. I have to go back tomorrow really early. I am sorry. I can't even stay for the lunch." Dad, not unsympathetic in his gaze, , accepted the turn-around, tight lipped, saying nothing. When we rose before dawn, to get to the 5AM flight, mom let me know she would go to the lunch, carrying on.

I walked back in the front door of our apartment at about nine in the morning. Richard, usually so slow and lumbering, dashed to hug me tight. He whispered in my ear, "You can leave me now if you want to. I will understand."

I playfully pushed him away and then kissed him, nuzzled his soft curly beard, and kissed him again. Determined to find heat, passion, life, I led him into the bedroom. It was after making love, on that strange, unreal morning that I began to learn what happened.

"Did you go over there right after you dropped me at the airport?" I asked Richard. He looked puzzled.

"No, was I supposed to?" he asked. "I was so angry at Mom that I went for a long drive. Did my thing of driving upstate, got lost, and found my way back. I didn't get home until about 5:00. There were a couple of messages from Mom on the machine and then one from Danny. When I called the house, they just told me to come over, it was an emergency. When I got there, they told me that Carrie was dead, and Michael was missing." This was all pre-cell phone.

"How did they know that?"

"Well, Mom and Carrie had been in touch all day about the plan to hospitalize Michael. Carrie had stayed home from work to help. The Crisis team was supposed to come in the morning, but they called to say someone had called in sick. Danny, who was staying with Mom last night, took that call and told them it was okay to come on second shift, after three. Mom called to speak to Carrie at about 4:00, to say the team should be on its way. When she called, Michael answered."

"Really?"

"Yeah, Mom was surprised to get Michael on the phone, too. She asked to speak to Carrie." Richard paused, and started to cry, his chest heaving, but no tears were in his eyes. I held him.

Richard continued. "Michael said, 'I think I killed her. Or maybe it was a great big wind-up doll and all the stuffing came out.' Then he hung up on Mom."

I was shaking my head, back and forth. *No, no, no.* "What did your mother do then?"

"She called the Hastings police and asked them to check on Michael and Carrie. It wasn't too long before the cops showed up at her house with the news."

I clutched Richard, speechless. We held each other for a long time. Finally, Richard got up to get a cold drink, and when he came back, he began to tell me things I couldn't grasp (or at least so badly did not want to believe) about his family.

"Dad used to chase Danny around with a knife," Richard said solemnly.

"Really?" I said, raising my head to my elbow. "What kind of knife?"

"A kitchen knife. He never caught Danny though, because Danny was too fast."

Richard adjusted one of the six pillows behind his head. This was hard to picture. Richard's father died before we met but I knew he was a tenured professor, a big shot at the synagogue, and a beloved unofficial "mayor" of the neighborhood shopping center where he would schmooze with people for hours.

"Why would he do that?" I shuffled my feet along the smooth blue cotton sheets.

"He couldn't get Danny to behave, and Danny would taunt him and run away." Richard was lying still, staring up at the ceiling.

"Do you think he would have really cut him if he caught him?" I asked, turning to hold his hand.

"Probably not, but when Dad lost his temper, you never knew. Dad would usually just scream a lot, but he might have hit him. If he could have caught him." Richard managed a chuckle at the thought of his bad middle brother's misbehavior.

The brothers were all seriously smart, wickedly funny, and graduates all of Ivy League law schools, but were variously known as the *weird brother* (Richard), the *mean brother* (Danny), and the *crazy brother* (Michael, after his breakdown at age twenty-four). Before that he'd been dubbed *the golden brother*.

"Wow." I was quiet for a few minutes after hearing about Danny and those knives. I pulled Richard close, again.

The next thing Richard said was, "My mother has Carrie's blood on her hands."

I knew what he meant. Richard had lobbied for weeks to have Michael hospitalized, but Ruth wouldn't hear of it. She hung up on him every time he suggested it. Her view was that would have to wait until Michael's psychiatrist returned. This delay, this unwillingness to act, this abdication of parental responsibility was a part of what had now happened. However, I knew it was complicated, far more complicated than just "blame the mother."

I could blame myself, too. I had wanted to warn Carrie to leave, and I hadn't. She'd told me plainly that knives had been drawn during their fights, and I ignored it. *Did I have Carrie's blood on my hands, too?*

And what about Richard's role? Richard was supposed to go to Michael and Carrie's apartment after dropping me at the airport and seemed to have forgotten that. I shuddered, thinking what his presence there might have prevented. Or precipitated. *Would Michael have killed Richard too?*

And Danny, not knowing any better, had allowed the hospitalization to be delayed.

Then of course, there was Murray. Was Ruth acting on the advice of Michael's psychiatrist to delay? Was Murray even fully aware of what was happening with Michael in New York while he was in France?

I thought then, and still do: We all have Carrie's blood on our hands.

Of course, Michael's were utterly the most bloodied and the most responsible, if not on that day, when he was completely psychotic, then in the decisions that he made, or that others allowed him to make, leading up to that day, to stop his meds.

Only many years later would I realize that on that clear June morning, by telling me about his father chasing his brother around with a knife, and the blood on his mother's hands, that Richard was trying to warn me off, again, just as he had when I first walked in and he told me I could leave him. Richard and his family were big, big trouble. This was not the first time someone in his family had brandished a kitchen knife at a loved one. However, at that moment, at that phase of "us," what Richard's family was or what his relatives had done didn't matter to me. We loved each other.

I thought love, like John Lennon, was all I would ever need.

Chapter 18

Wake and Funeral

Rain fell as we set out five days later for Carrie's wake and funeral, the dim, gray day befitting the journey. Richard and I drove alone up to Newton, just outside Boston. Ruth pleaded for us to all ride together, but Richard refused. He claimed that doctor's orders dictated he not spend too much time with his mother.

"Did you ever meet any of Carrie's family?" I asked Richard as the highway stretched in front of us.

"No. I'm not sure if I were in their shoes if I would want us there."

"No kidding."

I hadn't met the Costellos, either, but I had heard a lot about them from Carrie and Michael. They sounded like good people, down-to-earth people, much more conservative than Carrie. As practicing Catholics, they were quite unhappy that Carrie's future husband was Jewish—apparently more difficult for them than Michael's illness. I did recall Michael saying that they had asked him once if his illness made him violent or if he would ever hurt Carrie. With his usual arrogance, Michael assured them that he would never, ever hurt her. That his schizophrenia didn't mean he was or could ever become violent. Carrie told us that her mother, a nurse, understood that she loved Michael and would come around. She was not so sure about her father, a career military man, whom she was used to arguing with over politics and most things.

Michael's best friend Tomas, as a non-family member, had contacted the Costello family priest, to say the Laudor family was grieving deeply for Carrie and would like to come to her funeral. They would, of course, respect the Costello family's wishes. Although their attitude would later change—as Danny took charge of the civil legal issues, including Carrie's life insurance, which left the money to Michael—the Costellos were initially open to seeing the Laudors. Perhaps they recognized Carrie's loss, and in some sense Michael's, affected everyone. Through the priest, the Costellos said we could and should come. Later, the Laudors would be banned from contacting anyone in the Costello orbit, including their priest.

We met Danny, Ruth, and Tomas at the hotel and drove together to the wake. It was dark, though the rain was letting up. At the funeral home, the parking lot was crowded and three red-faced, beefy guys in black suits directed the cars. The door to the building was open and light spilled out, a bit of brightness in an otherwise grim scene.

Danny asked, "Everyone ready?"

Richard answered. "Sorry, Dan, there is no fucking way to be ready for this."

Tomas, in his slightly Czech-accented English, replied archly, "We will get through."

After taking a deep breath, I said, "I plan to call on my midwestern WASP upbringing to hold it together." Everyone laughed, but the expressions all around quickly shifted back to somber and strained.

Inside, the wake, well underway, was packed with mourners and noisy with chatter. Carrie's open coffin was at far end of room. I tried not to look. I needed to work up to seeing Carrie, dead. I stayed as close to Richard as I could because I knew this was an absolute torture for him. He saw his presence in these rituals as a moral requirement, to be there and take whatever came his way—almost as punishment for Michael's deed— and to stand in for his dead father, as the eldest son, the responsible party.

Waves of emotion surfaced in me—shock, indigestible terror. Carrie's murder began to seem most real and violent in those moments. Yet I felt I had no right to surrender to these feelings, to show them, as they mattered so little compared to those of Carrie's family. As we started introducing ourselves and shaking hands around, many people pulled back at seeing us, just a little, grimacing.

I talked with Carrie's sister Joyce, a short woman with eyes like Carrie's. Her husband hovered around, with their young son Tyler on his shoulders, holding a cowboy hat—a gift, I knew, from Michael and Carrie.

I held out my hand. "Hi, I'm Liz. I'm engaged to Michael's brother, Richard." I pulled Richard towards the group.

Joyce said, looking at Richard, so tall and round, "Carrie talked about you. She said you were the big teddy-bear brother."

I laughed. "Sweet and cuddly, yes," and shifted tone. "How are you holding up, Joyce?"

"Okay. Not good. I'm mostly worried about Mom and Dad. Mom can talk. Dad doesn't talk."

I nodded and looked straight at her, trying to be as empathically in tune as possible with how hard this was for them.

"And this guy?" I shook my head at Tyler.

"He doesn't understand. He really loved both Carrie and Michael. We told him that Michael's illness killed Carrie, not the Michael he remembers." She turned to the next person approaching to shake her hand.

As Richard and I moved on, we came to the family priest. After introducing ourselves, he asked, "So, you saw Carrie all the time?"

Richard answered, "Yeah, she was really a part of the family, all the family holidays. She took a yoga class with my mother. And she and Michael had been together almost eight years."

"So, she was family?"

We both nodded. The Priest had very blue eyes, which he trained on my face. He said, "You know, even if you are angry, you can talk to God about this. I am often angry with God and have those conversations."

Why did he think I was angry? I felt misinterpreted, but maybe he knew that this did seem cosmically unjust. Or, that I didn't believe in a god of any kind. Not wanting to get into a religious dispute, I said, "Thank you for that thought, Father."

He kept looking at me, seeming to sense something from inside of me. He clasped my hand and said, "Really."

In response to this, I smiled as authentically as I could made full eye contract.

Finally, we joined the receiving line to file past the open casket and shake hands formally with Carrie's parents and other relatives. I had only seen three dead bodies before—my three grandparents. In the coffin, Carrie was dressed in a long-sleeved, high-necked white blouse and a dark skirt. I realized there must be stab wounds on her neck and that was why they had chosen that neckline. Although disguise had been attempted through cosmetics, I could still see a wound mark at the edge of her face. Carrie had been a minimal makeup kind of girl, and with her corpse so formally painted, she didn't look like herself. The only way she looked like the real Carrie was in how petite she seemed, so much more so in that big casket.

As I stared at her tiny body, something I had read in the papers or seen on TV flooded into my mind—an account of what finding her body was like for the cops. Someone, somewhere, was quoted as saying, "He was a really big man and she was very small. She tried to fight back but didn't stand a chance. There was a lot of blood." That image was dizzying; it literally dazed me, to think of how she died, bleeding through the wound I could see and many others. Carrie was so tiny and so dead, right before me. I didn't fall over, but it took every ounce of strength to stay vertical.

The image of her corpse kept reverberating. I kept seeing her dead face in eyeglasses, but Carrie never wore glasses. Her face had to have glasses, somehow. I realized that my mind was trying to superimpose the images of my two dead, bespectacled grandmothers on the image of Carrie. Although seeing my grandparents' corpses had been shocking for me, their deaths seemed to somehow be right, the natural time for them to die. Better to paste their images over the image of the dead Carrie, to block her young face in my mind's eye, than to really see her in that coffin—the wounds inflicted by someone I knew and cared about—partly covered by a high-necked collar.

As we passed through the line, I spoke to Mrs. Costello about the trip Carrie and I took to the mall, how we had talked about both marrying into the same family, the fun we'd had choosing wedding registry gifts. She was a practical, almost masculine-looking woman, and though she tried to smile a little, her eyes were deadened as she shook my hand. Mr. Costello didn't look all there either and though we had never met, he quite awkwardly hugged me. I'm not sure if he realized who I was.

Later, in the milling about, Richard and I came upon Ruth talking one-to-one with Mrs. Costello. I was surprised to hear Ruth speaking in an injured tone as if she were the victim.

"Never, ever would I have expected that something this horrible could happen. I couldn't imagine. No one told us there… We had no idea. We are in shock, and in grief," Ruth gurgled.

Richard interjected, "I doubt O.J. Simpson's mother thought she was raising a murderer, either."

Both mothers recoiled, abruptly jumping away from the other. Mrs. Costello walked off. Ruth stared at Richard, speechless for a few seconds, and then sputtered "Huh? What? What?" with a tone of wounded child.

Then her voice changed, and with unmodulated fury and revulsion, said, she said, "What are you *saying*, Richard! Richard!" She seemed to expect only the worst from her first-born—and in this instance, he had delivered. Revolted, Ruth marched away from us, too.

Did Richard understand how publicly wounding his words were? Maybe he did. Though I had witnessed tense mother-son exchanges before, this was my first contact with the blistering hatred smoldering between them. Back at the hotel, I confronted Richard.

He replied, "She will never take any responsibility for this. She has never taken any responsibility for anything."

That night, neither Richard nor I slept well. As usual, he kept the TV on full blast all night long as well as the air conditioner, though that June night was reasonably cool. These were the constant nighttime tactics he used to fight off his chronic insomnia, which fueled mine. In the morning we found Danny and Tomas in the hotel coffee shop. Danny had been a professional comedian before law school, and usually he could be mockingly funny but not today. We all said very little at breakfast.

Ruth joined us shortly before we needed to leave. She wanted to plan strategy for the funeral, her main goal to avoid all the press and photographers. (A deeply unflattering picture of her taken with a tele-photo lens at home had been printed in one of the New York tabloids.) We planned to arrive five minutes before the funeral mass started, to walk in pairs into the church, and to sit in the middle pews, all to avoid calling attention to ourselves.

At the church, there was a huge turnout with men directing traffic, motioning us to a spot in a large parking lot across the street. We waited in the car for several minutes then walked quickly, in a slightly different route than most people, across the far side of the lot and the street to the church, the farthest we could manage from the press and the photographers who were congregated on the opposite corner.

We found places in the center of the large, full church by climbing over some people sitting on the aisle. We recognized only a few faces in the crowd, Carrie's relatives from the wake, a couple of friends of Michael and Carrie, and Benno Schmidt (the infamous former president of Yale, sometime actor in Woody Allen films, and Carrie's official boss at the Edison Company). Richard whispered in my ear, "He's a drunk and gay, you know." Schmidt had been Dean of Columbia Law School during part of Richard's time there.

During the funeral service, a full Catholic mass, the priest spoke of God's mysteries and acknowledged our presence. Some faces turned to look for us, not all friendly. Mrs. Costello gave the eulogy. She spoke of her daughter's intelligence, drive, and beauty, her opinions that led her to argue politics with her father, and of her love, tragic love, for Michael. I cried. The pallbearers included Carrie's sister and small nephew Tyler, who held his hand against the polished wood as the coffin passed out at the end of the service.

Since we had been outed during the mass, after the casket passed, we held a whispered conference about how to get back to the car as quickly as possible. Tomas, a type-A guy, wanted to escort Ruth out. I insisted that if there were photos, Danny and Richard should be on either side of Ruth, with Tomas and I behind. I won the argument, somehow, though in the end, all the photographers focused on the casket. We stepped out of the line following the coffin and veered off to the car without being spotted.

Chapter 19

Days After

Back in Riverdale, the next morning, we slept in, until nearly 10:00, until Annie demanded to go out. I stopped at the corner drug store and bought all the New York tabloids and the *Times*. Were there any pictures of us at the funeral? The story was there in all of them, but no photos. Ruth's wish had been granted.

Richard was awake when I got back, and we sat with coffee in the living room. We both had the day off, as I was supposed to still be in Illinois, and Richard had put his new life as a graduate student on hold when he heard that Michael had killed Carrie. Richard did not do well with change, and it was only six weeks since he had moved from Albany. He was shifting his career from attorney to grad student and had been in classes for just two weeks at the NYU Wagner School of Public Policy. Richard hated being a lawyer and wanted to transition to government or public policy work. He was nothing if not a policy wonk, full of facts, history, and figures. He had just started classes and it had been hard, before this, as it involved meeting new people, a new role, with lots of open time on his hands, which all fed his anxiety; his social awkwardness was making it all a significant challenge. *How could he ever do this now?*

Over coffee Richard expressed his own doubts about school. "I can't take it, Lizzie," he said. "I need structure. I need work. Especially now."

"The NYU people should understand that this changes everything." I gestured into the air. "But it's your dream so you shouldn't give up altogether."

"Yeah, maybe I can go part time, but I don't know what that will mean for my scholarship."

"You'll see. Nothing has to happen today. What do you want to do today?"

"Nothing, really. But we are not seeing my mother, no matter what."

"Agreed," I laughed. I could see lazing around all day, but there was also a lot to do—so many details to take care of for the wedding, about ten weeks away. *But given the tragedy, should we go through with a big ceremony and celebration?*

"Richard," I said quietly, taking his hand. "Do you think given all this, that we should go ahead with the wedding as planned? I mean maybe it's too much."

He looked directly into my eyes. "You said this didn't make you want to leave me."

"No, no. I don't mean not get married. I just meant the big party part."

"In my religion, life always has to trump death. Life wins. The wedding goes on."

This brought tears to my eyes. "So, you still want to marry me?" I asked.

"More than ever, babe," he said, his dark brown eyes glowing. Then we were quiet again.

The phone rang.

"Don't answer it!" Richard yelled as I started to get up. "It could be the press."

"Don't you think they will have another story to move onto by now?"

"We should ask Randi who else has been calling her."

Richard, a former reporter, had asked his friend Randi, also a former reporter, to handle the press on behalf of the Laudor family. In addition to dealing with an *Inside Edition* team chasing us down the street for information, she had fielded interview requests from all the major networks and had spoken several times to both Diane Sawyer and Barbara Walters. Randi's husband Jim Estrin, Richard's best friend from childhood, was a photographer for the *Times,* and he was the real reason the first story about Michael the genius schizophrenic graced the pages of that newspaper. Just before we left for the funeral, Randi had orchestrated a "positive" story about Michael and Carrie's relationship for the *Times,* in addition to taking on the talking heads.

"Let's call Jim and Randi," I said. "They would probably like to know what the last couple of days have been like. And I would love to go over and see their kids if they are up for it. That would feel kind of normal."

Richard made the call while I got a legal pad to make yet another wedding list. Both the return from the funeral of someone Richard's brother murdered, and the wedding to come seemed surreal. I did not feel grounded, mind floating, outside my body, foggy. Maybe I could distract myself by getting practical with the list.

Wedding Invitations/pick up and address
Dress
Flowers
Food: make the rest of the Caterer appointments
Music—get that harpist?
DJ
Bridesmaids' shoes

Uh-oh. My three best friends were supposed to walk down the aisle ahead of us, next to Richard's two brothers and Jim. Now there would only be one brother and one friend. Put that problem off somehow, my brain said.

Then, the memory of Carrie telling me that Michael had drawn a knife on her resurfaced. I had to remind Richard of that. Did anyone else know? Would it affect the clear insanity defense the new lawyers were planning? Maybe Michael didn't pull knives only when in the throes of a psychotic delusion or hallucination.

Richard reported, "Randi says Barbara Walters is still trying and they invited us over for dinner. They'll just order pizza and Jim thinks he can be home fairly early. He's working City Hall today."

"That's a good plan." I smiled at Richard. "I just thought of something," I said, nervous but resolved. "You know how I told you Carrie said Michael had pulled a knife on her before?"

"No," he said sharply. "You didn't tell me that."

"Yes, I did. You just don't remember."

Richard shook his head no.

"Well, anyway she did tell me that. I wonder if that is something Michael's lawyers need to know."

"It's hearsay," said Richard immediately. "You did not see him pull a knife. You don't know that he actually did that. Not admissible in a court of law."

"Yeah, okay, but what if she told other people? Don't you think his lawyers need to know?"

"I'll take that under advisement," said Richard, behaving like the lawyer he still was.

The phone rang again. Again, we didn't pick up. We could hear from the answering machine that it was another journalist. I was suddenly very exhausted, even though I had only been out of bed for an hour. "I need to go back to sleep," I said. Richard, always up for a nap, followed me into the bedroom, and we both lapsed into unconsciousness in the middle of a beautiful day. Our nap lasted until late afternoon and even then, I was still exhausted. A lifelong insomniac, I thought I knew what it meant to be tired, but for the rest of that summer, I felt a new kind of fatigue—a tortuous, unrelenting exhaustion, that no amount of sleep or rest would ameliorate.

Normal life, or some approximation, had to resume. I went back to my part time job at a social work agency and to school.

Richard stopped classes full time and took temp lawyer jobs, went back working long hours, though he left those too in time for the wedding. After, he'd struggle on for a semester or two, taking classes part time at NYU, but eventually give up. Richard's dream, to change professions, to be something else, was also murdered.

I was trying my best to pull the wedding off, without much help. My own mother was far away and entering the early stages of dementia. Ruth had her own ideas, but her plans loaded even more stress onto my addled brain. The worst was when she wanted to have an invitation-addressing party at her house, turning the simple process of getting the invitations out into an ordeal. She also wanted us to come to her synagogue on Friday night, for a special blessing before our Sunday wedding, as we were not using the family Rabbi or shul. This meant asking my parents to change their flight plans; they refused. Families. Weddings. Exhaustion. And a few moments of exhilaration. I was going to get married, after all, to my dear sweet Richard.

We learned, just one week before the wedding, that the first most hoped-for outcome for Michael had come true: he was found incompetent to stand trial and sent to a forensic psychiatric hospital for treatment, until he was sane enough to understand any legal proceedings. Richard and I didn't see him until after the wedding. We were told Michael didn't believe that Carrie was dead.

Chapter 20

Amazed, We Get Married

The wedding was the Sunday of Labor Day weekend, not quite three months after Michael killed Carrie. Even though there had been threads of turmoil and sorrow woven in everything all summer—for me, September 6, 1998, was close to pure joy.

That hot, early morning in Riverdale I walked to the corner hair salon to get my hair done and my makeup applied, a first for me. Then I retrieved the female cohort who had stayed the night with me: Mollie, her sister Georgia, their mother Gayle, and my "second mother" Mel, to head to Brooklyn. Richard had been banished to a friend's place the night before. We packed the big white wedding dress in the trunk of the car service vehicle and were off to the Picnic House in Prospect Park, for a once-in-a-lifetime adventure.

I'd have been happy getting married barefoot on the beach somewhere, in an informal ceremony, but Richard wanted a big family Jewish wedding, him in a tux, me in white. I wanted what would make him happy. His friend, Rabbi Jonathan Rubenstein, had agreed to marry us, even though I had dropped out of conversion class.

By New York City standards, it was a long drive from Riverdale to Park Slope. As usual, I was behind schedule and the car service driver got lost. I was starting to get incredibly nervous, but Mel held my hand, smiling with her usual serenity. Pulling up outside the Picnic House, just a little late, I spied Richard looking frazzled and impatient. We locked eyes and giggled. Neither could believe this was happening. I hurried off to change for the signing of the Ketubah, the traditional Jewish marriage contract.

There had been some wrangling which Ketubah. Richard, for some reason, wanted to pretend that we were still in the tribal holy land and use a Ketubah in Hebrew that spelled out who got the goats after the ceremony. Jonathan talked Richard out of this; besides, he could not say, exactly, that he was marrying us by the laws of the Torah. He could say, "in the spirit of" the laws of the fathers. Richard agreed, but not without some lawyerly and religious exegesis. I did agree that Richard could stomp the glass at the end of the ceremony but I required that we circled each other, to symbolize equality in our relationship, an update to the traditional "the bride revolves around the groom." Jonathan had also agreed that some elements of my choosing—not from my religious tradition but my American-English heritage—could be part of the ceremony. This included poems by Shakespeare and Elizabeth Barrett Browning; the early American tune, "A Gift to be Simple" performed on the harp; and the walk back down the aisle to "Ode to Joy" by that German guy Beethoven. I wanted to have everyone sing the "Internationale" in honor of Labor Day, but neither Jonathan nor Richard thought that was funny. It was to be a Jewish ceremony, not a communist one.

I changed into my wedding dress for the Ketubah signing, as there would be photographs taken, and the shorts and t-shirt I had arrived wearing would not be appropriate. (Note to self: if you ever have a Jewish wedding again, plan an extra outfit for signing the legal contract.) I felt like Cinderella, stepping into the soft, full, and fluffy white dress, with a deep, lace-trimmed, off-the-shoulder neckline. I thought Richard especially would like that, and I wanted so much to play bride to his groom.

Just outside the entrance to the Picnic House a table had been laid with the Ketubah, some flowers and pens. My parents and Richard's mother gathered around. My father had found a yarmulke to wear, likely a first for him, covering his still-black hair. As a student of the history of religion, he was intrigued and listened intently as Jonathan described the meaning of this document—a contract: one that outlines the responsibilities of the groom to the bride and the rights of the bride in marriage. Ours was on two-foot-wide parchment paper, edged with a colorful block design, the text in calligraphy speaking of love and equality and our commitment to a Jewish life.

I loved seeing my father's interested face and Richard's lit-up face as we participated in this ritual. Our two witnesses were Randi and Leslie. My hand shook a little as I signed, praying inwardly that this step would not involve submission, only connection. Afterwards, my mother, never known for any display of feeling, hugged me.

We processed down the aisle to the traditional "Here Comes the Bride" on the harp, with Elizabeth, Jim, and Randi's daughter walking first as flower girl. She was a methodical soul even at four and carefully placed one rose petal at each row of chairs. The audience smiled enthusiastically at this, though I hoped they were partly smiling at me, all done up in a white poofy wedding dress. My three best friends, accompanied by Jim, Danny, and my cousin Stephen, standing in for Michael, followed Elizabeth. Mom and Dad were on either side of me, and I saw beaming Richard in his tux under the chuppah. I felt so happy.

I don't remember the vows, but I do remember the warmth and sincerity in Jonathan's bearded rabbinical face and Richard, swaying intently with joy throughout. Mel and Richard's cousin Paul recited poems, and the harpist played a credible "Simple Gifts" during the Tingley interlude in the Laudor Jewish service. We circled each other at the appropriate moment, Jonathan pronounced us husband and wife, Richard stomped the glass, and shouts of Mazel tov rang out. When we kissed, Richard made the grand gesture of sweeping me backward for a dramatic first married embrace. With him, I felt alive and so utterly delighted to be committed to my dear sweet Richard.

Chapter 21

Without Rest

Two days later, I went right back to classes, clinical work and part time job at the Infant, Child and Family Institute. My mood was lifted by the wedding, but the grief and pain of the murder lingered. The exhaustion continued, compounded the rush back to everyday life with no downtime post-wedding. The honeymoon would wait until winter break. I was now a second year at City. The first year had been all classes and adjustment to my new life as a student, not the professor. One thing I concluded early on is that it is easier to be the student than the prof. You could sit and listen without having to run the show. Now, I was about to meet my first patient, a sacred moment in the training of a psychotherapist.

Benson, a slight seven-year-old African American boy, looked nervously at me in the waiting room. He had been coming to the City College Clinic before and was transferred to my care. His prior therapist, Ms. B, gone on internship, was much beloved. We students hadn't received much practical advice given about how to conduct this first session, or any sessions. I knew the goal was to play, to follow the child's lead and try to make sense of what he meant, as he created fantastical worlds, using small props and toys. I walked Benny, as he told me his name, back to the same playroom he had worked in before. His eyes lit up as he saw the room but he was somewhat avoidant of me. I tried to shift my exhaustion and grief into the background and be present in the moment with my young patient. Wordlessly, Benny got some Legos and small figures off the shelf and began to construct something, solo. After a few minutes, I said, "I think you might be missing Ms. B." He gave a tiny, almost imperceptible, nod.

"It's hard to get used to someone new," I offered.

No reply. Benny was here because he had uncontrollable angry outbursts his parents did not know how to handle. When he became most upset, he would turn into "the subway," standing stock still, running his hands in front of his face as if they were subway doors, and uncannily mimicking the dings and beeps that accompanied the subway doors' action. Benny was unreachable when he was the subway. His mother was disabled from a car accident in childhood; his father was unemployed, and a sometimes drug addict. Benny lived with a lot of turmoil, even violence at home. Benny was incredibly bright, at the top of his class, but he could not stop his own attacks of rage, hurting himself and others.

Benny stood abruptly, went to the small table where the children always had a snack, opened the apple juice and slurped it down, eyeing me with some suspicion.

"What's your name again?" he asked.

"Ms. Tingley."

"Ms. B would sometimes get me better snacks. I don't like graham crackers."

Knowing that I was lapsing into a concrete, less than therapeutic mode, I asked, "What kind do you like?"

"Ritz."

"Okay. I can try to bring those for you." Trying to return to a therapeutic mode I asked, "What else did you and Ms. B do together?"

Benny went back to wordless playing. I knew the first task was to find a way in. I stayed quiet and mirrored his play action with my own small figure, jumping mine up and down as he moved his. When his guy fell from the Lego tower, I made a k-boom sound. Benny laughed. I had my guy rush over and waited to see what would happen next between our characters, noticing a slight release of tension in Benny's body. What would Benny's next play move reveal about his inner state or his unconscious ideas of self and others? Of course, he began to play of danger and rage, his small character attacking mine, with zest and glee in his eye as we got down to the business of play therapy. Surprised, I did know how to follow his lead into meaningful, affective engagement with the play material.

Afterwards, I had to write a process note, getting down every move and nuance in the play to read to my supervisor. By the time the notes were done, my fatigue returned.

Maybe I could do this, even with a dark exhausted haze my now constant companion.

Chapter 22

Razor Wire and Nazis

We carefully planned the trip up to Mid-Hudson State Hospital, the state forensic psychiatric hospital where Michael was being held, for a Saturday afternoon. This would give us enough time to recover from the pain of seeing Michael, essentially behind bars and still completely psychotic, before returning to our real and work lives on Monday.

While preparing for the one-hour drive north, I noticed Richard's hands shaking while buttoning his shirt. This would be the first time seeing his brother since before the murder.

"Oh, Richard. It'll be hard. But it will be okay," I said as I hugged him. "We'll be together."

"I know, babe." He paused. "I am just gonna hate to see him like this. Not that I haven't seen him crazy before. But still."

I hugged him tighter. Richard, who could cry, had not really allowed himself to sob since his brother's descent into mad violence. I thought he was going to break down, finally, at this moment, but instead he abruptly pulled away.

In a monotone, Richard said, "I always promised Michael that I would never let anything hurt him. But I couldn't protect him, could I?" Bitterness edged into his voice.

"Sweetie, what could you do? There was no danger to Michael from the outside, just the inside."

Though I said these reassuring words, I remembered what Richard seemed to have completely forgotten: that he was supposed to be with Michael that day—a plan we'd discussed that very morning at the airport—spending the morning and afternoon of the murder with Michael while waiting for the intervention team to arrive. Instead, his mother insisted that Richard only go to Michael's place later that afternoon to help Carrie get him into the hospital. They had argued and Richard refused to go to Michael's at all; he would not be ordered around or treated like staff by his mother. This was not the time, nor would it ever be, to remind Richard of these details. And if he had been there, Michael could have killed Richard too. For that I was selfishly grateful for the crazy dynamic that kept Richard away.

Richard finished buttoning his shirt. I grabbed his hand. "Let's get this show on the road. You carry the bagels." We were bringing Michael kosher food he liked. "I'll drive both ways," I added. "You can relax."

The cloudy, humid, fall day, held the potential for drizzle, not cold, not hot, but not bad for driving. As I made the turns through the Bronx to the New York State Thruway, which we could take most of the way there, the mood in the car was somber, a change from the last month, when we were coming down from the high of our wedding.

Now, for the first time, my husband would be facing his brother as a confessed killer.

As I drove, we discussed thank-you notes to distract us, with me insisting that Richard write some of them. We exited the Thruway in Orange County, more than an hour from home, and drove along a two-lane, state road, littered with small, rundown houses, fast-food joints, and used-car dealerships. The clouds had descended and, though it wasn't raining, the air felt thick with moisture.

"We're in the middle of nowhere, now," I said, joking, trying to raise Richard's spirits. He continued staring out the window.

"The turnoff to the hospital should be just a little way up from here," Richard said a few minutes later, consulting the directions from Ruth. Richard was sweating and very pale. He often felt sick when it was humid. I reached over to pat his hand.

"Are you feeling sick with this weather?"

"Yup. And the occasion," he replied, managing a smile.

"Yeah, no fucking kidding."

"I think that's it," he said, pointing to a sign. A winding driveway led to a series of dingy, one- and two-story, institutional buildings, all surrounded by a huge chain-link fence, topped with coils of barbed wire. Mid-Hudson looked like a prison, not a hospital.

I was suddenly scared.

The place seemed foreboding and spoke of violence that needed to be contained, though the rural setting was full of green grass, with some red and yellow from the autumn trees. I had somehow thought this little trip to the country would have an element of the peaceful or pastoral, but seeing Mid-Hudson shattered that illusion. It was grim.

We were on time, a few minutes before the start of visiting hours on Saturday, between 2 and 4 PM, and a line of people waited outside the fence to get buzzed in. Richard carried in the bag with bagels, lox, and cream cheese. We were buzzed inside the fence to face a solid door, also controlled electronically, to wait again to enter the building. When it was finally our turn, we entered a small waiting area, where a tall, burly man behind spoke through a microphone from behind a thick glass door and window. He asked whom we were there to see.

"Michael Laudor," said Richard.

"Laudor, okay," said the guy. "First time here?"

"Yes."

"No weapons of course. No keys, no money except for coins, no wallets inside the visiting room. You can leave those items in a locker

171

in the next room." He buzzed us through the next door where we found a metal detector and another, even more burly guy.

"Who are you here for?" asked the guy in a uniform.

"Michael Laudor," Richard repeated.

"Family?"

"He's my brother. And this is my wife," Richard said proudly, as he was still thrilled to be calling me his wife.

"Sign in. Name, address, and relation to the patient. What's in the bag?"

"Food," I answered. The officer peered into the bag. He picked up one of the small plastic knives we had brought from the bagel shop and ran the blade over his hand.

"No good," he said and put the knives aside. "Ask the guy at the counter inside for utensils." Then he put the bag through the metal detectors and waved a wand over us. It buzzed at Richard's pocket.

"Oh, my keys. Sorry." Richard pulled them out. The officer gave him a stare, wanded him again, and waved us on. We placed our possessions into a locker and were given small plastic tags with numbers.

"Wait 'til you get buzzed in, one at a time," the officer said. Then, speaking into a microphone, "Two coming for Laudor."

This was our third locked door and when we were buzzed in it was to a small four-by-four-foot area, with yet another door to pass through. When the door behind me clicked shut, two more large men watched to be certain that the door behind was completely closed; then they buzzed us through to what looked like a cafeteria, except that the chairs and tables were bolted to the floor. Small windows high up on the walls allowed some light into this otherwise gray room, but the windows were tiny and far out of reach. No one was going to break or crawl through them. At one end of the room was a counter, the guards were mostly standing behind, and some vending machines along a side wall. Again, we were asked to write our names on a sheet of paper, along with the number on our tags, and to put Michael's name down.

"Have a seat and we'll bring Michael down soon." This man smiled a little at us; perhaps he could tell we were freaked out at this first visit.

Richard surveyed the room and whispered, "Let's sit at that far table, because I bet Michael is going to be paranoid that we'll be overheard."

The visiting room was not full but there were about seven or eight other tables of patients and visitors. Nearly everyone had brought food; the family next to us was passing around a full fried chicken dinner. I could mostly tell the patients from the visitors, even though the patients were wearing street clothes. The vacant look of over-medication, the silence, the friends and family leaning toward the person they were visiting. There was a little laughter now and then, but it was not a happy place.

After about ten minutes, the door at the far end opened and there was Michael, accompanied by yet another big, tall man. As Michael stepped in, his escort nodded to the guards in the room and reversed course. Michael stood blinking, looking out across the room for us. When he caught sight of Richard, he walked toward us, slowly. Richard stood and embraced his brother with a bear hug. Michael clung to him for a few seconds longer than seemed natural. I also stood to hug him.

If I hadn't known we were there to see Richard's little brother, I might not have recognized him. In the nearly five months since I had seen Michael, he appeared to have aged far beyond his years, transformed from a robust and healthy, handsome thirty-something man into a thin, ugly, mental patient. His head was shaved, as was his face, which had always been bearded. His skin looked unhealthy, pale, and somehow scarred. A pair of huge, brown-rimmed institutional glasses unattractively covered his face, and though he wore his former favorite uniform of khaki pants and button-down shirt, the clothing appeared worn, frayed, clearly never ironed, unlike his former immaculate sartorial state. Michael was slack jawed and his whole body drooped and sagged awkwardly. Michael, the varsity volleyball player, was gone. His eyes darted around, even as he sat across from us at the small table, probably scanning the room for danger. I had no idea what he was seeing, perhaps hallucinating fire and other visual dread.

"How are you, Mike?" I asked.

He smiled and made eye contact with me, and seemed glad to see us, even in these circumstances. "Not bad, considering." He laughed a nervous laugh.

"We brought food," I motioned to the bag of bagels. Michael raised his eyebrows and looked sort of happy at this.

"Bagels," said Richard. "How's the food here?"

"Not Kosher, that's for sure."

"Could you ask for Kosher food? Surely, they could honor your religious beliefs," Richard said.

I began laying out the bagels, cream cheese, and lox. They guard outside had left us one plastic spoon.

"This looks good. Thank you," said Michael, who turned his gaze to Richard's face, perhaps searching for something there. Then he went back to sweeping his eyes around the room, nervously, before leaning in, whispering to Richard, "I am not sure they know I am Jewish. I don't want to tell them."

Richard and I glanced at each other; of course, by now everyone in the New York metro area who read the newspaper or watched the news knew Michael was Jewish. Michael leaned in farther and said very, very quietly, "There're Nazis on the unit."

Richard took this on, seriously. "How can you tell, Michael?"

Again, Michael whispered. "I saw a swastika on the wall in the bathroom one morning."

174

"Was it there the next time you went to the bathroom?" Richard asked.

Michael shifted nervously and didn't answer.

"Think, Mike. Is it still there?"

Slowly, Michael said, "No."

"So, someone erased it, yes?"

Again, Michael nodded very slowly. "But—"

Richard interrupted him. "There probably *are* Nazis on the unit. There are Nazis everywhere. But I don't think everyone is a Nazi. Right, Michael? Think, Michael."

Michael appeared deep in thought. He took a bite of bagel and lox.

"Is there anyone on the unit that you think is not a Nazi? What about Scott, your social worker? Mom thinks he is a good guy."

"Yeah. Scott is okay. He talks to me when he can."

"How about the nursing staff? Do any of them seem good?"

Michael stared at his brother's face, clearly trying to believe that Richard was telling the truth and that he was not completely surrounded by the Third Reich.

Richard took a deep breath. "Mike, do you think I am a Nazi?" This came from what Richard knew about Michael's delusion when he was first hospitalized, years before. Then, Michael had thought everyone in the family was being impersonated by aliens and Nazis. Michael looked Richard up and down and then directly again at his face. He broke into a smile.

"No. You are so weird, no one would make you up," Michael said, and laughed.

I chimed in, "You're right, Michael. He is still my Richard."

Michael turned to me. "Congratulations. I heard you guys got married. Liz, you prove there is someone for everyone, including my weird-as-hell big brother." He glanced over at the TV, showing the Yankee playoff game silently above us.

Richard spoke calmly and directly, again to his brother, "So, your job, is to figure out who is and who isn't a Nazi. Okay, Michael?"

Like a small, vulnerable child, Michael nodded yes; he would try to follow these instructions.

"I think the Yankees are going to go all the way this year," Richard said, injecting some normality in the conversation.

"Yeah, I only get to follow it a little. The guys don't always want to put the baseball on in the unit."

"Jeter is having an incredible season," I added and went on, mischievously, "Your brother has almost converted me back to the Yankees from my days as a Red Sox fan."

This made Michael laugh, and I felt I had succeeded, for that day, in some small way, in helping Richard and Michael. We ate our bagels, and Richard filled Michael in on who from the extended family had attended the wedding. Michael seemed to follow this conversation for about twenty minutes and then appeared utterly exhausted, and started to sag into himself, growing less responsive. I thought about the metaphor he used to use, about keeping reality on the screen in front of him. When the psychosis was strong, this took more energy than he had, and I could see he had used up his ability to stay with us in the noncrazy world. Richard could see this too and wolfed down his bagel, so we could leave Michael before he stopped functioning altogether.

"Time for us to go, Michael," Richard said, standing up.

I hugged Michael first and then Richard did and again, Michael did not want to let go of his brother. Richard held him close for several minutes. Then Michael turned to the guards and one of them walked him out.

When we had passed through all the secure doors again, and were back in the parking lot, Richard began to shake, silently. We put our arms around each other and I helped him into the car. He sat wordlessly on the trip back. Back at our apartment, early Saturday evening, Richard climbed into bed and didn't get out again until Monday morning, when the alarm chirped.

Chapter 23

A baby is not too much to ask

I wanted to move further out of my long-term sense of aloneness and the current crazy ecosphere and reclaim at least a morsel of normal. I wanted to try to make a baby with dear, sweet Richard. Wasn't baby making what you did after getting married?

I was 44, and it wouldn't be easy or likely even possible. I discovered early on that Richard did not like children, was in fact not good with children, and did not want them. Richard's dislike of children got in the way of many of my friendships as most of my friends were "kid people," too. The first time he met my friend Hattie's two small children, he had been hostile and disagreeable about their noise and their demands to be the center of attention. Richard wanted to be the center of attention. He had been tortured and bullied as a child by other children; thus, he didn't like children.

We did talk about having kids before getting married. Richard didn't want to be a father because he felt his gene pool was contaminated. His grandmother had been psychotic; Michael had schizophrenia. He felt his dead father had been "crazy" and he hated his mother. He did not want to continue the Laudor line. Between his own difficulties with depression and having been labeled "weird" as a kid—what I later got diagnosed as Asperger's Syndrome—he would be content becoming an uncle, and as his grandfather had been to him, a source of unconditional love, taking his yet-to-be nieces and nephews to Broadway plays and baseball games.

I told him about my possible infertility but that I hoped to try maybe once to have a baby, even with assisted means, though I didn't want my life to be consumed by not having a baby.

This was a lie. Becoming a mother was all I had ever wanted, but this was the most I could admit about how much I wanted kids, even to myself.

As a child, I dreamed of growing up and having a large family, with six or eight or even ten children of my own to fill the empty space created when my brother died, and my mother retreated into her grief. I created pretend families from the model photos in the Sears, Roebuck catalog, and each cutout child, named something like Rob or Ben or Susie, had lavish cutout outfits and mountains of cutout toys. I created drawings of these families' house layouts, carefully considering which children would and would not get their own rooms. I wrote stories about them, and each family had boundless fun and exciting adventures with so many lively children.

This desire to fill a house with noise, mess, emotional chaos, and love loudly demonstrated, so unlike the cold silent one I grew up in, stuck with me into adolescence and adulthood. I loved being around small children. Babysitting a group of seven children at the "commune" during high school had made me happy-ish. I was a kid person. I was the adult who found kids at parties and got them screaming, throwing balls around in the house, leading a game of sardines or feeding them extra dessert behind their parents' backs. In some ways, my first career as a childcare teacher, spending my day with 10 toddlers, was an effort to create this kind of family for myself. And I had Mollie, my unofficial "goddaughter," the child of the friends I had lived with after my nervous breakdown in the 1980s. She and I shared a special closeness and when I moved from Boston to Texas, she wrote me a letter on the occasion of her sixth birthday that read "This is the first birthday in my entire life that you have not been with me." She was thirteen when I met Richard, and for her, he made an exception of his "I don't like children" rule, and my relationship with her continued.

This was not enough, though. Being a real mother, having my own child, was all I really wanted; it felt like it was the only way to fully heal the family destroyed in my early childhood and my own broken sense of self, to become a part of life. But I also thought I was unworthy of motherhood, because I was so apart, weird, damaged, depressed. I could not speak this wish aloud, let alone formulate a plan to make it happen. Whenever I felt like I wanted to die, to give up, the thought that came into my head was always, "I'll never be a mother." And then, of course, although I had occasional serious boyfriends, I was never close to or trusting of anyone until I met Richard at age forty. Gynecologists had been telling me, since I was in my mid-twenties, that it would be difficult for me to conceive. My medical history pointed to infertility—irregular menstrual cycles—so the doctors said I should have kids young or I might not have them at all. This fueled my depression and suicidal wishes. By my thirties, when Mr. Right wasn't coming along, some of my friends had children on their own, through assisted reproductive technology or adoption, but this was not for me. Given how important my father had been to me, I wanted a father for my children. And the experience I really wanted was to be pregnant, to feel a baby grow inside of me, to birth my own child or children, to carry on the family line, for a child to be a Tingley.

How had I chosen someone who didn't even like children? I hoped he would change; I had friends whose partners had been reluctant and then been good parents. Richard had wanted to "grandparent" Michael and Carrie's kids. Naively. I thought a baby that belonged to him might actually make him happy.

One night, after we became officially engaged, not long before we moved from Vermont to Riverdale, we sat up in bed talking about what it meant to get married. I started crying. I turned to Richard, and with a fierce desperation in my voice, said, "Promise me. Promise me. Promise me that we can try to have a kid." I broke down, sobbing, loudly.

Richard held me close and kissed me with passion. "Yes."

Years later, in couples counseling, we would discuss this moment. It came down to a rather legalistic definition of "try." By considering it, putting the idea on the table, discussing, thinking about it, pondering it, opening the topic up—this to Richard was the definition of *try*. To me, *try* meant to physically try to make a baby, to find ways for our sperm and egg to meet and become one to grow inside of me, either through conventional or artificial means.

This is what I thought we had agreed to, when we gotten married, that we would try—my definition of try, that we would try to become pregnant.

Six months after marrying, I got around to transferring my medical care from upstate to the city and made an appointment with a new gynecologist. Though a routine visit, I told the doctor that while I recognized the long odds, I hoped to become pregnant, and she immediately referred me to a top specialist, Dr. David Barach at the Fertility Treatment Group of Montefiore Hospital and Einstein School of Medicine out in Hartsdale, in Westchester County. I expected more resistance, but Richard agreed to see the fertility expert. He loved me, he said, and would do anything to make me happy.

I went alone to the first appointment., thinking I didn't need Richard to get the ball rolling. When I made the appointment, no one told me the typical protocol was for both partners to appear for this interview.

Dr. Barach, a thin man with odd affect, cold and yet intensely pene-trating in other ways, asked in a hushed tone of gravitas and condescen-sion, "Are you not married?"

I assured him I was married. We discussed many issues and I brought up the genetic one—that Richard was the brother of the genius psycho-killer Michael Laudor. He immediately knew who I meant.

"That kid from Yale?" he asked. I nodded.

When we got to our sex habits, which also might have an impact on our efforts to make a baby, Dr. Barach closed the door. I had thought it was odd that the door had not been closed before then. (Later, after we completed our treatments with Dr. Barach, I got a strange letter from him, letting his patients know that he was taking a leave from the insti-tute, not for reasons of his choosing, to do research in biochemistry. A little online snooping revealed that Dr. Barach had had his medical license suspended for sleeping with a patient. He must have been under investigation for these charges and so had to keep the door open most of the time so as to not fall under further suspicion.)

At this point in the summer of 1999, nearly a year after we married, Richard was still working temp jobs as a lawyer, which was decent money, but our health benefits were through my part-time job at the Infant, Child and Family Institute, which I held while a full-time grad-uate student at CUNY. Dr Barack recommended, given my age and other factors, that we go right for the most aggressive treatment, in-vitro ferti-lization. Miraculously, all of the fertility treatments were covered, except for the hormones that we would have to inject daily into my butt before the in vitro fertilization procedure. The reality that Richard, terrified by needles, would have to do the injecting, and the money, were stum-bling blocks: between $3,000 and $4,000 out of pocket. After discussing the injection issue with his friend Leslie (in whose apartment he had proposed), she offered to travel daily from Manhattan to Riverdale and do it for him, but finally Richard decided he would just man up. He also said that we could find the money.

Contrary to any romantic ideas of baby-making, undergoing *in vitro* fertilization was an arduous process, full of poking, prodding, examining, analyzing the inner organ world, an operation to harvest eggs, and daily early morning forty-five-minute trips out to the lab in the Westchester suburbs to monitor progress. I also had to go off all of my antidepressant and sleep medication. Dr. Barach and my psychiatrist did not communicate well, thus leading to a more rapid withdrawal than was probably best. This, plus the hormones, made me feel entirely crazy, in a way that made the world around me seem unreal.

Like with much previous in our lives together, I managed it all.

I picked up the first round of medicines from the pharmacy. After an initial squeamishness, Richard did okay at jabbing me with the hormone-filled hypodermic needles. Then it was Richard's turn to get them a few days later to put on his credit card. This involved some logistical planning, as the little pharmacist-owned shop in Westchester was not open 24 hours and Richard was working way downtown. One of Richard's favorite chants was, "I don't do logistics." Thus, I organized his trip, making him drive to work, park in a very expensive garage, and called him at intervals to make sure he would leave on time so he'd get to the shop before closing.

That evening, I was home after a long day of classes, patients, and my part-time job, feeling completely crazy, in my hormone-fueled state. The evening light was fading through the western window of our living room while I sat at the dining room table, fingering the mail, yet unable to open any of it. I tried to take a deep breath. Nothing felt real and I was pretty scared. I petted the dog but failed to get up to make dinner. I just kept sitting there, wondering, worrying, and hoping that we could have a baby. Yet it all was out of kilter and illusory. I heard

Richard's key turn in the door and felt some relief. He would be there, with the medicine, and I would have something to focus on besides the bizarre, detached state wrought by antidepressant withdrawal and high doses of hormones.

He came in with a bang, looking enraged, threw a large bag on the table in front of me and said loudly, flailing his arms around, "Do you know how much that cost? This is going to ruin us."

Stunned, as this was not typical Richard behavior, I asked, "How much?"

"Almost thirty-five hundred dollars," he shrieked, fishing the receipt from his pocket, and throwing it at me. But this was the price range we knew ahead of time. I was so confused and addled.

"I told you this was a bad idea even before Michael killed Carrie. Now, there's a murderer in the family. I should not pass on my genes!" he continued, yelling angrily at the top of his lungs before stomping off to the bedroom, shedding his clothes, and diving under the covers.

The room was now dark. I sat there, feeling the most intense fear of my life. I could see that I was on my own in this. On my own. I had never wanted to be a single parent, but I knew that if we did succeed in making a baby, and staying married, I could never count on Richard for anything. And I would be subjecting a child to a father who couldn't cope, who wouldn't come through. Was he right about the genetic risk? I had looked it up; having an uncle with schizophrenia only increased the odds of having a child who would become schizophrenic by six percent. This had seemed like odds I, —or, I had thought, *we*—were willing to take on.

For the remainder of the fertility treatment, I was filled with terror and knew we should not go through with it. I did not get pregnant. In the days spent mourning the baby we didn't have, Richard was the most active and most gentle in tending to me of all the time we were together.

I wondered if we should try again, in spite of the revelation I'd had about Richard as partner and father. We consulted with the obnoxious Dr. Barach, who said he would do another round for the sake of "closure," but the odds were against us. We went to Boston to see another specialist, who agreed the odds were very, very small but didn't tell us, so I thought, *not* to try again. I was now 44, after all. We took this dilemma to our couples' counselor. Richard was dead set against trying again and claimed the Boston doctor had told us not to try again. He felt he had more than fulfilled his part of the bargain. The therapist clearly took his side—a man, of course. In that session, I realized my hope for a family was dead.

As we walked out, Richard looked at me with concern. He kissed me. He told me he loved me. I didn't care. I pulled away, and unfairly, hated him and the therapist. We both had cars in the city, and I drove alone back up towards Riverdale, along the Westside highway, the George Washington Bridge looming above. The depressive urge, the thought that I would never have what I wanted most in life, overtook me. The despair was so enveloping that I headed toward the bridge, to jump off it, right then. The "right then" in my suicidal thinking was new and different. Usually, I was able to cling to some hope that things might change, that somehow, I could get what I wanted out of life. This usually allowed me to postpone offing myself.

That night, I knew for certain that I would never have a family of my own and to me this meant I could never be a part of normal, real life. At the last second, I swerved left to stay on the Westside Highway and go home. But for a long time, the option to jump off that the bridge never completely left my mind.

Chapter 24

Competent?

Over the next year, we visited Michael at Mid-Hudson every few weeks. Each time, after suffering seeing his best friend and brother crazy, Richard became completely incapacitated, in bed for at least twenty-four hours. We had to see Michael, but I was of two minds. I would never see him as the true mensch Richard, his family and *The New York Times* claimed, though Michael's charm, intelligence, and vulnerability remained lovable.

Seeing him was also terrifying; I worked hard to keep out of my mind the bloodied knife in Michael's large hands, stabbing tiny Carrie over and over again. This made the visits so peculiar. Michael's general demeanor was sweet, gentle, kind, and yet he had done something so grotesque and evil. My head pounded trying to put these two Michaels together. I felt fragmented, becoming spacey, aloof on the outside and full of colliding, fierce emotion on the inside after each visit.

What a strange way to live the first year of a marriage—joy filled, yet often overridden by tragedy, with many weekends taken away from us by these visits. In addition, the perpetual buzz and angst in the family about Michael's legal case proved stressful. Richard and Danny, both lawyers, never agreed and Richard's family generally perceived the eldest brother as incompetent, giving Danny more authority over legal strategies, which infuriated Richard. Occasionally, Richard prevailed—like his idea not to use a big-time Manhattan criminal attorney. Believing that all politics are local, he counseled the use of the best Westchester Country attorneys, as they knew the area judges and DA, how local juries worked. Danny had walked away from practicing law at a big downtown law firm just weeks before the tragedy and behaved as if he had the full burden of the case and made it his full-time job. Richard believed this arrangement existed for Danny's benefit. Ruth paid him, so he wouldn't have to return to work. In fact, Danny would never really work outside the family again. On repeated phone conferences about the case, Ruth and Danny frequently hung up on Richard.

Richard's professional life was unsettled, as he continued to work temp legal jobs. He'd dropped out of NYU, the career change jinxed forever. Richard felt enraged and hopeless and helpless, and began to experience serious psychiatric troubles, the kind he hadn't since we'd met. It grew harder for me to pull him along, as I was so engaged by my own career change and new city life.

At first, given how strong his paranoia was, Michael refused all medications and remained completely psychotic. Theoretically, as a mental patient in New York State, he had this right. Though charged with second degree murder, he was assigned to Mid-Hudson by the court in order to become competent for trial. His doctors there sought a court order to force him to take medicine to reach this goal; there was a court onsite at Mid-Hudson. Per standard procedure, Michael was appointed a Mental Hygiene attorney to argue his case in the hospital court—that the medicine was poison. Michael lost, the judge ordering him to take antipsychotic medication. Now, if Michael refused a pill, he would forcibly be given an injection of Thorazine. Terrified of needles, he complied. In the early winter of 1999, he started taking all his medications and began a slow climb back to at least semi-reality. Even before this last descent into utter madness, no medicine had ever worked well enough to completely take away the delusions and hallucinations. Since the onset of his schizophrenia at age twenty-four, at his best Michael had only been clear headed enough to think *around* his psychosis, but never been entirely free from it.

By late spring, as we sat in the visiting room at Mid-Hudson, spooning out the Ben & Jerry's brought as a treat for Michael (and to soothe my soul as an ice cream fanatic), Michael wore a glum expression. He had been at Mid-Hudson for almost a year and was now certain that Carrie really was dead and that he might never have any kind of life. Paranoia radiated as his eyes continually darted around the room searching for danger. Then he focused on Richard's face.

"You are getting kind of grey, bro," he said, gently teasing. Richard's beard had greyed considerably in the last year.

Richard smiled softly at Michael, seeming to savor a moment when Michael was well enough to just act like a brother. He started rubbing his chin. "World affairs have added some of this grey. Mom always ages me. Danny, too. And there might be a strand or two put here by you, Michael."

We all chuckled, although Michael also looked slightly sad. I leaped in: "Am I off the list of stressors, Richard? I mean, now that you are an old married man, maybe your wife is stressing you out too."

Richard gently reached out his bear paw of a hand and put it on top of my head. "I just love you, Lizzie," he said. All three of us exchanged happy looks for a moment.

Richard turned to the real matter at hand. "Are you taking all of your meds Michael? Like a good boy?"

Michael nodded.

"To get out of here you are going to have to promise to always take your meds."

Michael nodded again.

"Have you talked to your lawyer lately?" Richard asked.

"Yeah, Andy Rubin came up last week. He says Jeanine Pirro is pushing to re-evaluate my competency."

The Westchester County DA, Jeanine Pirro, flamboyant, right wing and reactive, wanted to pursue the case vigorously, likely to prove she was very tough on crime.

"Yeah, now that the publicity about the case has died down, she wants to stir it up and go back on Larry King Live," I said. Richard shot me a look: *shut up*.

Michael appeared puzzled. I had forgotten how little he knew about the media hype around his case. The family was intent on protecting him from this, so I changed the subject.

"How do you like your psychiatrist? It's someone new, right?"

Michael shrugged. "She seems nice, okay. Her English is not very good."

"How often do you get to see her about your medication??" I asked.

"Every couple of weeks, maybe."

"Are you getting any talk or supportive therapy from a psychologist or counselor?"

Michael laughed, sounding cynical. "No. Scott the social worker is a nice guy and he tries to talk to me, but he has a huge caseload and therapy is not part of his job description. He also might be transferred off my unit."

This wasn't good news; from the family's perspective, Scott was the only one with any sense about what, aside from medications, might help Michael.

"What is the program for you?"

"Lining up for meds twice a day. We get occupational therapy once a week, where we can do crafts and things like that. And the psychologist pretends he sees everyone once a week, but really, he sees all of us on the unit in a group at the same time for thirty minutes. Other stuff, like the swimming pool, is closed due to lack of funding. I usually do get to play basketball with the guys once a day if the weather is okay." Michael laughed. "I show these young black kids that this old white guy still has a little game."

"That leaves a lot of time on your hands."

Michael bearing turned grim, perhaps scared. "Yeah, we sit in the day room a lot and there are two TVs, one at each end, that are on all the time. It's loud. Sometimes there are fights over what to watch."

I knew Michael in the past claimed psychotic messages came to him from TV. "Can you go in your room to get away from it?" I asked.

He shook his head. "No, only on Sunday afternoon when they let us take a nap."

This meant there was no escape from the noise and chaos of the unit, which were psychotic stressors for Michael. *What a non-therapeutic place.*

The burly men standing guard behind the counter called out that visiting hours would end in fifteen minutes. Saying goodbye, Michael hugged us both, gripping tightly before approaching the door to the yard leading back to the unit, where he waited resignedly for the guard escort.

After Richard and I were buzzed out of the three locked doors and made our way to the parking lot, I said, "Michael really seemed a little better today."

"Yeah," Richard replied bitterly. "He's probably well enough to stand trial for murder. That puts him in a really good spot."

"I know," I said, as empathetically as I could. "I know. But hopefully the insanity defense will work and he won't be found guilty of murder and have to go to prison. That would be worse than Mid-Hudson."

"Remember what our dear friend Jeanine Pirro told Larry King and F. Lee Bailey on national television? 'Mental illness is not a get-out-of-jail-free card.'"

191

"Well, she will try to prosecute the case, given what a conservative sleazeball she is but I think it will be hard for her to win."

"Hope you are right, babe."

By the end of August, Michael was declared competent to stand trial. His attorneys argued that Michael should not be sent to the Westchester County Jail to await trial, as his mental health was still fragile, so the judge ordered he be kept at Mid-Hudson until trial. Though Mid-Hudson was very jail-like, and wasn't a comfortable or therapeutic environment, it was safe place where Michael could reliably get his medication. His continued placement there counted as a significant victory.

Chapter 25

I Just Wanna Have Fun

Other weekends, I tried to ensure that Richard and I had some fun—like driving up to Cambridge to visit my dear old friends. We arrived to just in time to watch Owen play soccer. Owen, aged eight, was the black-haired, younger son of friends, the boy Michael had dug in the sand with on Block Island. No longer the toddler who loved to sit on his mother's lap, sucking his thumb and, with the gentlest, kindest demeanor, stroke her hair—"tweedling," he had called it—Owen was now a bigger boy, still sweet, who played sports and other bloodthirsty games. He liked Legos and superhero figures and had friends. He adored my dog, Annie.

Richard and I arrived at Cambridge Common with the game well under way on a late fall afternoon. Soccer in Cambridge was a very politically correct game. Children played to learn how to work together, to harness their competitive urges into cooperation and teamwork, and all children got equal playing time, constantly rotated in and out, regardless of who might score the most goals.

I joined Connie and Jeff, Owen's parents, on the sidelines. I always thought that I might know some of the other parents; perhaps I might have taken care of their older children at the Harvard Law School Child Care Center during the 1980s. This day, I didn't know any extra parents, although they were types I recognized.

We talked and watched the children running up and down the field in the cool, autumn air, as the afternoon light edged away. Suddenly, I had one of those moments where everything felt whole and golden: children in joyous activity and I surrounded by people I loved so much.

Richard had taken a spot right at the edge of the field and was following the play intently. Whenever Owen come close to the ball, he started to yell for Owen. Then, Richard, who couldn't move very well in the best of times, began that now-familiar activation of his whole body, where his arms trembled, following the players down the field, lurching and stumbling forward in whole-body awkwardness. One child fell; Richard yelled, "Kick him while he's down, Owen. Get him. There, he's down. Go, Owen." The words spun as wildly out of control as Richard's body.

I ignored this, tried not to listen, and kept talking to my dear friends. *Well, Richard, who does not like children, is maybe trying to relate to Owen, trying to connect.* Owen, when he had first met Richard at the beach, had been confused by his sarcasm. Richard had hurt his feelings, Owen said, adding, "Richard tells mean jokes, but then Liz explains them and it's okay."

When the game was over, one parent, a casually but perfectly dressed Cambridge father, turned to Connie. "Who was that man? A friend of yours?" he asked, voice dripping with disdain and incredulity. Connie nodded. She was one of the few friends of mine who saw the good in Richard and never stopped hanging out with us (although eventually she did stop going to restaurants with us, because she was seriously embarrassed by the demands and flirtatiousness Richard foisted on waitresses).

That night, Richard and I ate at one of my favorite restaurants in the world, Sol Azteca, with Connie and Jeff and other friends, Cathy, and Jack, who drove in from Western Mass. We started going to Sol Azteca together in fall of 1980, when we had all first met in our twenties, working as day-care teachers together. Back then, a meal at Sol Azteca, complete with enough Sangria to get us reasonably drunk, seemed a fortune—I think about $30 each—and so we only went there on very special occasions. The price hadn't gone up much, but we all earned middle class salaries now.

Parking at Sol Azteca could be challenging if there was a baseball game at nearby Fenway Park, or if Boston University was in session, and we had to park about five blocks away. Richard hated walking that far, so I stayed next to him, to keep him cheerful as we ambled along while the others walked ahead. I held his hand and got him to laugh. Even though we had a reservation, there was a line and we were herded to a little waiting area, down some stairs. Richard was too big to fit down there. I could tell he was going to start complaining soon but was determined not to let that ruin things. This was my special place, with the best, dearest of friends, where we always felt magically close and confessional as the Sangria flowed.

Once seated, we ordered Sangria and chips while Richard pored over the menu; he didn't really like Mexican food and never knew what to order. I understood that novelty was so stressful him, given his Aspergers. I tried to find him something mainstream he would like. He asked for soda instead of Sangria, taking time to ask the waiter carefully about each kind of soda they had, and engaging him in conversation, wishing they had Pepsi instead of Coke. The waiter tried to be patient. When the chips were mostly gone, Richard started snapping his fingers, searching for the waiter. I tried to reassure him, knowing this was his anxiety, and not meanness.

"Richard, they will come in a minute." He looked down, seemingly unaware that his behavior might be seen by the group as annoying.

We got more chips, more salsa. We talked about their kids, their extended families, and Mollie, my goddaughter and Connie's niece. I told stories about my new work as a therapist and the classes I was taking. Connie and Cathy shared anecdotes from their work, also with children. The conversation between Cathy, Connie, and me was fun, funny, and loving, an aura of openness among us, here in our place to talk. Richard tried to talk to Jeff and Jack. When the bill came, we all kicked in money equally. Richard started to complain, but I managed to dissuade him, and paid for both of us. For the first time ever, I was a bit relieved to leave Sol Azteca.

It's hard to bring these worlds together. Richard, soulmate of mine, can also be difficult, even though he doesn't mean to.

Chapter 26

Jeffrey Dahmer was Sane at the Time of the Crime

The next step in Michael's case was the evaluation of his mental state at the time of the crime. To be found "not responsible by reason of mental defect" was a high bar. The examining psychiatrists, hired by the defense and prosecution, and new to Michael, would have to determine if Michael knew right and wrong *at the moment he stabbed Carrie*. It seemed clear to me that Michael had mostly believed, at that moment, that Carrie was some kind of evil force out to harm him, that he must have felt so threatened because of his delusions and paranoia about who she was and what she was trying to do to him, that he killed her out of "self-defense." But Michael had always used the "two TV" metaphor about his psychosis and so perhaps even *while* he was in the act of brutally killing her, objective reality was still somewhere in his view. The psychiatrists hired for the defense would be sympathetic to this and perhaps not push too hard to find that other screen in Michael's head.

The psychiatrists hired by DA Pirro surely would push to show that the psychosis defense was a lie—that Michael knew what he was doing *at the moment,* and simultaneously that he also knew he shouldn't be taking those actions. They could also twist his behavior after he killed her—his purposeful flight in Carrie's car, to Binghamton where he ditched it and took a bus to Ithaca—as evidence of a functioning, devious mind trying to escape capture. He was charged with second degree murder; even Pirro's office could find no evidence of premeditation.

I wasn't sure what I thought about Michael's culpability. When he stabbed Carrie, he surely was in an alternate universe and not responsible. When he had made the decision to stop his meds, I thought he—and his psychiatrist—were responsible. When telling Carrie all those weeks that it was not safe to sleep in the same apartment with him, he was effectively saying, "It's not safe to be with me and my psychic demons." He knew there was danger, though he could not accurately locate it. *Didn't that make him responsible?* We knew that too, and no one, including me, had stepped in to save Carrie from Michael's paranoid perceptions. In spite of all of this, I still had some compassion for Michael because his life, no matter the trial outcome, was effectively over.

There was some discussion of not using the insanity defense at all. If Michael pled guilty, or even if he stood trial and was found guilty, second-degree murder carried a fifteen- to twenty-five–year sentence. He could earn some time off that sentence for good behavior and there would be a limit to Michael's time locked up. Thirty-five now, he would likely get out before he died. On the other hand, if he was found not legally responsible by reason of mental defect (the insanity defense), and did not go to trial, he would be committed to Mid-Hudson or some other forensic facility indefinitely without any clear mechanism to get out. Either way, he would likely never live outside of a locked facility.

At moments, Michael leaned toward pleading guilty, but the family and attorneys were strongly opposed. Besides, we all agreed that he should not be free unless he was well; he was so ill we feared he could kill again, the next time, perhaps, one of us. The best bet was to hand the decision-making over to even the not highly skilled mental-health professionals in conjunction with the Mental Hygiene courts. After the initial arraignment and competency hearings, the case was being handled through communication between attorneys and the recommendations of the forensic psychiatrists.

Pirro was a colorful character whose personal life was somewhat scandalous as her husband was convicted of tax evasion on forms she signed. He went to prison while she faced no charges. Pirro loved publicity. After leaving the DA's office, she launched a television career, first as a television judge on the show *Judge Jeanine Pirro* and then as a commentator on Fox News—years later, often defending President Trump. She was a strong law-and-order prosecutor who believed the insanity defense was never justified. A couple of years after Michael's case concluded, she wrote a book called *To Punish and Protect: A DA's Fight Against a System That Coddles Criminals*, in which she discussed Michael's case:

> One of the greatest travesties in this rush to forgive and excuse is the use of the insanity defense. I have believed for a long time that the insanity defense has no place in a criminal trial. It should only be a consideration once the verdict is reached. In the fact-finding portion of the trial, the issue should be: Did he do it? Did he commit the crime? If he did, find him guilty. Convict him. Then deal with his mental illness at the sentencing phase. Insanity should not be used as an excuse for getting away with murder.

With these views, she set out to hire the most pro-prosecution psychiatrist she could find to examine Michael and hopefully find that he was sane (knew right from wrong) at the exact moments of the crime.

She settled on the nationally known forensic psychiatrist, Park Dietz, who rose to prominence in the John Hinckley case, where he testified for the prosecution, claiming that Hinckley was not schizophrenic, but rather "personality disordered" and fully aware of how wrong it was to shoot President Reagan. Ultimately, the jury disagreed, and found Hinckley not responsible for his actions. Dietz went onto pronounce the serial killers Arthur Shawcross, Jeffrey Dahmer, and Ted Kucinzski sane—and should all be legally held accountable for their crimes.

I had seen TV interviews with Dietz, mostly about his evaluation of Jeffrey Dahmer, and he seemed to me a cold, clammy, and bloodless man. As his TV appearances focused on his analysis of the minds of murderers, I couldn't tell if it was just his subject or if he himself was creepy. I heard him say on TV that he liked Jeffrey Dahmer, the Michigan man who had killed several young men and eaten some of them. He said that Dahmer, unlike most killers he interviewed, was motivated to understand *why* he killed. This affection did not, however, stop Dietz from concluding that Dahmer should be held responsible.

I doubted Dietz would approach his examination of Michael with empathy when he came to Mid-Hudson early in 2000 to interview him. We heard through the family grapevine that Michael had been cooperative and obliging.

We visited Michael shortly after. This time we brought a pizza, a token of the real-world Michael was missing. By now, I was used to the barbed wire, the multiple lock check in, and the grim, institutionalized feel of the visitors' room, but was still shocked every time I saw Michael. He was so reduced, so far from the person I had known before.

As we ripped into the pizza, I asked Michael how he was. He hung his head and shook it slowly, then looked up with a fake smile, answering, "Okay, I guess," before shoving almost a whole slice into his mouth.

Richard bemusedly regarded his little brother. "When we were teenagers, Mom was always surprised that between us we could eat three whole pizzas, right, Mike?"

Michael swallowed and grinned. "Yeah, she never ordered enough pies. When Richard and I had at it, there was none left for Danny or Mom or Dad."

Richard said, "I can't actually eat like I used to."

Michael laughed and gestured around the room, as if to say, "Do you think I could ever eat like that in here?"

Richard chose this somewhat light-hearted moment to ask the real question on our minds.

"How did it go with Park Dietz? Mom said she thought he was done with the examination."

Michael grew quiet. He reached for another slice of pizza but this time his hands were shaking. In a tone just above a whisper, he said, "I don't think he liked me."

"What made you think that?" I asked.

"He made it clear he thought I was arrogant."

Uh oh. Did Michael try to be the genius, not in the least bit humble or remorseful? That would not go over well.

"What did you tell him, Michael?" Richard asked. This was interesting. Richard had never asked Michael directly, at least in my presence, what happened when he stabbed Carrie to death.

Michael replied, "I tried to answer all of his questions honestly."

"Okay," I nodded, trying to be empathetic. "Good strategy."

Michael went on, "I had to tell him it is hard to remember. It was so long ago." He paused again, taking in the visiting room with a vacant stare. "I can see my hands, hurting Carrie." He started to sound like someone was strangling him. "But they were not my hands." Michael's whole upper body started shaking. He looked me in the eye but then his eyes darted away. He fell silent.

Richard, in the kindest, gentlest tone, said, "Okay, Michael. Okay. You told the truth. That's what counts."

Looking like a small child hoping for a mother's absolution, Michael nodded slightly, his eyes on the floor. He seemed to fully retreat into himself and leapt up and away from us when time was called on visiting hours, no hugs this time around.

Two months later, Danny called for Richard. I listened in.

"You are not going to believe this, but Park Dietz found that Michael was insane at the time of the crime."

"You are shitting me. Really? Jeannine Pirro must be livid."

"Yeah. Michael's lawyers said the report he issued doesn't look very professional. It's one page, single-spaced, and full of typos. They wondered if Dietz and Pirro had a falling out and this was his payback. They don't have any proof of that, but it is a weird outcome."

"Can she go ahead and prosecute anyway?"

"She could but without a single medical or professional witness saying he was responsible for his actions when he stabbed Carrie, she will not have any real way to counter the insanity defense."

"So there still could be a trial?"

"Maybe, theoretically, but I really bet there won't be. What would be the point?" Danny said.

Tears of relief welled up in Richard's eyes.

In her book, Pirro would write that Dr. Dietz:

…then called me on the phone.

"I have to conclude in my report that he was suffering from a mental disease defect at the time of the killing," Park told me apologetically.

"Damn." I shook my head in disgust.

"He thought Carrie was evil. In his mind, it's all about good and evil," Park mused.

Why or how Dietz decided to come to this conclusion is not clear, except that this opinion conformed to the truth as we understood it.

Chapter 27

After this, how could I ever leave you?

On our wedding day, the very happiest of days, Richard didn't have a fulltime job. I wasn't worried—then—because the story Richard told about his work life was that he always got a better job than the one before. It took a few years, when the glow of being newly in love no longer vanquished every speck of Richard's darkness, until I understood Richard had been fired from almost every job he ever had, except his last gig in Albany, where he was hired for just one case and the job ended.

For the next five years, Richard worked at temp jobs or for a friend's law firm in New Jersey, but none morphed into a full-time, steady job. Finally, in spring of 2003, he landed a job, through a neighbor in our coop in Riverdale, working for a tiny but powerful commercial land-lord/tenant firm in Manhattan. It was essentially a one-man operation, Rozenholc and Associates, located in a brownstone on East 84th Street. The proprietor was an eccentric guy who paid very little and kept the three attorneys under him busy and off balance. He yelled a lot. Though always on the side of the tenants, Rozenholc liked to live both on the inside of New York real estate and on the outside, having begun as the equivalent of a legal-aid attorney for low-income tenants in the Bronx. Once he took Richard to a hearing where the other side was Donald Trump. As they approached, Richard pulled out a tie. Rozenholc stopped him. He told Richard, "If I had a tie on right now, I would take it off to meet this guy." Richard believed that Rozenholc had some fatherly feelings toward him. In spite of this, Richard was terrified of losing this job and toiled long, long hours to keep it. I was terrified too. We needed the money until I was completely finished with graduate school.

When it came time for my annual summer visit to my parents, Richard felt he couldn't ask for time off so I went alone. It was 2004, and I was looking forward to talking to my father about the just-concluded Democratic convention, where John Kerry and John Edwards were nominated to top the ticket, and a young Barack Obama, the Senatorial nominee from Illinois, had delivered an inspiring speech. The Democratic Party was the true religion in my family. Although we were Methodists, with church and Sunday school every week, elections, more than Easter or Christmas, were our main seasonal organizers. Voting day was the most sacred of days.

As we got settled in my parents' tiny apartment in the assisted-living facility, I asked, "What did you think of the Edwards pick?"

Dad looked pained. He said, with some effort, his breath labored, "I like Kerry. Always have, ever since he was head of the Vietnam Vets against the War."

"Me, too. But what about Edwards?"

"I don't know much about him." Dad seemed almost disinterested.

"What did you think of Obama's speech?"

Weeks before, Dad had first opined that Obama had no chance to win the Illinois Senate seat—with a name like that, he wouldn't get a single vote outside of Chicago. But when he saw a video of Obama talking with a group of old white farmers in a cornfield, Dad realized that he might do well with the downstate vote.

"I didn't see the speech," Dad said. I was dumbfounded. He didn't see it. Dad had watched every minute of every convention that he didn't attend since 1952, when he and a friend rented a television for the sole purpose of seeing the convention. It turned out he hadn't watched one minute of the 2004 convention. Something was terribly wrong.

While Dad's face often appeared unhappy and angry, usually he lit up around me. Now, his expression was different, his eyes hollow. He seemed somehow defeated.

"Dad, are you okay?"

"Me? I'm fine." He paused. "Jeanne, why don't you go check on the mail?"

I knew from prior visits this was one task my mother could still sort of do, because she kept the mail key around her wrist on a bright orange coil, and if she forgot what she was doing after she left the apartment, the wrist key would remind her.

"Oh, is it time?" she asked.

"Don't know. Just check." I could see this was a ploy to get her out of the apartment so my father could speak more frankly.

When she left, Dad turned to me. "It's your mother. She can't do anything. And I can't really take care of her anymore. She's getting up in the middle of the night and going out and then falling and getting hurt. I don't even hear her." He paused, "and, I hurt."

"Oh, Dad, I am sorry. Can you move to a unit with a higher level of care, so someone would see right away if she got out?"

"Those are just rooms, not an apartment. We would have to eat all our meals with the other people. If something happens to me, you are going to have to put her in a place."

"Dad, of course I will take good care of Mom in any event, you know that."

My father nodded. "I trust you, Liz." Then he held up his arm. "Look at this."

I hadn't noticed earlier, but his arm was bright purple, all up and down, and in fact his shoulder and chest were similarly discolored. He laughed as I gasped.

"Dad, you have to go to the doctor."

"Naw."

"What do you mean 'naw'? That doesn't look good at all." I knew Dad was battling some kind of pre-leukemia condition. I had flown out some months before to take him for a bone marrow test. "I am going to call right now and make an appointment."

The first one available was the following Monday, but I would be back East by then. "Dad, will you keep this appointment, or do I need to stay?"

His anger showed, not used to his only living child giving him orders. He thought about it for a minute. "I will go," he said dryly.

"Really? I can stay." I caught his eye, but he nodded affirmatively and I understood our conversation was at an end. We sat silently for a few minutes.

"Where do you suppose your mother has gotten to?"

"It has been kind of a while. Should I go look for her?" Again, he nodded, looking resigned.

I left Illinois three days later to attend a memorial service in Vermont for two friends, killed together in a car accident. I didn't really mind that Richard hadn't come; he would have needed a lot of attention and taking care of because he always felt so out of place in the country, with my friends. I was freer without him.

I called Dad from my room in the inn in Vermont on Sunday evening. The cell phone reception was bad. I asked about the doctor's visit. He said he would still go. When I asked about Mom, he just said, "Don't ask." I begged off the call quickly on the grounds of the poor cell service, but I was really feeling that it was all just too much, between the sadness of the memorial service and my parents' decline. I told Dad I would call when I got back to New York. And then I didn't call for three more days.

Back in the city, I called Wednesday evening after 8:00. The phone rang and rang; my parents didn't have an answering machine. Where in god's name could they be? They never went anywhere or did anything. After about 40 rings, a stranger with a serious Midwestern twang answered, "Tingley residence."

"Who is this?"

"Who is this?" the stranger replied.

"This is Liz Tingley, their daughter. Where are my parents?"

"I'm Betty. I work for Josie." Josie ran the home health aide service. "Here's your mom."

"Mom?"

"Liz? Liz. Liz. Big Problem here. Big Problem here. Big Problem."

"Okay. Mom—where is Dad?"

"Big Problem."

"Okay, Mom, can you put that other lady back on the phone?"

"Hello," said Betty.

"What is going on? Please tell me."

"Well, your mom kept coming out in the hall and pacing around. She told the front desk that her husband couldn't find his car keys. But then she kept looking around sort of crazy like and walking up and down the hall and I knew that wasn't normal for her. So, I came in and found your dad unconscious on the living room floor. I called 911 and they are just loading him in the ambulance now."

Oh, Jesus Fuck. "Okay. I am going to see if I can get there tonight. But I doubt it. Can you get to Josie and see if there is anyone who can stay with Mom overnight?"

"Yes, Ma'am, and I will stay here with her 'til somebody comes." She lowered her voice. "I don't know how long he was unconscious for. I think the guy at the front desk ought 'a done more."

I gave Betty my cell and home phone numbers and then said, "Put my mother back on, please."

"Mom, I am coming. As soon as I can. I don't know if it will be tonight or first thing tomorrow. Someone will stay with you. They are taking Dad to the hospital." By then I was already looking for flights online.

"Oh," Mom said. I started to panic.

Richard, hearing this shift in my voice from the bedroom where he was watching the Yankees, lumbered in. He hugged me, so I was totally enfolded in his big bear self. He put his hand on my head and gently asked, "What, Lizzie?"

"I knew something was really wrong. I should have stayed." I burst out crying. Richard held me and let me cry.

"Your dad?"

Between sobs, I briefly explained. Then I went back into action mode, the tears stopping immediately. "Let me call the hospital and see what they have to say."

I got through to the emergency room quickly, and a nurse told me it didn't look good, that they had Dad on life support. Anger flared. Dad had made it clear for many, many years that he did not want his life prolonged by artificial means.

"Do you want us to take him off?" he asked.

Now I had a dilemma. Snap judgment called for. Slowly, I said, "No, we'll wait until I can get there. I am in New York. I'll be there early tomorrow at the latest."

"Okay," the nurse said and slammed down the phone. He apparently had other emergencies to figure out.

"What? What?" Richard asked.

"He's unconscious, on a respirator. They don't think he's going to make it. We have to get out there as soon as possible. You are going to have to come with me."

"I don't know if they will let me out at the office."

"Richard, just tell them it's an emergency." He could see that I meant it and nodded, though clearly scared of his boss's reaction and uncertain what to do.

"I do have work at home. I can bring it and we can fax and email," he said, "but I will need computer access."

"Look, if we have to, we will buy a laptop out there, on Dad's credit card. And that motel we stayed at last time has free internet access." Richard seemed unsure; technology was always beyond him. I went back to the computer and flights. We could leave LaGuardia at 5:30 AM, be in Indianapolis by 7:30, rent a car, and arrive in Urbana by 9:30.

"Do you think I should call Rozenholc at home now?" Richard fretted.

"Well, we will get off the plane at 7:30. You could phone then. Or call him now. Maybe that would make you feel better."

Richard went off to call. I started packing, wondering if I would need a black dress. Better take it, in case. I got my things together and then started thinking what Richard would need. He was a useless packer. I put in a grey suit for him, along with the tie I always chose for him for funerals.

Richard reported on his call. "Rozenholc was not too happy to hear from me, but we worked out what I need to get done ASAP. I will have to find a computer and a fax machine there as soon as I can."

"Jesus, Richard, can't it wait a day? This is not going to be pretty." *This is going to be a pull-the-plug scene.*

"No, it can't," he said. Then, begging for approval, whined, "But I am going."

"I know. It's just that I am really going to need you. I started to cry again.

Richard lumbered over and held me. "It will be all right. It will. We will be together. I'm here for you, babe."

I knew this was a lot for Richard, to put aside his work anxieties, to try to even pretend that he was going to be strong for me. I loved him a lot right then. We went to bed soon after and I curled up next to him while he sang to me.

The early morning dash was stressful, but we made our flight, and Richard made no scenes. We arrived in Indy on time and soon were off across the prairie in our air-conditioned rental car. I drove because I drove faster than Richard and hopped out at the hospital door, instructing Richard to park.

In a small room in Intensive Care, Dad lay on a hospital bed, cranked halfway up, connected to a lot of tubes and a respirator. Mom sat near the foot of the bed, head down. Marge Tingley, Dad's cousin's wife, who I had contacted to take Mom to the hospital, sat next to her, patting her hand. Marge left after a hello, and I sat with Mom, quietly observing my unconscious father. The man in the bed still looked like my dad and I wanted to touch him, to find him, even though my guess was that *he* was already gone. I touched his bare foot. No reaction. His feet were old and gnarled and discolored, like his arm the week before. I remembered how often Dad liked to go barefoot, inside and out. This brought me nearly to tears.

Richard joined us a bit later, grumpy but not complaining. I was so grateful for his presence. This would have been impossible to do all by myself—in the lonely days before Richard, confronting my father's mortality, losing him, was something I had ruminated about often. The awful sense that I would be on my own, having already lost my only sibling, and with Mom half lost to Alzheimer's, had haunted me. Now Richard was here, and I hoped I could count on him.

After several minutes a nurse arrived and I asked to speak to the doctor in charge of Dad's care. Richard put his arm around my mother. She leaned into him. There was a still rhythm from the ventilator and a kind of snoring noise coming from Dad. The room had no windows and we were all alone. Waiting, though we weren't sure for what. Finally, the doctor entered and I asked to speak to him privately.

At the nurses' station, I asked him, "How bad is it? And do you know what happened?"

"Well, I don't know the specifics but somehow, he got a bump on his head and bled into his brain. I don't think he has much brain function left. I'll show you the brain scan." He turned to the computer and pulled up images that I, the psychologist, pretended to understand.

"Does he have any chance to wake up and be sort of okay?"

"If he were to wake up, the quality of his life would likely be seriously compromised."

That was it. Dad would never ever want that. He already had been in such pain, so disinterested in the world, not himself, and now his brain function basically gone. We had to pull the plug. *Why hadn't they let him die naturally last night? That would have been his wish.*

"We need to explain this to my mother," I told the doctor. "She has Alzheimer's but gets some things."

"Has she been declared incompetent? If not, we need her permission to do anything."

"Oh, Jesus, I have health care proxy rights, but I have no clue at this moment where that paperwork is. Hopefully, she will remember that he never wanted to be kept alive by artificial means."

Away from Dad's bedside, the doctor explained Dad's situation to Mom.

She said, "I want him to wake up and have a happy life." I got down on the floor in front of her and took her hands. Before I could say anything, she said it again. "I want him to wake up and have a happy life." This was one of her longest sentences in a long time and she said it twice.

"I know, Mom. I do too, but the doctor said that's not possible. And you know how Dad didn't want to live as a vegetable. We have to let him go."

She hung her head and nodded in assent. "Okay."

The doctor said, "Give us a few minutes to prepare and then you can come back in as we unhook him."

Richard's phone rang when we got back to Dad's room. He mouthed, "the office," but valiantly let it go to voicemail. We watched the medical staff unhook all the machines. Mom let out a yelp of agony and said, "No, no!" and became very agitated.

"Mom, do you want to wait in the other room?" She nodded vigorously. "Richard, will you stay with her?"

He held my mother up and mostly carried her out of the room. *How could I have done this without Richard?* If I had had to leave my father just then, I would have hated my mother, but I would have given her what she needed. What *I* needed was to stay with Dad through his last breath. Even though many, many things had been difficult in our relationship, I knew my father. I could feel him. We were alike, with the same intelligence and sense of humor. My mother often said with some disgust when we were kidding around, "The two of you are like two peas in a pod." I also knew how much my father loved me and wanted only the best for me my whole life. I knew how much his life had been about giving me things he wished he'd had, like those childhood French lessons, a trip to Europe when I was fifteen, and the most extended education any person had ever had, college, a master's degree, and two Ph.D.'s He had thought that was all grand. Now, with Richard's help, I could stay with him as he died.

Dad breathed on his own for about 40 minutes. They said his brain stem was the only functioning part of his brain. I thought there was a small chance that Dad could recognize me there, in that most primitive brain level, so occasionally I said, "Dad. It's Liz. I am here." This was probably futile, but it made me feel better. Then the breathing stopped.

I found Mom curled up in Richard's arms, as he gently held her close. I loved Richard more than anything at that moment. He had held my mother while I watched my father die. Richard made it possible to get what I needed in this terrible situation and give my mother what she needed too. For years after, when things got hard, I remembered Richard in that moment.

How could I ever, ever leave someone who would do that for me?

Chapter 28

Trial, and Other Legal Afters

When Park Dietz declared that Michael was insane at the time of Carrie's murder, Jeanine Pirro decided she could not get a murder conviction at trial, a decision she loathed having to make. As payback, she got the judge to agree to allow the Costellos to make victim impact statements, which Michael would have to hear; he still had to go before a judge and formally enter the plea.

Danny, Ruth, and Michael's lawyers thought that the Laudor family should show up to support for Michael at the hearing. My feelings were mixed; I did care about Michael, but I also knew the Costello family's pain was intense and enduring. I did *not* want to appear to support her murderer, over their pain. Richard, of course, wanted me with him. I went.

Nearly two years after the tragedy, Michael was getting his day in court. We filed in: Danny, Ruth, Uncle Lewis, Richard, and me. I was last in the group to be seated, and so was closest to the Costellos, sitting just across the courtroom aisle from Carrie's parents and her sister Joyce. After a short conference at the other end of the row between Danny and Ruth, I was instructed to make sure that at the end of the proceedings I was the first to pop up and begin the Laudor family exit, before the Costellos. This felt aggressive to me. I objected but was overruled. Richard refused to switch places with me. I was not happy to be the leader in this plan but, compared to the unfolding events, I decided while this was bizarre, it was trivial.

Tension filled the space as we waited for the judge and for Michael to be brought in. All three Costellos stared straight ahead, sitting behind the assistant DAs who were presenting the case. Jeanine Pirro was dressed to kill as usual in a grey power suit, heavily made up, hair stiffly coiffed, sat with the Costello. Her hand, nails garishly painted, rested on Mrs. Costello's shoulder. She murmured words, but it looked to me like she was feigning concern.

To our left, another courtroom door opened, and we saw Michael, handcuffed, head shaven bald, a hint of a beard, dressed in neatly pressed khaki pants and a button-down shirt. He was brought to the defense attorney's table, uncuffed, and he momentarily tried and failed to smile back at us. Michael looked terrified and paranoid. His eyes blinked rapidly. He sat down next to his attorneys and hung his head, while the lawyers tried to prop him up with whispered reassurances. In front of the Costellos, the assistant district attorneys laughed and talked among themselves.

It seemed an eternity until the bailiff called us to rise, as Judge Daniel Angiolillo entered. Though Michael's lawyers had told us that the judge would accept the plea, nothing was guaranteed.

The judge called on the district attorney's office to present their evidence and recommendations. One of them read a summary of the events of June 1998, ending with Michael flagging down an Ithaca College cop and telling her he thought he might have hurt his girlfriend. Someone should check on her, Michael had said. The DA then switched to the history of Michael's mental illness and the conclusions of three forensic psychiatrists that Michael did not know right from wrong at the time of the crime, that he believed he was killing an evil force, not Carrie, when he stabbed her to death. They recommended that the judge accept the plea of "not responsible by reason of mental defect" for the crime of killing Carrie.

Judge Angiolillo stated that he would consider this plea, after hearing from the family of the victim. Both Carrie's mother and sister described Carrie—a bright, vibrant young woman who had so much to offer, who was carrying an unborn child, their grandchild and niece, and that both Carrie and the child had been taken from them in the most horrible way. Joyce said even more about how her sister's murder affected her—that now she lived constantly with a kind of anxiety, irrational she knew, but she even saw her husband in a new fearful way. After all, Michael had supposedly loved Carrie and he killed her. This was so sad, so hard to hear, and I knew their words were so fully true. I cried a little bit, but I tried to do so as discreetly as possible. I was on the other side, after all.

The Judge then asked Michael to speak. Michael stood, with the reddest face I had ever seen. When Michael was well, he was extremely articulate. Now, he stammered and spoke in a very low tone, and he kept his body turned slightly so he would not make eye contact with Carrie's family. He thanked the court and uttered a few words; the only ones I remember made me angry: "I want the court to know that I too lost the most important person to me." This statement was so self-absorbed and lacked any apology, remorse, or recognition of the pain of Carrie's family. I bet, though, that Michael and the Laudors would not see it that way. They would see that Michael was trying to say his illness had cost him the most important thing—not his freedom, but Carrie. He may have said more, but I got stuck on those horrid, self-centered words.

The Judge thanked everyone for their comments and said he was prepared to rule on the motion regarding Michael's culpability by accepting the "not responsible" plea. Michael would be remanded to the State Department of Mental Health and Hygiene to determine appropriate treatment. Michael asked that he be returned to Mid-Hudson as he was comfortable there, but the Judge interrupted to say that the Department of Mental Health and Hygiene would now be in charge of Michael's destiny, not the judge. This was likely terrifying for Michael, as he had heard stories, from people he'd met at Mid-Hudson, who he believed were transferred away from families and their legal team, as punishment. Michael would be on a locked ward indefinitely, with no control over his fate, unless the psychosis abated.

As the hearing concluded, I stood to lead the Laudors out of the courtroom, uncomfortable yet determined not to fail. But as I put my first foot out, I came face to face with Jeanine Pirro. She glared at me, because apparently, she had decided the Costellos should be escorted out first, by her, to leave us cooling our heels behind them. There was nothing I could do, but shift back, face forward, feeling I had failed the Laudors, but pleased that the Costellos got to have it their way.

This should have been the end of legal proceedings, the end of inter-actions between the Costello and Lauder families. But earlier in the year the Costellos had filed a five-million-dollar civil lawsuit against Michael for wrongful death. Now, there appeared another weird complication. Because Michael had been found "not responsible for Carrie's death," instead of guilty of her murder, he was legally entitled, as the beneficiary of her life insurance of some millions, to collect the payout. To me, there was no other moral choice but to hand that money over directly to the Costellos, without any stipulations, caveats, or further legal action.

Not so, for the Laudors. The story I was told, through Richard from Danny, regarding their legal strategy concerning the lawsuit—and Richard was slightly involved in this effort, picking the attorney to handle the case, and giving advice from time to time—was that they would give over the insurance money as soon as the civil lawsuit was dropped. Given what I knew about how Danny operated, I doubted this was fully accurate. Danny was now spending his life, full-time, on Michael's case, and like everyone in Richard's family, he never saw straight lines, and created endless complications. Also, the Laudors maintained another narrative—that the Costellos' legal representation was inept and chose to keep the case going. I wondered the same about the Laudors. Were they fighting technicalities just to fight? In the end, most of the insurance money was used up in legal fees, and the suit was settled, giving the tiny bit that was left to Carrie's family. In some circles, the belief persisted that the Laudors wanted to keep the life insurance—that is not exactly true. No one ever said in my presence they wanted to keep it, but they did use it as leverage to make the civil suit go away.

Chapter 29

Sturdy Ladies

In the six months after Dad's death, I flew from New York to Central Illinois repeatedly, and finally, every weekend. Mom was dying now, too. Despite her dementia, she still recognized me, always. On my previous trip she had been dozing in her hospital bed when I arrived. When she awoke, her face brightened into a big grin.

"Why, it's Elizabeth come all the way from New York." We talked a few minutes and then she went back to sleep. When she woke, she repeated, with just as much pleasure, "Why, it's Elizabeth come all the way from New York." This happened four times before she became fully awake and then didn't doubt my presence.

Now, she was back in the nursing home, although not the Alzheimer's Unit that had been her home since Dad died. There she needed to be mobile and to take rudimentary care of herself. She was so weakened by her hospital stay that she required a higher level of care. When I got to town, I found her new room, a small double. She had the space in the back, behind a curtain. It smelled simultaneously of disinfectant and urine. The fluorescent light was too bright in an otherwise dim room. The March sun was setting and grey, still-wintry light edged in from the windows at the back. I woke her up, gently placing my hand on her shoulder.

"Mom, I came back to see you."

Her eyes opened, and she studied me, intently, smiled and said very softly, "Liz," without moving or trying to sit up. I could see she loved me, in that quiet tone of voice and the little bit of shine in her eyes. After a few moments of quiet, the regular Mom appeared and she struggled to sit up, annoyed by her weakness. I pulled her up by both her arms, pushed the button to change the hospital bed from prone to upright, and arranged the pillows so she could sit back.

"How are you getting along, Mom?"

She gestured, somewhat forcefully, something I took to mean, "Don't ask."

"The last time I saw you, you were in the hospital. The doctors must think you are a little better to be here."

Mom was being treated for a urinary tract infection, often fatal for elderly women. When they first called to say that she had an infection, they asked me what I wanted to do. I was puzzled and only later realized they were asking me if I just wanted to let her die. Pope John Paul II had just died from a UTI. I had instructed them to treat the infection but to take no other heroic means to keep her alive. She was so much more fragile now than just a week before.

My mother was never comfortable with weakness, hers or in others. About four years before, she fell and fractured her pelvis in April, a very painful break. She said she didn't need to go to the doctor then, as her next appointment was scheduled for October. Dad and I did persuade her to go, and with the diagnosis of a broken pelvis, she was sent to a rehabilitation center. The physical therapist did not know what she was dealing with. She urged Mom to do several sets of pull-ups using a bar over her bed. Mom did, and then kept going and going, surprising the therapist with her strength for a nearly 80-year-old woman. Mom always did what she was told, calling on her days as a gym teacher when she made the girls do *just a few more* push-ups. Aching, she was so much worse the next day, having weakened herself by pushing so hard. The physical therapist said they would have to go more slowly from then on.

Just a few moments after Mom sat up, they brought her supper, the delivering aide displaying what seemed like a fake, perky cheerful attitude for my sake. "How are you doing, Jeannie? Are you hungry?"

If my mother were in her right mind, she would have patiently explained that here name was Jeanne, from the French, not Jeannie, and that the American habit of spelling it "Jean" was incorrect. That meant John in French and was a male name. But Mom was not in her right mind, and I decided not to make an issue of it. My mother was dependent on the aides.

Surprisingly, Mom was hungry and ate what was in front of her, although she started with desert and worked her way backwards. I thought I should have brought her some "green ice cream," her favorite. She had had it every night at dinner in the assisted living facility, before my father died. When I had first brought green ice cream to her in the Alzheimer's Unit, she spit that out and informed me that the pistachio I'd offered was not *green ice cream*. She wanted mint chocolate chip.

The meal over, she leaned back, looked at me and spoke clearly and directly of her feelings, an extraordinary event. "I feel my life is over."

I took a couple of seconds, so unused to direct dialogue with her. "I can see how you could feel that way, Mom. I mean Dad died, so that part of your life is over. But maybe if you get to feeling better, you can still enjoy things, go back to your regular room. I'll bring you the right green ice cream next time." This felt stupid and concrete to say, like something my mother would say and I'd find wanting.

Her nostrils flared. "I want to go home *now*."

I couldn't tell her there was no home to go to. Did she mean the house in Charleston or the apartment she had shared with Dad at the assisted living place?

225

She looked stonily at my face, this not apparently addressing her wish sufficiently.

"Do you want to come to New York and live with Richard me?" I said feebly, trying to think of a homelike option.

Her lips moved, but no sound emerged. I swear she mouthed, "That's not home." Then she audibly said "Okay," turned her back to me and didn't turn around again before visiting hours ended. I bid her goodnight without seeing her face.

I was furious. *That's it, Mom. Turn away from the hard stuff; leave me over here dealing with it by myself. And besides, aren't I here? You will still have* me. This was what she had always done: turn away—when my brother died, when I was sexually abused, when I was suicidal. True form until the end.

But then I thought of something that had never crossed my mind before. My mother was tough, really tough. This news that there was no home to return to, meant she just had to bear it, and to her, bearing it meant *bearing it alone.* That took guts, an inner resolve. One of her favorite phrases, whenever one of her friends was facing adversity, to convey her belief that they could make it through, was, "She's a sturdy lady." Well, my mother was a sturdy lady herself.

It slowly dawned on me: after a life of trying not to be like my mother, we were the same. I was tough, too This quality—this sturdiness, this toughness that led her through adversity—I also had it. When I had to, I put my head down, and pushed through what often felt like insurmountable odds: to be alive, to be connected, to fight my depression, to find any sort of happiness. And it came from my mother, not my father.

I didn't know it yet, but in the days ahead, I was going to have to be even tougher.

Chapter 30

He Does Feel Guilty

The trip to Mid-Hudson was never a picnic, no matter how often we made the drive. That late fall morning we were headed to "Family Day," the only family programming or intervention the hospital offered. Ruth, Danny, and Uncle Lew and his wife Judy would meet us there. As we turned off the Interstate onto the county highway, I watched Richard who was at the wheel. His mouth was turned down and his eyes narrowed, a look I knew meant he was raging. And, hurting; only his love for Michael had the power to sustain him through these visits. Not only would we have to see a very sick Michael, but also Danny and Ruth, Richard's least favorite people. Mine too.

"Maybe having Lew and Judy there will take the edge off," I offered.

Richard shot daggers at me. I had said something idiotic. "Nothing will make this feel like anything but torture." After a pause, he continued "For once, I do agree with Mom. It's important that the staff see that Michael has family who care about him."

Hopelessness washed over me. Why-the-fuck would I try to put any positive spin on this? The day would be tense, stressful, and likely stupid and absurd to boot, sitting through a program about how Mid-Hudson looked after our loved ones so exquisitely.

As I opened my car door in the parking lot, I could hear that Ruth and Danny had arrived. Danny was screaming full blast at his mother; when he saw us, he only slightly lowered the volume of his invective.

Richard snorted. "And he is her favorite."

I laughed. Danny had tried screaming shit at me exactly once, over the phone. I made it plain that no one ever treated me that way. He hung up on me.

Behind the first razor wire fence. Lew and Judy were already waiting. Judy, body held stiff, still managed to smile kindly at Richard and me. Lew remained gracious, glad too to see his sister's family. He patted his two un-incarcerated nephews on the shoulders. There was a long line, and we had to wait about 20 minutes. Buzzed in, we were directed down a path towards the gymnasium/pool area—the pool that was never open to the residents: "budget cuts." Round tables fille the gym, most already occupied. Up front there stood a lectern, with a microphone, projector, and big screen. Fluorescent light harshly illuminated the windowless dark space. The Laudor party wound our way across to a table, quite close to the front. The program was to begin before lunch, when Michael and the rest of the patients would join us. That way, I realized, the inmates couldn't challenge the rosy view of their care put forth by the institution.

The Chief Medical Officer welcomed everyone to Mid-Hudson, noting how much family support for patients means to their recovery.

Ha! Michael has been here for almost seven years, and I hadn't seen any efforts towards recovery or even rehabilitation, only some medication adjustments.

A slide show detailed the current patient population, their diagnoses, and staffing levels. We heard briefly from the heads of nursing, social work, and psychology how the patients were kept protected and busy, and viewed statistics about the safety of each ward, and the institutional goals for the next year.

From Michael, I knew these facts about his care: He did feel reasonably free from the threat of violence. He perceived that the nursing staff and mental health workers (guards) were essentially benign. Thus,

Mid-Hudson was better than prison. After much negotiation he was allowed to play his guitar one hour per week, during occupational therapy. He found comfort in this. He did not get any regular psychotherapy, or counseling. The psychologist led a once weekly half-hour group for all patients on the unit, though rarely was there an opportunity for a patient to speak. Michael did take advantage of any opportunity to speak to any denomination of clergy, as he remained spiritual and religious. He had recounted to us that he told a Catholic priest he "used to be a good person," the priest had talked of forgiveness and held out that Michael might still be "a fine man." Michael appreciated this as the most therapeutic experience in his time there. A Rabbi came every few weeks for religious services. Michael would not ask for Kosher food, as he was still scared of being widely known as Jewish. (Nazis might get him, even inside.) The psychiatrists tended to be an everchanging group of not-yet-certified foreign physicians who spoke little English and tried new medications every few months. None of the med changes had much effect on Michael's delusions and hallucinations. On days without snow or rain, Michael could play basketball or be in the outside yard for about an hour. In spite of being in the care of Mid-Hudson for nearly seven years, Michael remained highly psychotic, with impaired understanding of reality. Apparently though, he did know that Carrie was dead and that "his hands" killed her.

As I listened to the presentation on the efforts to move patients forward, and hopefully out of this hospital, I added up the number of hours per week that anything therapeutic actually happened: 90 minutes. Perhaps if Michael saw a clergyman once per week, this moved up to 2.5 hours per week; counting basketball, perhaps up to 7 hours per week. This left 161 hours per week for warehousing, and oh, sleep.

After the presentation wrapped up, it was time for questions. The first person, an elegant looking older African American woman, asked if visiting hours would ever be changed to match the once-daily bus from the New York City, so she could see her grandson more regularly. The head social worker fielded the question, without actually answering it. "We do like to make visiting hours accessible to all families," she said. Next, a Latino man, and a young women of color asked particulars about their family members. They were told to contact their social worker on Monday.

A petite, white woman tastefully dressed in neutral-colored slacks and matching sweater with a coral-colored scarf, stepped to the microphone. I knew her from our last visit. Michael had leaned in to say that she was the wife of "Todd," a prosecutor from upstate New York, who had killed someone in a drunk driving accident. Michael reported the guy did not seem in the least bit crazy, and thought he was in the institution because prison would not be safe for him, as he had put so many criminals behind bars.

The woman spoke boldly: "I would like to know why none of the patients here receive any individual psychotherapy. I know my husband's care would be enhanced if he could talk through his situation with a professional."

The Chief Psychiatrist responded. "The research indicates that psychotherapy is not helpful for patients with personality disorders. As you saw from the slide earlier, most of our patients have personality disorders, and so it would not be of any use to give them individual psychotherapy."

I gulped.

He was generalizing from the empirical research on antisocial personality disorder, to all personality disorders, an inaccurate conclusion. Besides, it was not clear that many of the patients we saw on visiting days had anything other than paranoid schizophrenia.

The woman persisted, appealing to his humanity, to see the patients are human beings and to recognize the needs of individual patients.

"Ah," said the speaker. "That is about your family member's individual needs. I suggest you call his social worker on Monday."

"I have spoken to him," she replied curtly, irritation filling her voice. She took her seat. Most folks had no questions; they were passive consumers of a dreadful service.

The Laudors sat quietly, feeling the best course was not to cause trouble of any kind; this might maintain the staff's somewhat benign view of Michael. Just then, a tired middle-aged woman approached us, introducing herself around as Michael's new social worker, since Scott, the one person Michael appeared to trust, had been transferred to another unit. Could we stay later after Michael returned to the unit for a brief treatment team meeting? Lew and Judy deferred, but the rest of us agreed.

Shortly Michael appeared in the entrance to the gym, looking quite disheveled and gaunt, dressed as usual, but his button-down shirt was frayed and khakis tired. He had a closely shorn head and bent glasses dangled from his nose. He approached, managed a smile, and embraced Richard, squeezing his brother. Ruth got a side hug, Danny a high five, and Lew and Judy a sweet grin. Michael met my eye and nodded.

As we all sat down, Michael asked, "What's for lunch? I bet they give you better food than we get."

"It's a buffet. Over that way," Richard pointed to the queue for cold sandwiches, chips, cookies, and soda. Michael was managing to carry on a conversation, wanting to know about all the relatives and didn't seem to tire of the news. Then he turned to Lew and they began a series of word plays.

"Do you have this one Lew: What's a dunderhead?"

Lew chuckled. "What?"

"A stupid storm cloud."

This was funny and very Michael before the catastrophe. A few years later, Lewis published a little book, called *Semantricks: A dictionary of words you thought you knew*. He credited Michael as one of his co-authors, a paeon to how things were when Michael was the golden boy.

After lunch, when Michael had to leave, he shrunk into himself, appearing exhausted and likely sad to step away from this approximation of family life. Lew and Judy left soon after. As the place emptied, the new social worker took us to a small conference room nearby, crowded with three other staff, including Michael's current psychiatrist and two mental health workers.

One of the male social workers took the lead. "We know that Michael is highly intelligent but he does not appear to be trying to get better. Do you have any insights into what is going on?"

The psychiatrist chimed in, in halting, accented English, "Yes, we have tried a range of medications and they should be enough to calm his psychosis but nothing appears to be effective."

I didn't want the spotlight, so refrained from answering. I didn't want to rile anyone up per family rules about dealing with the folks at Mid-Hudson.

Ruth spoke up. "He is grieving for Carrie. He needs help to process his grief."

I wondered what her basis was for saying this.

Richard added, "It hasn't been too long since he started believing that she was really dead."

Suddenly, I perceived we were having this meeting only because Michael was making them look bad. He was the sort of patient they were supposed to make better, not the usual patients the institution could dismiss, those deemed antisocial, unintelligent, and members of a racial or ethnic minority—groups, it seemed to me, they believed, though no one would ever say this out loud, could not be rehabilitated.

Ruth suggested they confer with Dr. Murray Shane, Michael's private psychiatrist before the murder, or Dr. Lewis Oppler, who had treated Michael when he was first hospitalized at Columbia Presbyterian Hospital in Manhattan in the 1980s, and now oversaw all of New York state's mental health systems.

"Dr. Shane did not do a very good job did he? Or Michael wouldn't be here," the most hostile-looking staff member replied.

I thought I better say something. "I'm Liz Tingley, Richard's wife. I'm a clinical psychologist. My best understanding is based on something Michael told me about nine months ago. He is punishing himself by not getting better."

"He told you that?" one of them asked with incredulity.

I nodded.

"What else has he confided in you?"

Suddenly all eyes were on me, as if I had some magical knowledge.

I glanced at Richard, not wanting to betray anything he thought might be confidential. Richard stared down at the table. I took this as an endorsement to continue.

"Michael has discussed this with his religious counselors, too, I know. In this case, as Michael does not have antisocial personality disorder, and he truly killed Carrie in the midst of a psychotic delusion, he feels very guilty."

The staff vigorously nodded their heads up. They were likely not used to their patients feeling guilty for their crimes.

"So, in this case, I think some psychotherapy might be helpful. It has been useful in the past and kept Michael functional for a number of years." Danny, Richard, and Ruth all chimed in to say this was an excellent idea.

Doubtfully, the psychiatrist, said, "We might be able to arrange that on a limited basis." This ended our audience with the staff.

Later, I drove us home, as usual. Leaving Mid-Hudson, Richard always collapsed the second the car door shut. I switched the radio on, needing something beyond the agonized silence of my husband. I felt weak.

Back to the apartment, Richard wordlessly undressed and climbed into bed. He clicked on some mindless TV sitcoms, to edge out whatever was in his head. I grabbed the leash and took Annie for a long walk, though it was dark and damp. I breathed—in and out, in and out—focusing only on the rhythm of my feet hitting the pavement over and over, trying to quiet the disturbed, suicidal thoughts running through my brain. Could this nightmare ever end? After nearly an hour of mindless walking, I discovered a new feeling.

I was angry. At Richard. Couldn't he ever protect me even a little from this horror show? Why was I the one always picking up the pieces?

I heard Dr. Grossman's voice saying "that's an old feeling" taken from my past into the present. His gentle reminder of this countered some of the despair, reminding me that this feeling began when my brother died, and lasted until I took my 1984 trip to the locked ward—when I let go of the perfect-child pretense I maintained for my parents. I recalled that feeling of profound relief, a physical sensation of that heavy burden toppling off my shoulders. I could and would no longer hold up the sky for my parents.

How long could I keep holding up the sky for Richard?

Chapter 31

Cats and Dogs

Richard and I had no actual children. This relentlessly fed the sadness in me, but over the years, our family was enlarged, and tested, by several cats and dogs, real and also, pretend. The contentious cat versus dog issue surfaced in our first emails. In Richard's story of his knotted childhood, his cat Dusty was a rescuer; Richard only learned to feel love because Dusty loved him. When I first met Richard, he was in a grief group, mourning his recently deceased father. One group assignment was to write about an earlier loss. Richard composed a stunning essay about Dusty's death while Danny was at camp. Danny was furious that no one told him about Dusty until he came home, and he stayed in his room for days. On the anniversary of Dusty's death, Danny wore a black arm band in remembrance for years. Richard, who rarely said anything good about his middle brother, felt this was a just acknowledgement of Dusty's value.

My beagle-something mutt, Annie, a tough little dog, ran free during her life in Hoosick. Annie was my first dog to live inside. All my childhood pets were never allowed in Mom's pristine house. Annie followed me around, wanting to be right next to me. She slept touching me. Initially, her need to be close was too much, but I learned to like, even need her presence, which brought some relief from the isolation. If I hadn't learned to enjoy the relentless dog presence, I doubt I could have gotten married and been able to tolerate a husband's relentless presence.

Richard was petrified of dogs. When he began sleeping over, I had to ban Annie from the bed and bedroom, though over time, he developed an appreciative, distant relationship with her. One of the most joyous times for the three of us came nearly every week as we celebrated Shabbat, singing over the challah, wine, and candles. (Richard sometimes serenaded just me before the official blessings, with the Sabbath Prayer from *Fiddler on the Roof*.) In the kiddush, when it got to a part with an up-tempo, Annie vocalized along with us, in rhythm and approximating the melody. She wagged her tale vigorously in time with the music. Shabbat guests were amazed. Every time, Richard got a kick from this, laughing heartily from the center of his belly.

Annie lived a good long life, until she got cancer of the spleen at age 12, and I had to put her down. I went by myself. I sat alone, my hands enveloping her, soothing her with words of love until she stopped breathing. Then I cried for two months. Richard tried to comfort me, but I needed to a new puppy to fill the hole. Against his wishes, I found a rescue beagle-something puppy that was being driven to Connecticut by some committed dog ladies from a kill shelter down south, early on a Sunday morning in November.

The pick-up point was a True Value store in the wilds of far suburbia. The beagle puppy had been too sick to travel but, the dog lady inquired, would I want one of the others? I spied a little fluffy red-headed guy and when I picked him up, he immediately snuggled into my neck and stayed put under my chin. Except for a minute when I put him in Richard's arms, I couldn't let go. He was mine.

We named him Charley in honor of both of our dead fathers and because of John Steinbeck's *Travels with Charley*, a book we both loved. Richard's father's name was Charles, though he went by Chuck and when we got home, he emailed his father's extended family to be sure they were okay with this name for our dog. When I was small a child, I would sit with my father, named Donald, on the front porch and watch the cars going by. Dad waved at every car and said, "Hi, Charley."

When I was little, I was amazed. "Daddy, you know so many people named Charley!"

When I was just a bit older and already cynical, Dad played the same trick. I yelled, "You don't even know that guy and he is not named Charley!" This made my father laugh.

Charley needed a lot of expensive veterinarian care at the start. The runny nose was actually pneumonia, and he required an operation to remove a straight pin from his belly. Charley was a very expensive mutt but I was in love with this dog that was so handsome people would cross the street to remark on his good looks. Charley slept snuggled under my chin, licking my neck as if he were nursing, my baby in so many ways. His only drawback was that he chewed everything.

The cats who initially played an important role in our family were Richard's stuffed toy cats. When Richard was first hospitalized for depression, his friend Alison gave him a stuffed gray Gund cat, which Richard named Andy. By the time we met, Andy was mostly retired from active cuddle duty, and sat on top of a bureau next to Richard's bed. The second or third time I slept over, when we were holding hands on the bed, fully clothed, I noticed Andy on the shelf.

"Cool. You have a gray guy sitting over there," I said, thinking how adorable it was that this big, six-foot bearded man kept a stuffed animal in his apartment.

"That's Andy," Richard said, reaching for the toy. "Alison gave him to me when I was in Four Winds." Richard held the cat up to me, as if I should talk to him.

"Hey, Andy," I said, playing. "You look well loved."

Richard smiled and took his big hand and stroked Andy's little head with great affection. Then he reached under the bed and pulled out an orange striped cat.

"Andy's kind of retired. He was getting worn out so I got Cinnamon. When you aren't here, she sleeps with me." I laughingly patted Cinnamon. This was unbearably cute and appealing.

The way Richard talked to both of these inanimate objects made them seem almost real. Used to hanging with small children, I was happy to play along. It was all play to me. Over time, though, I realized these cats were actually alive to Richard, not simply pretend. This was a little spooky and complicated. Over time, Richard acquired several other stuffed cats, until he had a whole menagerie in the years after Michael killed Carrie.

I wondered if I got Richard a real cat, the bizarre attachment to stuffed ones would evaporate, but he resisted. He didn't want to change the litter box and if it was his cat, I was clear that would be his job.

Our neighbor down the hall took in a pregnant cat, and Richard fell in love with one of her litter, a lively, grey-striped kitten. When he was old enough to leave his mother, he came to stay in our apartment. We named him Ash, because his grey markings reminded me of campfire ashes. Ash was a sweet kitty, but Ash did not diminish Richard's attachment to the stuffed cats.

One Saturday morning a couple of months after Ash came to us, he was exploring the windowsill in the living room and appeared transfixed by something outside. Within seconds, he found a hole in the screen and got out but then could not figure out how to get back in. He tried to crawl up the screen and fell off backward from our sixth-floor apartment. I screamed to Richard "Ash is dead!" and ran down six flights of stairs. Ash, however, was not dead. I found him lying in a bush; several neighbors who had seen him pass their windows as he fell were gathered around him, surprised by his loud meowing. We rushed him to the vet and discovered there was not a bone broken. Forever after, Ash was known as the miracle cat. The litter box, however, was a source of ongoing tension. We tried many solutions, including an "automatic" litter box. In the end, the litter box was cleaned only if I "helped" Richard with the task.

Charley chewed and chewed—through several of my best pairs of leather shoes and so many pieces out of the coffee table that we had to get a new one. One evening in December, a month after adopting Charley, I arrived home from work before Richard to find Charley in the bedroom, one of Richard's stuffed cats in his mouth. Charley shook the cloth cat violently back and forth, as if trying to kill a rodent. This was not good.

I yelled at Charley, but he just wanted to play. I grabbed the cat toy away from him. Too late. He had eaten the eyes off the cat. Then I saw that Richard's whole collection of cats strewn over the bed. Charley had gotten to all five, and they all had big holes on their faces, eyes all gone, chew marks on each body, even Andy, who Richard usually kept on the shelf. How did Charley do all this damage? What the fuck was I going to say to Richard? Would he want to get rid of Charley? I felt nauseous watching Charley happily chase his tail around on the bedroom floor. I decided to hide all the cats, and hope Richard didn't notice their absence right away.

When Richard came home about an hour later, he went straight to bed, as usual, after shedding his suit. He was rooting around on the bed and asked if I had seen his current favorite stuffed cat, Minimum, the little orange one that had replaced Cinnamon, lost some months before. I could play dumb because I knew Richard would not get up to search, but he would lie there and complain petulantly that he couldn't find the cat.

I took a deep breath. "Well, there's a problem with Minimum and, actually, all the cats." I decided a good defense was an offense. "I told you not to leave the cats on the bed now that we have Charley the chewer."

"What do you mean? Where is Minimum?"

"You don't want to see her," I said. And perhaps with a touch of sadistic joy, I continued, "Charley ate her eyes out. In fact, he ate the eyes off all the cats you left in the bed. I told you not to leave them there." At that moment, Charley bounded onto the bed, wagging his tail. I scooped him up immediately.

Richard stared angrily ahead. "I told you he can't have soft toys! You have to train him to not touch my cats!" He turned to the real puppy. "Charley!" he yelled, rigid with rage.

I left the bedroom with Charley and closed the door. *Let him stay in there to watch some stupid TV. He is not going to hurt my boy.*

I searched online to find a service to put the eyes back on stuffed cats. Sure enough, on Lexington Avenue, on the Upper East Side of Manhattan, there was a listing for a doll animal hospital, claiming to have been in business since 1900, and able to fix all doll and animal damage, Monday through Saturday. I resolved to take Richard's eyeless cats there the following weekend. Maybe this would restore peace in our household. Meanwhile, I would try to keep Charley away from Richard.

Saturday morning early, Charley and I headed to the dog run where I shared his chewing sins with my fellow puppy owners, who all laughed. I took Charley back home (and prayed Richard would not harm him), boarded the Eastside Express Bus into Manhattan carrying a shopping bag filled with eyeless cats. *Let's hope I don't run into anyone I knew on the bus.* How could I explain the contents of the bag or the purpose of my journey? I was a little embarrassed about how much these pieces of cloth meant to Richard and that I had accepted and played along for years.

D.W. Winnicott, the brilliant British psychoanalyst who first called security blankets and teddy bears "transitional objects," meant that the object took on the meaning of comfort found first in the primary caregiver. The one-year-old child has not fully internalized this, but rather projects that feeling onto the blanket/bear. He described this as "partially hallucinatory." I knew Richard was weird and odd, but this episode showed me Richard's true psychic underdevelopment. Nonetheless, I had to save Charley from Richard's wrath.

The Doll Hospital, advertised on a big awning and window signs, was on the second floor over a restaurant, and getting in required buzzing and then climbing a narrow set of rickety, dirty stairs. As I entered, the place took my breath away. It was like something out of a horror movie. Doll parts, heads, limbs, hair, torn clothes, and other smashed bits littered the floor all around. There appeared to be no order, and some doll parts could have been a hundred years old, antiques, but damaged. I saw nothing intact in the whole place. Though the aura did not inspire confidence, I was in the right place, as the animals in my bag were damaged too. The shopkeeper was carrying on a loud conversation with a tall, decrepit-looking man about bills not paid and how to collect them. He eyed me suspiciously but did not stop talking, so I nervously explored a little, examining some of the headless dolls. Finally, the man concluded his conversation about collections and boomed, "Yeah?"

"Uh, do you fix stuffed animals too?"

"What do ya need?"

I held up one of the cats from the shopping bag. "They need eyes and some repair around the eyes." He took the cat and then the whole bag.

"These need a lot more than that. These are all filthy," he said.

This was a little funny, given the state of his grimy establishment. Besides, for little children and Richard, the unwashed smell of the transitional object was part of the charm. Indeed, sometimes after a long hard day I would find Richard lying in bed with one of the cats draped over his face so he could sniff it.

"Look, I don't care if you clean them. They just all need eyes," I said.

He rummaged through the bag, counting the eyeless cats. "It will cost you."

"Whatever it takes," I said. He wrote out a receipt.

"We'll call you when they're ready. It'll take about three weeks."

"Okay," I said. "Just please don't lose them." *My loony husband really needs them back.*

I went from there over to FAO Schwartz to buy Richard a new Gund cat, just to tide him over. It didn't make him very happy, but he desperately hugged it to his chest. Sometimes I thought he liked the stuffed cats more than me. But by then, I was starting to like Charley the dog more than Richard.

Three weeks later, the guy from the Doll Hospital called. The cats were ready. "Cash only."

"How much?" I asked.

"Twelve hundred dollars."

I practically fell over. There went more of my parents' hard-earned savings to pay for this lunacy. But it never occurred to me not to pay it. We'd paid nearly five thousand dollars when Charley the real dog had needed an operation. Partly real cats could cost nearly the same.

Chapter 32

The Yard Sale

Having fetched Mollie from the Metro North train, we were on our way to help Ruth with her yard sale. This was a monumental step for Ruth. Even though her house sold in January, she had been trying to avoid actually moving to the retirement community. Getting rid of things was a key step forward.

"You know your mother is going to be at her worst today," I said to Richard.

"She will be. I know. That's why I'm not staying."

"Wait a minute. I need your help."

"You have Leslie." Richard's childhood friend loved yard sales and was already at the house, organizing. We were supposedly going for moral and practical support and Mollie's strong young arms.

I sighed. "Well, I guess at least if you leave, you and your mother won't get into a fight." Richard smiled.

Mollie, now 21, studying for the MCATs and about to go home to Cambridge for the summer to take organic chemistry, piped up from the back seat to scold us. "I can't believe that she is as awful as you say she is." Mollie had had hippie parents and adored her grandmother who taught her to write thank you notes and other essential life skills.

"On that one, you will see," I replied.

"You'll see." Richard laughed.

"Really!" Mollie protested. When Richard pulled up, signs of yard sale activity were underway, some tables already spread with clothes.

"Keep your phone on. If we need rescuing, you had better come back right away."

I was still more than a little scared of Ruth, though I had known her for 10 years by this point. In addition, one of her elderly friends Rachael had called, enlisting my help encouraging Ruth to let go of more things. She mistakenly believed I had leverage with Ruth. It was a mission impossible, but I was roped into trying. Ruth would be at her most crazed, given how controlling she was and how rigidly she held onto the past. She was leaving the house she had shared with her idealized dead husband,

"Yeah," Richard answered.

"I mean it. Do not go on a drive to get lost so you can't get back here." Richard's favorite thing was to drive back roads until he was lost and then challenge himself to find his way home.

"Yeah, yeah," he said again.

I looked him sternly in the eye. "I mean it."

"Let's roll," I told Mollie, as if we were entering battle. Richard's tires squealed as he made his getaway.

I sighted Leslie with price tags and called out to her. She whispered, "Thank god you are here. Ruth is really hyper."

Inside. I noted the hideous blue shag carpet again. *The new owners will get rid of that ASAP.* Ruth was with her two friends, Rachael and Geri.

"Hi Ruth. You remember Mollie, don't you?"

"Hi, dear." Ruth, red faced, seemed far away and twitchy.

"How can we help Ruth?" I asked.

"I think there were things in the basement that Leslie would like outside," she shrieked, so agitated by this process that she could not control her voice.

"Well let's go see." I knew this would bring us past the tool bench, where the items her friends wanted me to help Ruth let go of were waiting. We all trailed down the basement steps.

"Ruth you could sell these tools for a lot of money," I said, appealing to her sense of avarice. Jeannie shot me a doubtful look.

"No. I have other plans for this whole work bench." Ruth's tone had gone from hysterical to hostile. Did she know her friends and I were in on this?

"Oh yeah? What are do you plan to do? Maybe I could help with sorting?" I said, trying to sustain a tone of reasonableness.

"Never mind," Ruth screeched, her volume escalating even more. "These are not going away today."

Who knew what emotional freight these tools, assembled and used by Chuck, held for her. I allowed a Freudian moment, the phallic tools, to slip across my mind and I grinned. She was not budging; I acquiesced knowing there might be some point in the future when we would have to pry her hands loose from each and every one before she moved to the Kendall assisted living apartment.

Ruth pointed to some things hanging on one wall and yelled, "These need to go out into the yard." Mollie, wide eyed, began to carry the items outside. As she filed past, I noticed the beach chair I had bought last summer. How did Ruth end up with it? I pointed it out, and asked that she not sell it, as it belonged to me. Ruth barely noticed.

"What about in the other part of the basement?" There Leslie was inspecting an old, furniture-size sewing machine.

Leslie asked, "Do you want to part with this, Ruth?"

"Yes, dear that can go," Ruth said clearly.

"Do you know it's filled with mold?"

"Oh well then even if we can give it away that would be good."

"You are sure?"

"Oh yes, dear. I'm not doing any sewing at this point in my life."

"Well, I hate sewing. Good riddance," I replied. Leslie chuckled.

"We better get out there. People are going to show up soon."

Outside Leslie had been busy. Tables were piled with books and clothes, old and dirty cookware, a strange assortment of glassware. Leslie gave Mollie some price tags and instructions, and Mollie got to work.

For the next two hours, we companionably greeted customers and collected dollar bills for an assortment of items. Things were selling well, and Ruth was staying in the house. Then a group of young and old Latina buyers all emerged from one car. We nodded as they purchased a few household items. They were smiling, polite, and spoke very little English. Some of them went into the basement, which was open to yard sale shoppers. I thought nothing more about it, continuing to work the crowd and adjust prices if I thought I could make a sale. Mollie got called inside to help carry a few heavier items out of the basement.

About twenty minutes later, the Latina ladies emerged from the basement, carrying between them the sewing machine. They seemed excited about this acquisition and were halfway down the driveway when Ruth came charging after them, screaming. "Did anybody give them a price? I saw them just take this from the basement." Oh no, she thought they were ripping her off.

The ladies froze. They could tell they were being accused of stealing. The one with the most English said, "But that lady…"

Leslie must have heard the commotion, came outside, and hurried over. "Ruth, I told them to take it. Remember? We talked about the mold and how we should just give it away."

"But they should pay something," Ruth said, venom in her voice. "No one gets something from me for nothing."

"But remember the mold? We talked about it. They checked with me and I told them they could take it for free."

This sunk in and for once, Ruth appeared slightly chagrinned. "Uh-uh," she sputtered. Then reconsidered. "But you should have at least tried to get something," she snapped.

Leslie remained calm, as if talking to one of the students she worked with. "But I told them to take it. They didn't do anything wrong." She turned back to the group. "My apologies. Mrs. Laudor was confused. You are very welcome to it." Ruth remained silent.

I approached, and with as much warmth, eye contact, and the gentlest smile I could muster I said, "It is yours. Please my apologies for the confusion."

The lady looked re-assured, but they walked sideways out of the driveway to their car to keep a steady eye on Ruth who glared at them until reluctantly heading back into the basement.

When we got back into the car with Richard at the end of the yard sale, immediately Mollie said, "I did not know people acted like that." She seemed stunned.

"Yeah," was all I could get out.

I felt guilty that I could not find it in me to have any sympathy for Ruth. She had just the wrong combination of selfishness, helplessness and rage, coupled with a lack of insight about herself that drove me crazy. I was scared of her, but I knew I would make a better wife to Richard if I could be more compassionate.

Chapter 33

Weighted Down and Lightening Up

By the middle 2000s, professionally, I was back working full-time. With sweat, blood, and tears I had completed my dissertation and internship and passed the licensing exam, opening a private practice with children and families on the Upper West Side in a terrific office space a colleague and I renovated using some of my inheritance. I still needed a day job as the practice developed and signed on as the head of the Infancy Program at the Bank Street Graduate school, my alma mater for my first graduate degree.

As my small practice grew and I was thrilled to be doing work I cared about. But for the first time in my life, I started to screw up big time at Bank Street. I was depressed and the insomnia intensified, rarely allowing me more than a couple hours of sleep. Richard too was depressed and extraordinarily unhappy in his work life as an attorney. Then, I contracted Lyme Disease and though this meant true physical exhaustion, I still couldn't sleep. Probably I should have taken a leave of absence but didn't. At Bank Street, under these strains, I couldn't remember things, get places on time, grade papers, or plan ahead. My boss called me in to discuss these lapses.

Not only was I having trouble bearing up under Richard's depression, my own was ascending. Not having kids continued to feel like I was missing out on being a normal human being and woman. My weight kept notching up, being married to a fellow ice cream lover and couch potato, and feelings of self-loathing and hatred of my physical self-re-surfaced with a vengeance. Suicidal thoughts erupted daily, I could not pull it together at work, and had to step down, a major humiliation. This kind of failure was novel and hard to take Eventually, in 2008, I was let go from Bank Street (ostensibly due to the George Bush's fiscal disaster), creating an unbearable financial stress.

When we first met, Richard reminded me that in the personal ad, I had described myself as *zaftig*, the Yiddish word meaning pleasantly plump. In those days personal ads did not feature photos, and I didn't want to meet someone who was only interested in a social x-ray. But I was not truly fat, not obese, maybe 15 pounds to lose. Looking back at photos of our early days, Richard too was only a little chubby then, having struggled since childhood with being overweight, probably eating to mask his vulnerability. As an adult, he actually took a certain perverse pride in his 3XXXL girth. When someone like Jackie Gleason came up in conversation, Richard would call him "one of the great, fat Americans." At the time we met, not long after his nervous breakdown and recovery, Richard had lost weight and was exercising twice a week with a trainer.

After ten years together, Richard did less and less physical activity, getting out of bed only to go to work. He ate more and more when at home, lying in front of the TV, and wanted me to keep him company. We both earned the medical label of morbid obesity, me at 250 pounds and Richard at 350 pounds. Richard developed Type II diabetes; my blood pressure shot up, and my feet hurt constantly. Walking for pleasure, something I had always done, was no longer possible. The physical pain and the effort it took to move any and all parts of me, contributed to a deepening sense of my life closing in. I ate too much pasta and not enough salad. I craved chocolate, cheese, or anything with large amounts of butter fat. I felt more and more hopeless and helpless about the situation. Though it was not fair to blame Richard for my own weight gain—

he hadn't chained me to the bed or poured the Ben & Jerry's down my throat—when I thought of fixing it, his weight, in all its senses, felt on top of me. I knew I could barely motivate myself, let alone both of us.

"Anything else?" Dr. Charap, my internist, asked as he finished my yearly check-up. I sat uncomfortably at the end of the exam table, the paper gown barely covering my round body, my toes and nose cold from the air conditioning, tissue crinkling under my butt.

I gulped. "Any advice about losing weight?"

Bespectacled, thin, and greying, Dr. Charap was a sweet but fast and efficient guy. He glanced at my chart, checking the weight recorded at the beginning of my physical, and then gestured to his office across the corridor. "Get dressed and come over."

As I sat across the desk from him, terrified, Dr. Charap asked my height and age.

For all the therapy in the world, for all that Richard loved me anyway, the childhood sense that my physical self was disgusting, persisted. Paralyzing shame rushed through me. *I was fat and ugly and bound to stay that way forever.* But I had asked the weight loss question and as humiliating as it might be, this conversation might point a way out. I rarely asked anyone for help.

When I replied five feet, five and a half inches, and fifty-four, he turned to his computer screen, entered in my age, height, and weight. Dr. Charap said, "You qualify."

"For what?" I asked, with a laugh.

"Lap band," he said in his usual staccato way.

Huh? Where was the standard advice to "eat less and exercise more"? Or the recommendation to join Weight Watchers, which my previous doctor advised (and had been a little bit effective for a few months when Richard and I went together.) Richard's doctor had recommended

251

weight loss surgery for him, and it was on Richard's far distant to-do list. Suddenly I realized that Dr. Charap's recommendation meant that I was as fat as Richard. Ouch. But it also offered a real and immediate course of action. Something *to do*.

Dr. Charap continued. "You could try the standard ways of weight loss, but I bet you've already tried that. I send a few patients a month down to George Fielding's office at NYU. He is the lap band guru. He's got a whole operation down there."

I knew immediately, with blinding certainty, that I was going to do this. And that I was going to become a thin person, or at least a much thinner person. I thanked him and left, clutching Dr. Fielding's number in my hot, sweaty hand.

Back at my office, I called right away. The first step was an evening orientation meeting at the hospital, and I signed up for a spot a few days later. Richard was not enthusiastic. "It's a big step," he said, before he changed the TV channel.

That Thursday, near the beginning of rush hour, I drove the FDR Drive on the east side of Manhattan to the downtown orientation, scared and exhausted after a long day of work but proud that I was going, not giving in to inertia by going home instead. In bumper-to-bumper traffic, I worried I would be late, holding in the beginnings of road rage—then felt an odd twinge in my abdomen. Next, I felt the worst pain I had ever had in my life. I doubled over, searching for a way off the highway. While I have a high pain tolerance, this was like nothing I had ever felt before, even when I was eleven and my appendix burst. This pain was sharp, unrelenting, and took my breath away. I found an exit and eased off, pulling up next to a playground.

By then my midwestern stoicism was in pieces and I was yelping. I called Dr. Charap's office and by chance he was still there and told me to go to the ER at Mt Sinai Hospital, where he was an attending. "Sounds like a kidney stone," he said. "I'll call ahead."

Richard didn't answer his cell but I reached him at the office. "You have to come. You have to help me," I shrieked. For once, he sounded ready to leap into action.

"Where are you?" he asked, like a good, concerned husband. To give Richard credit, he had taken me to the ER several times. My weird relationship to my body and my midwestern belief that enduring pain was a virtue often meant I ignored warning signs of illness or pain. When I finally admitted that something was wrong, I would panic and need treatment immediately. Richard always willingly accompanied me on these ER trips, though he sometimes complained about the wait times or ER staff. I gave him the intersection, and before he hung up, he said, "I don't have the cell so I can't call again, but I will be there. Coming up in a cab."

I got out of the car to see if standing up would lessen the pain. It didn't. I doubled over against the car and began to moan. Some teenage boys playing basketball in the playground noticed and asked, "Are you okay, miss?" I could barely answer. "Do you want an ambulance?" they persisted. Sweat was pouring off of me. This was a crazy kind of pain. My psychoanalytic brain shifted into overdrive. *This is pain to keep me from going where I need to go—how amazing the resistance my body is putting up to a change.*

"No, no," I said. "My husband is on the way."

They looked dubious but went back to shooting hoops. Constant pain intensified in waves while I tried to stay still and waited. After some time passed, I began to wonder why Richard wasn't there yet. I squinted at the street sign ahead and realized I'd given him the wrong intersection. He was going to be looking for me a block away and didn't have his cell. And

I knew he would never find me. Richard wasn't resourceful; he would stand and wait in the wrong place. I began to wave at the basketball kids. One of them noticed, and I pulled out a twenty and said to him, tersely, as it so hurt to speak, "Go down one block and look for a tall fat guy with a beard getting out of a cab. Bring him here." The kid eyed me, as if he might just run off with the cash, but he took it and loped off in the right direction.

In just a few minutes, Richard came huffing up with the kid, looking worried. "Lizzie. Lizzie!"

"Get me to Mt Sinai ER. Please!" I yelled. This was less than 10 blocks away but I knew I couldn't walk.

"Get in. I'll drive," he said. For once, a practical solution.

I gripped the side handle of my door and screamed until we got to the ER entrance and I hurried in as best I could, leaving Richard to park. Several levels of bureaucracy stood between my pain and seeing an MD, so I tried to return to midwestern stoicism, though it was not easy. I stopped yelling. Holding my belly, I spoke as calmly as I could. I described the severity of the pain, handed over my insurance card and explained that my doctor, an attending physician, had called ahead. The initial triage desk must have taken me seriously because quite soon I was called for the initial consultation with a nurse. By then, Richard had parked and was with me, though pacing and muttering under his breath, "They better do something for my wife." He always had a hard time seeing me suffer. Soon, we were ushered into the inner ER waiting room, so packed there was hardly a place to sit. Richard continued pacing.

The mental control over my involuntary yelping waned and I turned my head to the wall, moaning again. This went on for more than an hour before anyone paid attention. Richard demanded to know what was taking so long. Someone said they were waiting to assign my case to a doctor. I could see through the haze of pain that we must have arrived at shift change, one set of residents replacing another set; no one wanted to be stuck with me in case I took too long. Finally, I decided not to be stoic and started screaming. That got me a gurney and a chance to lie down, but no real relief.

Richard finally strode up to a computer terminal and began scrolling for my name to see where I was in the queue. Suddenly, an older man flew over to Richard's side and they both were yelling, Richard ranting about how his wife needed attention now. The guy called security and Richard was escorted out. I felt defeated, worried for him, but also like I was about to pass out. About that time, a young woman approached and asked a couple of questions. I told her to call my internist, whose cell number I had in my phone. Somehow Richard snuck back in, and phoned Dr. Charap but started cursing *him*, yelling for him to do something. I summoned what strength I had, sat straight up, grabbed the phone, and apologized.

"My husband just gets a little bit nuts when I am in pain," I told the doctor.

I lay back down, but not before telling Richard to get the fuck out, to sit in the waiting area, and if I ever got better, I would find him there. He slunk out. About a half an hour later, I got a shot of morphine, and within minutes the pain was gone, and they sent me home to follow up with my doctor in the morning. There was never a definitive diagnosis for the pain, but likely I had passed a kidney stone. So much for beginning a weight loss program.

I finally got to an orientation two weeks later. A lap band operation was major surgery; they'd insert a small band around the top of the stomach that could be loosened or tightened but never taken out. It created a pouch above the stomach, and I would never be able to eat more than the small pouch would hold; I could still eat almost everything, but in tiny, tiny amounts at one time. It was scary learning all it entailed, but a panel of patients reported on the after results and they all looked damn good. It was less invasive than another new procedure, gastric bypass.

I was in. After clearing all the hurdles my insurance company put up—I had to prove that I had tried regular diet and exercise for six months, and that I had been overweight by a specific percentage for five years—the lap band procedure was approved.

Richard was scared. Three weeks before the operation and one week before I needed to begin a nonfat, liquid protein diet to prepare, we were lying in bed, having a consumed an entire pizza between us.

He turned to me. "If you lose all that weight, will you leave me?"

"Of course not," I said. "Maybe you will have the operation, too."

"But do you have to give up soda?" Richard was a soda addict, although since the diabetes diagnosis a few months before, he had mostly stuck to diet soda.

"I asked Dr. Fielding—he has a lap band himself—and he said he still drinks soda, though he can't chug it."

Richard nodded soberly and turned the volume back up on the ever-present television.

I was worried about something else. Richard was not sure if he could get away from work on the day of my operation; that probably meant he was afraid to ask, but he wouldn't give me an answer. Things were tense at his job and he was increasingly worried about getting fired. He said he wouldn't know until the last minute. I could get friends to come, probably, but it would not be easy for anyone. Diane, with a tiny baby, would need a babysitter. Hattie would never be able to get away from patients. Lesley was similarly busy. The most reliable person was the other Leslie, but the operation would be on a Friday and she worked in a school and had a child. My goddaughter Mollie, all grown-up and in med school in New York City, might be able to get there depending on her (often unpredictable) schedule. Up until the last minute, Richard couldn't, or wouldn't, tell me. He blamed his boss. I was scared and unsettled. *What was the point of having a spouse if I had to face everything on my own?* When I had been alone for so many years, one of my main dreads was filling out the emergency contact information on medical forms. In those days, I had no one to put on that line. Now I could put Richard's name there, but I had no faith that he would show up, or that he could make any decisions or know what to do in an emergency.

In the end, both Mollie and Richard came with me to the hospital. Richard had the day off, begrudgingly given, he claimed, and he seemed morose and distant. He was going to have to go in both days over the weekend to compensate. As we were waiting, a nurse began explaining the procedure and what would happen next. One part was that I needed to get a prescription filled for a liquid opioid to take when I went home, as I wouldn't be able to get down anything solid for a while, including pills. She advised that the prescription be filled right then, at the hospital pharmacy, because it was hard to obtain in the outside world. It was Friday and the hospital pharmacy wasn't open on weekends. Richard took the prescription. I suggested he go right then but he shrugged and said he would do it later. As I lay waiting to enter the surgical suite, my feet started to get cold. Mollie sweetly found my socks in the bag of clothes and put them on me. I never felt better taken care of in my life than in that moment.

When I woke after the operation, it was dark outside. Richard was there and I was grateful, but he still seemed distant and irritable. I told him to go home and get some rest; he would be coming back in the morning and help me home. Though still drowsy from the anesthesia, I could not sleep well in the busy, beeping unit and by first light, my head started to ache. I felt sore around the incisions in my midsection, but that pain was manageable. The headache was not, and it slowly turned into a migraine. The overhead fluorescent lights were too bright, even with my eyes closed. Nausea overtook me, but I was supposed to try hard not to vomit, which would stress and possibly dislodge the newly implanted lap band. I was miserable, trying to control the nausea, head pounding.

At 6:00 a.m., a nurse told me I had to get out of bed and start walking. She was not sympathetic about my headache. "Get up," she said, "Or you are never going home."

I started walking, blinding pain throbbing through my head. I walked and walked. I wanted out of there. I called on my newly found inner toughness. Back in bed, I was still in incredible head and body pain though the nausea subsided a bit. By noon, I had not seen or heard from Richard, and reached him at home. Clearly, I had woken him and he sounded confused.

"What am I supposed to do?"

"Weren't you supposed to go into the office this morning?" I asked.

"Umm…"

"Come and get me," I said and hung up.

Richard showed up three hours later, looking exhausted. Wordlessly, he gathered my things and we drove home in silence. Before crawling into my own bed, looking forward to a quiet, dark snooze with Charley at my feet, I asked for the liquid painkiller.

"What prescription?" he said.

Rage and despair flooded over me. Drugs they had given me at the hospital would wear off soon.

I didn't yell. I didn't cry. I just reminded him, and he said, "Oh, right. I'll go fill it now."

But he couldn't. He tried three pharmacies and two said they didn't carry the medication in liquid form and the other said they needed direct verbal authorization from a physician to confirm that Richard and I were not addicts. The incision hurt over the next few days, but I toughed it out, without a painkiller.

And then I lost 82 pounds. I could walk again.

Chapter 34

Help by the end of the week!

On a Monday evening, around 10 p.m., I was utterly exhausted, and on my way home after a full day of patients, students, and teaching. I found Richard, naked in bed, eyes glued to television sitcoms. He did not look up, merely said, "Hi, Lizzie."

Charley and Ash appeared glad to see me. If there was to be any dinner, I had better do something. First, though, walk the dog. Charley jumped high; his red puppy self utterly excited when he saw the leash. His energy was uplifting. For the last walk of the night, I always let him run around the block, off the leash. He never tried to go in the street, and he got triple the exercise, because he would run away half a block and then run back to me as I called him before he ran forward again, totaling the equivalent of six blocks while I walked one. That night was still warm in late September, and I felt a little better after.

I found some cold pasta in the refrigerator and got in bed next to Richard. I handed him a fork, so we could eat from the same bowl.

"How was your day?" I asked, not really wanting to know. Richard was still working at the same small commercial landlord tenant firm, where he did not fit in and was not appreciated. His boss had called me more than once to say that Richard was acting "strangely and inappropriately" on the job. Most days Richard described working there as "torture."

Richard slowly turned to me and said in certain quiet tone, "I hope I die by the end of the week." He seemed more determined, more serious than usual.

The only thing that was new about this was "by the end of the week." A wave of helplessness washed over me. I didn't know what to do about Richard's depression anymore. He had a new therapist, James Ogilvie, a man he liked. Dr. Ogilvie had come on board after the senior psychoanalyst, Dr. M.—whom Richard had seen twice a week for ten years—had thrown Richard out of his office, cursing him, and telling him never to come back. I had met with Richard and Dr. M. once after one of those phone calls from Richard's office. Dr. M. had that utterly faux tone of concerted neutrality that actually reeked of contempt. I saw in one instant that he hated my husband. So, the change of therapist had seemed positive.

But now, here Richard was, wanting to die by the end of the week. He also had a psychiatrist, Dr. Asnis, a senior researcher in depression and anxiety, who had put Richard on a cocktail of complicated medications. None of it was helping. I felt like I had been my husband's therapist 24/7 for ten years. And that wasn't helping either. For the last three or four years, he had not really done anything except reluctantly get out of bed each morning, take the car service to the office, work—sort of—come home, and get back in bed. I had started taking vacations without him and living a parallel life as best I could, but it seemed Richard only approached a state of semi-contentment if I too climbed in bed or was asleep beside him or depressed along with him.

That night, I turned my back to Richard without even answering and cried myself to sleep, comforted a little by Charley at my feet. When I woke in the early morning, the sense of defeat remained; I looked at Richard sleeping inches away, yet I felt so alone. Richard had once been the relief from my lifelong sense of isolation. But after more than ten years of marriage, I was almost lonelier than ever. And then it came to me. I could not handle this "dying by the end of the week" by myself. I needed help—for me, for him, for all of it. I had a lot of help, spending years in psychotherapy that saved my life. If I could get the right help, maybe therapy would save me again.

I began my first real therapy at twenty-nine with Dr. Larry Seidman, two or three times a week for seven years, working through desperate depression. What I mostly learned was how, when I most felt like withdrawing in anger and or terror from human contact, to reach for it instead, even when something inside of me said not to. This was a critical step out of my isolation. In the 1990s, while living in Texas, I was again in therapy twice a week, for four years. There I worked with a very empathic woman, Dr. Laurel Wagner, although I never learned to trust her (a female therapist) because I couldn't fight through the negative transference engendered by my difficult mother. But I learned there that I brought shadows to my everyday life and I needed to find my way through.

At Bennington, I saw a very seasoned and thoughtful therapist, Dr. Richard Ford, who had the bushiest eyebrows I ever saw; he also had a dog in his office. We sat side by side, in two armchairs, and looked out into the woods as we talked. He helped me fall in love with Richard. And then there was Dr. Joyce Steingart, the analyst I saw twice a week for 10 years after moving to New York with Richard. In some ways I felt she did not help me—that negative transference to women thing—but, again, she did. She was steadying and I got steadier. But she never let me question being with Richard. He loved me and I think she thought that was enough.

I thought about a dream I had as I was beginning my first real psychotherapy experience with Dr. Seidman, in the fall of 1983, before my nervous breakdown. The dream fragment I recalled was walking in a dimly lit hallway, like an uphill tunnel. I am dressed in my 1980s uniform—jeans, t-shirt, Birkenstocks—and wearing two very heavy backpacks. Just ahead, a door opens and out pops Dr. Seidman. At our sessions, I mostly remember him wearing comfortable shoes, sweaters, and cords, but in the dream, he is dressed in the well-fitting gray suit and tie he wore the first time I met him. He was very, very tall, and lanky and as I approached, he smiled slightly. I slipped off one backpack and gave it to him. I kept the other one on my back as I continued along the tunnel by myself.

I realized suddenly that I was still carrying that second backpack after all this time. In fact, Richard and his family had added a few more stones to the pack. I needed to put this backpack down, open it, and get rid of those stones.

It was hard to know what to do. I didn't want to go back to Dr. Steingart; I had ended sessions with her several months before. I had wanted to finally try to live an unexamined life, counting on myself for a change. Now, this was urgent and there was no time to work through a negative transference. I needed immediate help. Dr. Grossmark popped into my head. He had been ahead of me by several years at City College and was married to someone I had known during my training. He was probably younger than me, but I had heard him speak about his work in group therapy and admired how he spoke about his patients—with respect, warmth, humor, and intelligence. I remembered him mostly because I had once thought Richard would benefit from being in one of his groups. I called and set an appointment for Thursday—before Richard's end of the week deadline.

Dr. Grossmark's office was on Central Park West, a few blocks from my own office. Once seated on his comfortable chair, looking him in the eye, I began talking about my despair over Richard, and I felt his compassionate presence. I began to sob and sob and sob. In his gentle

English accent, Dr Grossmark told me I was right to come, that I didn't need to bear this all on my own. Relief and hope returned to me.

Chapter 35

Happy birthday, not

Two weeks later, Richard was still alive, having forgotten all about his deadline. We were running late to my mother-in-law's 80th birthday party. Being late was not unexpected as we both dreaded any contact with that woman but she had asked for us to come early to help with set-up. Richard showered first and went down to get the car, urging me to hurry. I took a shower as fast as a boy and put on the only appropriate outfit I had and ran out. As I got into the car, Richard held a paper cup filled with spoiled coffee. It could have been sitting in the car for a couple of weeks. In helpless distress, he turned to me as I settled in. "Here. Do something with this," he said, handing me the gross, stinking cup.

"Why me? Haven't you been sitting here for ten minutes?"

"I don't know what to do. You just deal with it. Besides, you probably left it here. I always drink all the coffee in my cup." Ah, the sibling rivalry problem—Richard still refusing to pick up a crumb that might belong to Danny or Michael.

Rather than argue, I took the cup, planning to dump out its gross contents out the window and then throw it into the backseat. As I lifted the lid off and began to open the window, I said, "Don't move the car," but at that very moment, Richard stepped on the gas. The spoiled cream-curdled coffee flew all over my outfit, the inside of the door and window, and the edge of my seat.

"Stop!" I screamed. I got out and threw the cup to the sidewalk. "Stay right here."

I went back inside to find a new outfit; not an easy task, as I had been considering potential dresses for weeks for this fancy party. When I returned with a towel for further cleanup, Richard was sitting silently, unmoving. I wiped off the seat and the side of the window, then sat and buckled in. Just as the seat belt clicked, Richard stepped hard on the gas, the car jerked forward, and the large reservoir of spilled coffee hidden in the well of the door handle splattered over me again. I began screaming but no matter how loudly I pleaded, shouted, or cursed, Richard refused to stop. He didn't want to anger his mother by arriving any later that we already would.

I spent the entire party nauseous from the smell of spoiled milk and wholly self-conscious about the huge dark wet stains all over my clothes. I even had to chat amiably with Danny who had come from California for the occasion. As a sexually abused child, I could feel contaminated and disgusting even on a good day but this was horrid for me. Richard was oblivious.

Richard and I had been fighting about cleaning and all that it symbolized for many years. Never meant to be a good housewife, I was not a proficient cleaner myself, in spite of my upbringing by my very tidy mother. But having to mingle among the guests while feeling so gross created a new kind of resolve. Perhaps, I thought, I was strong enough to start cleaning up my own mess, but Richard's mess was another story. I would never have control of his helpless mess that splattered on me.

I felt a shift. There, at my mother-in-law's 80th birthday party, I saw with utter and certain clarity that I was going to leave my husband. I wouldn't say this out loud to him or to anyone, or even really to myself, for a long time to come.

The hell of Ruth's 80th birthday didn't end there. The next day, because she wanted all "her boys" together for this major event, we travelled up to the hospital to see Michael. I felt very numb and withdrawn. It was such a fake "happy occasion." Ruth had gotten special permission to take a photo in the visiting room. I didn't want to be in the photo but she insisted. Here we were in a building encased in chain link fence topped by razor wire and heavily guarded. How could Ruth pretend this was a celebration of any sort? I felt dazzlingly alone.

Chapter 36

Money isn't everything

"Where's the checkbook, Lizzie?" Richard bellowed from the living room couch as I was making the breakfast coffee.

"What do you mean, where's the checkbook?" I yelled back. "It's where it's supposed to be."

I had recently bought a bill organizer, with slots to file bills by days of the month they were due, and two little drawers for the checkbook and stamps. I thought this might help us tame the disaster that was our finances.

"If it's not in plain sight, then it's not where it's supposed to be," Richard answered loudly, furiously.

I thundered out of the kitchen, grabbed the organizer, and waved it in front of Richard's face. "It's in here," I screamed. "Don't you remember that we discussed this on Tuesday when this thing arrived?"

The bill organizer was heavy wood, but I kept waving it about. Our finances were in dire shape and nothing seemed to help us get on track. I knew the bill organizer was grasping at straws but maybe if we could agree on where to keep the checkbook, and how and when to pay bills, we could begin working together to find a way out of the financial morass.

Richard looked stolidly ahead. "If I can't see it, if it's not in plain sight, then it's not going to work. I never agreed to that thing," he said, swiping his hand toward the organizer so I didn't hit him with it. Richard insisted that the coffee table, where we ate most of our meals and which sat in front of the couch, the only place Richard ever occupied in our apartment besides the bed, was his surface to command. There, he kept all the important papers in our lives out for all to see, though not in any organized way that made sense to me. He had a real desk, taking up valuable space in the living/dining room, and filing cabinets, but these did not interest him.

I sighed, and brought out cups, the coffee pot, and the half-and-half, placing it all down among the bills and paperwork. I sat sipping for a bit in silence, our usually companionable morning routine. Then Richard began shuffling papers and looked pained.

"I better check the balance in the checking account. I don't think we have enough to pay the mortgage."

"What? I just put a few thousand in that account from my private practice income and besides there should have been some from the last time I sold off some of Mom and Dad's stocks."

My inheritance had been helping to keep us afloat. I knew this was not a sound strategy, eating up the principle, but our money woes were intractable and filled me with paralyzing, intractable shame. I just did what needed to be done in the moment.

"I used almost all of that to pay the American Express bill," said Richard.

"What the fuck? That wasn't due until the end of the month. How are we going to pay the mortgage and the maintenance?"

Richard shrugged. Despair flooded over me. There was only one account left to tap from the inheritance, which I had wanted to hang on to as an emergency fund. But I would have to cash it in so we weren't homeless. We had made so many bad decisions— me going to graduate school at age 43 and not earning much money at all for seven years, though now I made three times what I made before; Richard's intermittent unemployment and now underemployment so that his salary

272

was less than what it was when we met thirteen years before. The layoff from my faculty job in 2008.

Then, of course, the daily nonsensical way we spent money without a plan or budget. Richard ordering take-out daily, me taking cabs home from Manhattan to Riverdale, a $30 ride most days, as I was always too exhausted to sit on the subway for an hour and then ride the bus up the hill.

We kept falling further and further behind. This bore down on me, and I felt so ashamed because to me it meant I had failed as an adult who couldn't take care of herself and her family. This ran so counter to the value of "self- reliance" so fiercely embedded in the culture I came from. Richard's solution was to file for bankruptcy, but I resisted. Couldn't we find a way? If we did declare bankruptcy, I likely would lose the only asset I had left, the small, forty-acre Illinois farm where my father grew up. When it was left to me, I promised my grandfather I would never sell. The prevailing ethos in the family was that if we hadn't lost it in the Depression, then it would be ours forever. I would be letting the generations down. Land, my father said, quoting Mark Twain, is always valuable, because they're not making any more of it.

Late one winter night, near the end of 2009, Richard and I were talking about our deepening money troubles, in bed as usual. But this conversation was so serious that I reached over, took the remote from Richard, and switched the TV off. He told me there was no other solution but bankruptcy. I felt a rush of deep, black despair and shame overpower my brain and I said, "Let's just kill ourselves right now. Then this is over. That's another answer."

Richard replied, "Okay."

We both lay still, many minutes, not touching.

Richard broke the silence. "You aren't serious, are you?"

"Yes, I am," I said, remembering the range of medicines and alcohol we had on hand, the tools to cease the struggle. As usual when my brain was at its most broken, my only fear was that in attempting suicide, I would fail to die and wake up impaired. But I was pretty sure that I knew what it took.

Richard, usually the more depressed, said, "No, not tonight," rolled over and went to sleep. But I couldn't, didn't sleep. I spent the night immobile, rigid in my body, aching to die, to end, and to reach the moment when the curtain fell and *I* was gone, no longer hurting, or hating myself. But then morning came. I got up, made coffee, walked the dog, and went to work, the midwestern stoicism and work ethic prevailing.

A year later, mostly because of Richard's inertia, we had not filed for bankruptcy and I started to plan to leave Richard. The how of it—given the slight, tenuously improving state of my finances now that my private practice was expanding and I had another day job, was uncertain. I was waiting to tell Richard until I had a definite plan, as I knew he would freak out. I was so frightened of how he would react.

Then one night on his way home from his new therapist, Richard rushed to catch the express bus and fell hard on his shoulder. He was helped up by a physician who happened to be at the scene. In excruciating pain, Richard was taken by ambulance to Bellevue, a public hospital. He called me from there, and told me not to come down, as it was late and raining. I think he knew how angry and done I was with him even though it was unsaid. I didn't go to Bellevue, a serious error in terms of medical next steps. Richard was sent home with some minor painkillers, in agony, and told to return to the Bellevue orthopedic clinic in five days for further care. He screamed, constantly, all through the night. Waiting five days was not a workable solution.

In the morning, I started calling orthopedists, to find one who would see him on short notice. His primary care doctor was not on Richard's insurance plan and was unable to give a referral to any specialist who was. The insurance company gave me names and I called seven, but none would see him. Finally, I got an appointment at a satellite clinic of Montefiore Hospital, across the Bronx from us. I had to take time off from my new job to get him there. When we saw the doctor, it turned out he specialized in knees. However, he took an X-ray and reported that Richard had a shattered shoulder, a very serious and complicated break, and of course would need surgery. He called a colleague who did know something about shoulders at another Montefiore site, and we booked an appointment the next day, another day off from my new job. Finally, surgery was set for five days later. In the meantime, Richard would be at home, unsteady on his feet, in serious pain. Now even more depressed and crazy, he cried continuously.

I broke down and called Ruth. Maybe she could come by to check on him while I was at work. I rarely called her as Richard was in no emotional shape to speak to her. They usually ended up yelling or hanging up on each other.

"Hello, Ruth?'

"Yes, dear, how are you?"

"I'm fine, but Richard's shoulder is really hurting, and he is not going to have the operation for few days."

"Poor Rich," she said. "I just talked to Danny today and he was telling me that Sam got an award at school." Sam was her eldest grandson, who lived in California with Danny and his mother (who was not Danny's wife).

"That's great news," I answered. "I have to go back to work tomorrow, and I am little worried about leaving Richard alone all day. I was wondering if you could check in on him—you know, stop by, maybe?"

I was always afraid to ask her for anything, but she still drove herself places.

"Oh, not tomorrow, dear," she answered. "I've got a whole day planned. Maybe I could come at suppertime on Thursday."

"Thanks, but I can be home in the evening so that won't really help. Okay. Bye."

I hung up, not surprised that she was as utterly self-centered as usual. No one in Richard's family ever helped me with him except Michael. Michael had. Michael was locked up and psychotic but Richard needed his brother.

I left for work, but not before I made sure Richard had his phone in his pocket; he agreed to call 911 if he got into trouble. It would be a long day for me—a full school day at City and Country and then four patients in my private practice. I would be gone more than twelve hours.

When I opened the door to our apartment sometime after 9:00 that evening, I called out for Richard. Silence. I rushed into the bedroom, and he was lying naked on the floor, seeming only semi-conscious. Richard roused himself and said, "I fell and couldn't get up."

"When did you fall?"

"Just around lunch time, I think."

"Why didn't you call 911, like I told you to?" I asked, frustration, fear, and rage surging through me.

"I knew I could just wait for you," Richard said with a feeble smile.

I said nothing, but the thoughts in my head screamed. *It's all on me. It's all on me, and it is going to kill me.* Then a blaze of insight caused me to start shaking in fear, but also relief. Dr Grossmark was helping me understand that I had unconsciously recreated one of the central realities of my childhood, the sense and burden that my parents counted on me to stay alive after my brother died. I felt I was keeping Richard alive, literally and emotionally, in the same way. More than ever, I needed to break free of this burden, an unconscious, until now, repetition.

I tried to pick Richard up. I pulled. I pushed, straining until little beads of sweat broke out across my face. With his right shoulder, arm, and hand completely out of commission, Richard was no help at all. He was 6 feet tall and weighed more than 350 pounds. No way could I lift him. I found his phone two feet from him and dialed 911.

Two cops arrived about thirty minutes later, and even they had a hard time getting Richard up, though they were strong young men. With Richard deposited back in bed, I could stop sweating, for the moment.

A few days later, the shoulder operation went smoothly, according to the surgeon, but Richard remained in significant pain for nearly three months, completely unable to function. He didn't go to work. He was even more passive and dependent. He wept a lot, completely undone. The injury seemed to have destroyed some sense Richard had about his body, making him feel thoroughly disabled. I thought he was having a complete breakdown, but no one else in his life—mother, uncle, therapist, or psychiatrist—seemed to realize this. I really was at a loss what to do. I just had to lie there next to him, until he got better, so I could tell him I was leaving him.

Night after night, I imagined my new life, on my own, without this strangling yoke. One thing that kept me going was thinking about my books. I had hundreds and hundreds of books. And in my new life, I pretended I would only take ten of them. But which ten? That was the problem I focused on, as I distractedly pretended to care about my deadening husband and to nurse him through his long physical and psychiatric convalescence.

Chapter 37

Dumb Luck

Then something of extraordinary serendipity occurred. One evening as I lay next to Richard while he moaned in front of the TV, I was thinking about which books came after *Leaves of Grass, To the Lighthouse,* and *Harriet the Spy*, the three that I was always taking, the phone rang. A Southern male voice asked to speak to "Miss Elizabeth Tingley." I was cautious, suspecting a bill collector.

"Who is calling, please?"

"This is Willie Ramsey calling. I live down in Florida, but lately I have been spending time up in Clark County, Illinois, to go hunting with my son and grandsons, and I am trying to track down the owner of a piece of property there. And I thought that Miss Tingley might be the owner."

"Well, this is she."

Actually, I owned two pieces of property in Clark County. One was the sacred family farm. The other was a twenty-acre strip of land that, shortly before he died, my father had called worthless. It had been adjacent to my parents' "country place" they had bought with friends in 1970, where they had picnics and cookouts and maintained a huge garden, a getaway from the "pressures" of regular small-town life. They sold the main property not long after moving to the retirement community, but my father retained this strip across the road for political reasons. Twice, investors had tried to put environmentally unsound businesses adjacent to this strip but were stopped in part because they needed more land. The first was a landfill for low-level nuclear waste. The second time, investors tried to put a commercial hog farm there, which would raise a horrible stench and the run-off would pollute nearby streams. So, Dad had kept this little bit of land as environmental insurance, not thinking it would ever do him or me or anyone much good.

"Is the land you are speaking about a twenty-acre plot in Parker Township or a forty-acre plot in Darwin Township?" I asked Mr. Ramsey.

"Well now, I don't know anything about a forty-acre plot but it's the twenty acres in Parker that I wanted to discuss with y'all if I could," Willie twanged away. "I got to be good friends with a Mr. Dave Shiver from church and he told me about the property that your parents had. Do you know Mr. Shiver?"

I knew who he was—a prosperous farmer, owning adjacent land where three large blue silos stood. They meant he could store a lot of grain on his own property waiting for the right moment to sell. The blue silos also figured prominently in the directions my parents gave to friends coming to picnic at their country place for the first time. I also knew that Mr. Shiver was a Republican, not a good friend of Dad's.

"I recall the name," I answered.

Willie continued, "Well I bought a house not far from his place, from the Halls." That name also rang a bell—an eccentric old guy named Buzzard Hall that my dad *had* liked. He would amble over to the country place from time to time and chew the fat with Dad. Likely a Democrat.

"Oh yes, Mr. Buzzard Hall," I answered, my own voice now regaining the Central Illinois inflection I had worked hard to shed, but that always returned when I spoke to someone from home.

"Well, ma'am, I was wondering what your plans were for that land?"

"I don't have plans for it," I said, stalling a little. I needed to consider this carefully. "I have no idea what it would be worth anyway."

"Oh, well, ma'am, it's not worth much, there's no tillable soil there, really, but to me, to have a place of my own to hunt, it would work well." Mr. Ramsey was beginning to sound like a shyster, or, at the very least, a bargain hunter.

"I am not sure I want to sell, and this is not a good time for me to make any decisions," I stalled. "My husband just broke his shoulder. It's a bad break and he's needing surgery."

"I am so sorry to hear that, Mrs. Tingley. I'll pray for him at church." *You do that, you Christian born-again. Pray for my Jewish husband.* "Thank you," I said.

"Would it be all right if I called you back in a while, next month or so, to see what you are thinking?"

"Certainly," I replied. "And I would be glad to take your number in case I come to any decisions."

Richard roused a bit from the overwhelming pain of his broken shoulder. "Who was that?"

"A guy named Willie Ramsey who is interested in a little strip of land out in Illinois that I inherited. I almost forgot about that property."

I said nothing more, but wheels began to turn in my mind.

A few days later, from work, I phoned my second Cousin Barbara's husband, Danny Gard, in Illinois—the only one left in the family who farmed. I told Danny about Willie Ramsey and he suggested I get the land appraised. And so, step-by-step, I found out what the property was worth.

Then I got another call, from a lady who identified herself as Buzzard Hall's granddaughter. She told me she had heard that Willie Ramsey wanted to buy my piece of land and wanted me to know he was a bad man, a man who had bought her grandparents' house deceitfully. And she would like to buy the land instead, because she would like to build a house out there, to be close to the place of her ancestors. She told me, though, that she could never pay what Mr. Ramsey could pay, but if I said the word, she would go to the bank the next day, get a mortgage, and start the transaction immediately.

I didn't know what to do. This posed a moral dilemma for me. Like Ms. Hall, I suspected Willie Ramsey was not someone I would approve of. And I wanted to support the locals. But I needed money. I tried to think what my father would want me to do. I could hear him saying, "Don't look back. If you make a decision, just make it, and go forward." I decided to listen to this voice, and not the one saying, "Stick with tradition."

I called my friend Diane and asked her if her husband Noah, who was a lovely man, a finance guy used to deal-making, could call Willie Ramsey on my behalf and play hardball. She volunteered him right away. Noah got Willie Ramsey to agree to pay $3000 per acre, which was $1000 more than the appraised value. I was going to have more than enough to get out. I just had to wait until I would not be walking out on an injured, acutely mentally ill Richard.

Chapter 38

The Stairs Up

By the time 2011 rolled around, Richard's shoulder was mostly healed, and though he had more physical therapy to do, he was able to go back to work. He had stopped crying all the time, and while still clearly depressed, he was functioning better. He could tell that I was distant, angry all the time. I stopped couples' therapy, because I had decided to leave, although I had not informed him or the therapist. I was waiting until the time was right. By February 1, I had opened a new bank account and had my paycheck deposited there, instead of in the joint account. This made Richard angry, my making a unilateral decision, but I didn't care, or explain.

Finally, one day, when we were sort of getting along, I just blurted out, "It's over Richard. We are over."

We locked eyes. The connection was still there and yet, it wasn't. He started to cry. I held him. After some time, I said, "I'm staying until I get the money for the land. When I get the money, I'm leaving you." Richard kissed me desperately and then we clung to each other for quite a while.

A week later, as Richard was falling asleep, he opened his eyes and closed them before saying, "If you leave me, I will kill you."

I was stunned, and terrified. Killing in this family was not an idle threat. Did I need to leave immediately to be safe? I slept on the couch, keeping Charley with me.

Richard believed he could woo me back. He made a big deal over theatre tickets for Valentine's Day—*A Little Night Music* with Catherine Zeta-Jones and Angela Lansbury. He had wangled them somehow from a client for free. This was the only time in our 15 years, except when we were initially courting, that he got tickets to anything—and we lived less than a 30-minute ride from Broadway. I didn't want to go to a play in the middle of the week. I was exhausted by work and by the internal effort this upheaval in my life required. But Richard seemed so happy and proud of himself. I tried to play along but did not want to hold his hand or smile at the show. All I wanted was to get away from him, and yet it wasn't quite time.

By March, the deal with Willie Ramsey was set, with an agreement on the price, a letter of understanding signed. Title search was underway, as was a land survey. I would have my freedom. Before it was completely signed, sealed, and delivered, one of my parents' last remaining dear friends passed away, back home. I decided to go to the funeral. The route from Indianapolis Airport took me right past the area where that strip of land was located. I took a little detour to see it.

I was not sure I remembered the way, but as I made the turns down several tiny country roads, I found Dave Shiver's blue silos and there was the turn down the lane. I could see there were signs posted along the road. In fact, a sign nailed to a tree every five feet or so: KEEP OUT. NO TRESPASSING. PROPERTY of W. Ramsey.

How dare he? First of all, it was not yet his property. Second, no one around here put-up signs like that, every five feet. Maybe one or two across the whole property, but this was violating the local way. Country people were friendly. This guy was not. What a jerk.

Could I back out on the deal? I called my local lawyer, but he wasn't in. If I did the right thing here, I would screw myself. I was tired of doing the right thing as I felt I had done by standing by Richard for so long.

And then I remembered my father's words: "Once you make a decision, don't look back." I turned the car around and didn't look back. I was going to sacrifice this little corner of the county my ancestors first settled to an outsider, not a moral, good outsider. I felt guilty but I kept going.

The check for $60,000 arrived in early May 2011 and the next day I started researching apartments. I wanted to move into the neighborhood near my private practice office in Manhattan—likely an arduous search, as apartments in that area were scarce and expensive. My credit rating was in the toilet and I had a dog. For months, I had scoured Craigslist and the *Times* website. I studied listings, prices, and photos but discovered most of the listings were fake, just links to lure renters to realtors' websites. I decided I needed to choose a realtor and I began looking at photos of the *agents* and not apartments, at Citi Habitats. Most looked like insincere, slick twenty-something men who would not be sympathetic to my situation. I settled on a normal-looking young woman named Cathy who seemed nice and she started to show me places.

None were inspiring—all tiny, mostly oddly shaped with no light, located in buildings that were not kept up, but my price range was limited. I bid on one and got turned down because of my low credit score. Cathy took my case to a supervisor at Citi Habitats. As we chatted in the office, another agent piped up.

"Show her one of Frank's buildings. He doesn't care about the dog and he doesn't care about credit. He wants a bank statement that shows how much money she has in the bank."

Off we went to West 91st Street—a little seedier than most blocks in the neighborhood. As we turned towards the brownstone that had three apartments available, a weird-looking guy out front in mis-matched clothing made odd eye contact.

So, the block has some homeless mentally ill people. Well, this is New York, after all.

The first apartment, a studio, was in the front of the building yet kind of dark, but there was exposed brick, and it was on the second floor, only up one flight. *Doable.* The next apartment was on the same floor, but at the back of the building and had one bedroom. But the agent's key didn't work. There was also an open apartment on the fourth floor, and although I had specified not above the second floor, I was a bit desperate, so we climbed the flights, me huffing. The stairwell was filthy and overhead a neglected stained-glass skylight covered in grime, let in little light. The glass, held in place only by some torn ugly wire netting, looked as if it could tumble down on my head. The agent's key worked on the door to 4B, a small apartment, with a tiny kitchen, a bathroom with original tile in bright pink, a wall down the middle of the main room to separate the living area from the "bedroom." The sidewalls were exposed brick though, painted white on one side of the room and left brick color in the sleeping area. Its southern exposure meant light. The apartment felt dingy, but perhaps had potential. As I walked into the sleeping area, I saw a sliding glass door.

"Where does this go to?" I asked the agent. He shrugged.

I slid the door open, and stepped out onto a small rooftop terrace, about 8 feet by 10 feet. It had a black tar-paper floor, iron grillwork, some wooden lattice painted dark green, and a very New York rooftop view of nearby apartment buildings, water towers atop them, and some trees in the courtyard between the brownstones. I took a deep breath, of what in New York approximated fresh air, and knew.

"I'll take it."

"Great," the agent said. "The office is right downstairs. We can stop in and get the paperwork started."

We did our business in the office and the tall, thin, African American man assisting us said the final decision was up to Frank, the owner; they would let us know. Then he asked, "Did you see the owner in your way in? He was just outside."

I thought back to the man I had pegged as a mentally ill homeless guy. *That* was the landlord? But I was going to have a place, in New York, New York, for just me and Charley the dog, a place with a terrace and a view.

Chapter 39

A Different Kind of Knife

Though it was a hot August morning, the humidity had inched down a notch and my terrace was gorgeous. The flowers I planted were in bloom. I sat drinking the first coffee of the day, my mind empty as my body was still slowly, moment by moment, releasing the weight and tension of my marriage. A little over two months since I'd moved in, I was feeling close to good.

Inside, my cell phone rang. Maybe I shouldn't answer, I thought, but in my newly single state, I did like to hear from people. I found the phone by the bed and braced when I saw that it was Richard.

"Lizzie?"

"Yeah? What's up?"

"I can't do this." He started to cry. Through loud sobs, he continued, "It feels like knives are cutting every inch of my body."

What was it with Laudors and knives?

"Okay," I said, lurching forward into crisis mode. "What do you need to do right now?"

"I don't know. Maybe the hospital."

"Okay. Does Dr. Ogilvie know how bad you are feeling? Or Dr. Asnis, for that matter?" I asked, about his therapist and psychopharmacologist.

"I can't reach them. I called you. I thought I was okay, but I can't really go on."

He sobbed more. I listened. "So yeah, I'm going to head over to the psychiatric ER at Montefiore."

"I'll meet you there," I said. "Call the regular car service now. They'll send a car right over."

Richard sounded like he was shivering.

"Or do you need me to call them for you?"

"No," Richard said, calmer, but still with a catch in his voice.

"I'll meet you at the hospital. It'll be okay, Richard. I still love you."

"I know," he said, crying again.

I kissed Charley on the nose and took comfort in his tail wag. I started searching for the car key and began to scan my memory for where I had parked the car—street parking in Manhattan being a new and stressful part of single life in the city. Walking down the three flights to the street, my body stiffened, a pain in my chest seized me, and any sense of well-being and relaxation disappeared. I ran down the street to Riverside Drive, where I hoped I remembered where the car was. *What would Richard need from me now?*

I knew the ER at Montefiore well—it had been the place to go when I lived in Riverdale with Richard and thought I broke my ankle and then my shoulder, or when I had that weird jaw thing which turned out to be Lyme disease. It was noisy, dirty, always crowded, but better than the other alternatives in the Bronx. Besides, Richard's psychiatrist was an attending physician there.

In the Psych ER, I found Richard in a gown that didn't fit his roly-poly body, in a back cubicle. His head hung; his eyes dulled. I leaned in to hug him, and he broke into choking, heaving sobs. I held him crying for several minutes, without saying a word.

He kept repeating, "I can't. I can't."

I wanted to scream, "I can't either," but didn't. I just sat there, touching him, and waiting for a professional—other than me—to assess the situation. Intense and conflicting emotion surged through me. Guilt, so constant in my life. *Maybe if I hadn't left him in June, he would have some semblance of mental health at this moment.* But I remembered how depressed he had been for years, and my staying hadn't helped. Then, rage. *This was just a way to get me back and pull me in.* No. And no. Sadness. *I had loved him so much, and he had been so much for me and now it was down to this.* Lightness. *I would get to walk out of there, without him.*

Finally, a nurse with a clipboard asked me to step out so she could interview Richard. I could hear her asking about suicide and Richard said he wanted to die. After some time, she came out to talk to me. I explained that Richard had a long history of depression, that he carried a diagnosis of bipolar II, (which I disagreed with) and that his psychiatrist was an attending physician at Montefiore. I gave her the name and phone number of his therapist and the number for his mother, who would have to act as next of kin, since we were separated. Leaving him to his mother's clutches—that I did feel guilty about, but there was nothing else to be done.

The nurse turned her gaze on me, which I interpreted as judgment. This must all be my fault. I just stared back.

Then I hugged Richard goodbye, and he tried to cling to me, but I said I had to go. They would take care of him, I said, and I walked out, terrified, drained, and so relieved that I could leave.

Outside, I left messages for all of Richard's psychiatric helpers, Uncle Lewis (as I no longer spoke to Ruth), and his two best friends, Leslie and Jim.

There was no inpatient bed for Richard at Montefiore. Instead, he was admitted to Four Winds, up in Westchester. Richard had been in a Four Winds facility much further upstate in Saratoga for his first long term hospitalization so I imagined that he wouldn't mind. Three days later after work I drove up to see him. I didn't want to, but Richard had begged. Why I complied, I wasn't sure. As I walked towards his unit, my brain yelled *turn around*. Suddenly, I saw a tall, slender older woman carrying some shirts on hangers walking unevenly towards the same unit. Her gait gave her away: Ruth.

I froze. *Why had Richard asked me to come tonight when that woman would be here?* She terrified me still. I should have turned and left but was immobilized for several minutes. Then, I walked on. I would at least let Richard know I had come when he'd asked me to. There were a few steps up and then a locked door. I buzzed.

"I'm here to see Richard Laudor."

"Just sign in here and you can go into the day room. He already has one visitor."

"No," I said, trying to keep the panic and rage out of my voice. "I hope he could just come here for a minute. I don't want to see his other visitor." No matter what, I was holding to my vow not to see or speak to his mother. That was part of what I was free from.

"Let me see if he can come to the vestibule." The man sounded irritated. After what seemed an eternity, Richard poked his head around the corner. His shirt, one I had gotten him from Eddie Bauer in size XXXL, billowed about him; he had stopped eating he was so depressed. His face broadened and he smiled. "Lizzie! Come in"

"No. Isn't that your mother in there already?"

"Yeah, but you can both be here."

"No. I'm not seeing her ever again. You know I don't want to see her. Why did you tell us both to come at the same time?"

"She called after I talked to you."

"I'm leaving."

Richard started to cry. "Don't do this to me. Don't do this to me," he sobbed.

"What am I doing to you? I came. But I can't stay now."

"What am I going to tell her now? She knows you are here."

"That is your fucking problem."

I left. On the drive home, that phrase "Don't do this to me" ran through my brain like machine-gun fire, only I was screaming it at Richard. "Don't do this to ME!" Richard stayed in Four Winds for about two weeks.

Chapter 40

Unbraiding

When fall began, I had a wonderful new day job, as the consulting psychologist at a progressive school in the West Village. I spent four mornings a week there, enjoying mostly joyful, healthy children, a thoughtful group of parents and the best team of my long career, professionals who understood children. Richard was completely unemployed and apparently still profoundly depressed but agreed to meet with a mediator to discuss how to proceed with dissolving our marriage and sorting out the finances. Since I was still paying the maintenance for the Riverdale coop so Richard had a place to live, while he allegedly paid the mortgage, I was drowning, financially.

The mediators' office was in the Chelsea area of Manhattan, in a relatively upscale building. As I rode the elevator, dollar signs went ca-chink in my head. Richard had arrived already and was sweating. The mediators, Abby and Elle, were both slim, professional forties-looking women, one shorter with darker hair, the other tall and angular; they seemed like nice girls who were also attorneys. We all sat around a long oval table. Richard looked so miserable that I took his hand across the table for a moment, whispering, "This will be okay." He made piercing eye contact—searching and angry.

We began with paperwork, a contract and the mediators' fees. I was paying the bill for now, although we agreed that ultimately the divorce fees would be negotiated.

When it was Richard's turn to lay out what he wanted from the mediation, he said, with something of his rusty lawyer attitude, "I don't want conflict. But this has to be fair."

"I am all for fairness and I do want this to work out for you, too," I agreed, "but I imagine what we each think is fair won't match up."

Elle replied, "It's our job to help you sort this out in a fair way."

"The main issues are financial, I think," I said. I feared at that moment Richard would say, "You ruined me financially," and I would have to say the same back to him. But instead, he just slumped down in his chair. He looked so dark and fragile, his eyes frozen.

After further discussion, the mediators told us the first step was for Richard and me to consult a forensic accountant to determine the current state of our overburdened finances. Until then, no details of the divorce could be addressed. As Richard was so paralyzed, I took the list of recommended accountants and agreed to make the calls.

Richard asked me to get coffee afterwards. I knew it would be on my tab, of course. We found a little upscale coffee shop, and Richard complained about how "chi chi" it was. *This is downtown New York, what do you want?* We discussed the pets. He was sure that the cat missed me. I lied and said the dog missed him too. After some awkward silence, Richard said, "I still love you."

I was quiet, unsure how to reply as I was so angry. Tears welled up in my eyes and I found the "I still love you, too. I do." I paused, realizing I did mean that. But we can't be together."

Richard looked down. "Okay," he said.

Leaving we shared a long, desperate hug but I had to get away, turned abruptly, and walked like a New Yorker down 6th Avenue, sadness filling me with every fast step. Once again in my life, I was so alone, and scared to realize it.

I had to make the calls, to all the accountants on the list, and rarely got through the first time. Most, it seemed, were after bigger fish than Richard and me, as we had only debts, not assets, to apportion. The best option was all the way out on Long Island. The accountant had a family connection to one of the mediators. The appointment was for an evening after work (not that Richard was working) in two weeks' time. Our instructions were to gather all financial records and arrive at 6:00. I conveyed this to Richard, who was nearly wordless. This was not a good sign, as when well, Richard tended towards long windedness.

Because the accountant's office was an hour outside the city, I worried I would have to drive Richard, as I had the car. Fortunately, Richard got his Uncle Lewis to bring him. This was okay. Lew was the only sane member of Richard's family.

Bruce Minna's office was in a four story, nondescript building, just off a main road. A short balding man extended his hand. "I'm Bruce. Are you Elizabeth?"

"Please call me Liz," I said as we shook. "Richard and his uncle should be here shortly."

"Come this way." He led me through a cluttered set of rooms to a conference room lined with boxes and papers. "Just wait here and I will come back when they get here."

I looked around; it was a remarkably messy space. But Bruce had a kind vibe. Who was I to cast stones over mess? That was why we were here, a mess of a different kind.

Soon Bruce ushered in Richard and Lew, waving them to sit opposite me at the table. I smiled softly to greet my still-husband and Lew, who I genuinely liked. Richard had a sheaf of papers in a red folder. Similarly, I had a stack of every sort of financial record I could lay my hands on.

Bruce spoke up. "We are here to look at all your assets and debts, to determine what is fair as you divorce. Agreed?"

We all nodded, though Richard looked down at his hands. And secretly, I thought none of this is going to be fair. We had different narratives; Richard thought I ruined him financially. I had the opposite view.

"Let's start with assets."

"We jointly own a coop in Riverdale, but it is heavily mortgaged," I said. "Since 2008, we probably owe more than we could sell it for."

Richard sighed.

"I have a small TIAA-CREF retirement account and own some farmland in Illinois, that I inherited from my parents. And the car, which is paid for, but I bought it with my inheritance."

Bruce nodded. "Make and model?" I gave him the information, and he went on. "As you inherited the money to purchase the car from your family, it is not considered joint property." An angry look crossed Richard's face.

"Richard, assets?"

"I have a 401K account but little else beyond the coop. All the other stocks have been sold to keep us afloat."

"Really?" I asked Richard, sarcastically. He glared at me.

"But I will check the account," he replied stiffly.

Lew, seeming peacemaker, interjected, "That is easily checked, Rich."

"Okay, debts?"

"Extensive," I said, thinking about the credit cards, student loans and medical/shrink bills. "One attorney thought we should file for bankruptcy. And we have not filed taxes for a while. Richard doesn't believe he has to file every year," I explained, rage filtering through.

"Okay, should I file for you?"

"Yes, please," I said.

"How much is this gonna cost?" asked Richard.

"I will pay for this as long as I can," I said. "Or we can sort out the fee in the divorce agreement. We have to do this."

Bruce added, "It depends on how much time I put in. Your wife has agreed to give me a $1000 down payment tonight."

Richard acquiesced with a shrug.

From there we each handed Bruce a pile of papers—credit card balances, student loan balances, tax documents. He madly typed into his accounting calculator, the kind that printed out a long receipt, which he studied for a moment. "This is just preliminary, but I think it's a wash. You both are about equally in debt. That is not a final accounting, just my impression tonight. I will have to run the numbers again and see what you owe in taxes. Richard, did you bring all of your tax information?"

"No. When do you need it by?"

"As soon as you can get it to me," Bruce said.

"Can I send it to you after the weekend?" Richard asked.

"Sure."

When we got up to leave, I could tell Richard wanted something from me. I hugged him and offered reassurance. "It's gonna be okay. And thanks for coming, Lew."

Driving back to the city, I felt phenomenal relief. Unlike what Richard believed, I likely did not owe him anything. Maybe, the financial strain would dissipate.

Chapter 41

Down we go again

A couple of weeks later on a Saturday midday, as I was walking back to the apartment after a few hours in my private practice office, I got a call from a neighbor back in Riverdale. Diane sounded agitated.

"What is going on?"

"The medics are taking Richard out now."

"What?"

"Yeah, his uncle came to take him to lunch and Richard didn't answer. When he couldn't get the super to let him in, Lew knocked on my door because I sometimes feed the cat. Turned out, Richard was having a seizure or something. I thought you would like to know. I think he is still unconscious."

"Thanks. Jesus, did he take an overdose?"

"No one knows but they took hundreds of empty pill bottles off the kitchen counter."

My heart sank. I didn't want Richard to die. I wanted him to go on and be okay. "Do you know what hospital they are taking him to?"

"I'll check." I could hear voices and traffic. They must have gotten him outside.

"Montefiore."

"Tell Lewis I will meet them there."

Angry and scared, I searched for the car, somewhere on Riverside Drive, while simultaneously leaving messages for Richard's therapist and psychiatrist. Finally, I drove off like a cabbie toward the Bronx, and that same Psych ER I'd met Richard at before. Lew was walking in just as I arrived and we found Richard, on a stretcher, with a medic and an ER staffer asking questions. Richard's eyes fluttered; he was quite pale.

Leaning over, to put my face next to his, "Richard?" I prodded. "It's Lizzie."

"Lizzie?" His eyes opened wider, taking in the scene. "Where am I?"

"In the ER at Montefiore. Lewis found you having a seizure." He looked surprised.

"Did you take an overdose of something?"

"No, no. I was lying in bed waiting for Lew."

I turned rapidly around to the ER guy. "He says he did not take an overdose. He doesn't usually lie."

This man pushed me aside and began questioning Richard. After he left, some color was returning to Richard's face, and he joked with Lew about standing him up for lunch. He was still Richard, and I felt better.

After waiting for what seemed like an eternity in the hallway, I decided to push my way into the ER to find out what was happening. I asked for the doctor in charge of Richard's case, and filled him in on Richard's recent history, including his last trip to the ER, and let him know that Richard's psychiatrist was an attending at Montefiore.

Since Richard had told the nurse that he was in the middle of a major medication change, the doctor thought this was likely what caused his seizure. They would do a full work-up and see if he could be admitted to the psych floor. He had already put out a call to Dr. Asnis who was on his way. *Relief. Dr. Asnis knows Richard.*

I relayed what I had learned to Richard and Lew and motioned to leave.

Richard begged, "Please stay a while, Lizzie." I felt so tired, but I stayed, holding his hand him for another 15 minutes, and then I left him with Lew. I cried on the way out, it was so sad to see Richard like that, but I couldn't do anything for him, and besides, *Always drama with this family.*

Richard was admitted to an inpatient medical floor and then transferred to the psych unit when a bed came open, where he stayed for nearly six months, unheard of in the era of managed care. When he was released, he was still too fragile to work on the divorce, and I lived in financial limbo, unable even to file taxes because Richard did not feel competent to read or sign anything.

Chapter 42

Two Tracks

Nearly two years after I'd moved out, the divorce was dragging on. Richard was still barely functioning but was able to do some of the work that Bruce had requested, and we were finally able to file tax returns. The bad news was that delinquent state taxes, accumulated over four years of non-filing, were high—nearly $14,000 in taxes and fines.

I got on the phone with the state tax bureau. Agent Morgan didn't seem to be an educated man and came across as rigid and mean besides. He was unyielding: we had to pay nearly $14,000 by the end of the week. I did not like him, and, in a fit of pique, told him he a "bad karma" job.

I had my lawyer call Danny, who was acting as Richard's agent/attorney. An agreement was reached: we would both take money from our individual retirement accounts to pay the $14,000 not by Agent Morgan's deadline, but only a few days late. When both funds were in my account, I cut a bank check and drove it out to Bruce's office on Long Island. He called agent Morgan, who told Bruce that I had told the tax bureaucrat he was going to burn in hell—apparently, Morgan's understanding of karma. Bruce said he was holding the cashier's check for the full amount. Should he FedEx it? This was on a Friday. Must it arrive on Saturday? Or would Monday morning be sufficient?

The fact that this was dragging on, and that I still had to deal with Richard and his family, was so wearing. Ruth kept trying to call me, and left messages: "This is your mother-in-law." I never returned any of her calls. Danny tortured my lawyer by keeping her on the phone for as long as he could.

I was trying hard to free myself, but nothing worked, nothing was finished.

I began to slide down into my own depression in a serious way. My horizons were closing in, a deep dark grey film covered all I could see—it wasn't all black yet, as it had been at times in my past. I spent that chilly weekend in bed, staring at the ceiling, crying, feeling weak, exhausted, hopeless. All I had done to make things better had come to naught. I walked Charley in a stupor. One day he only got out once. Little tears all day; hard to eat, hard to sleep. I didn't call a friend. I spent that weekend fully alone. Monday, I cancelled my private practice patients, something totally out of character, so I could stay in bed.

Tuesday, I went to work at my day job, hoping that seeing some young playful children could evoke a spark; my colleagues, a real team, were warm and funny. Contact might move the depressive needle back a notch. But when I got there, I hid in my office, unable to fake a smile or find any warmth to share. I checked my bank account; I was stunned. There had been a few thousand dollars in there after I'd withdrew the $14,000 for the tax check; now it showed nearly an eleven-thousand-dollar deficit. Upon inquiry, it emerged that because we had technically missed the state tax payment deadline, Agent Morgan had put a lien on all of my accounts, cleaned out my checking and savings account, which left me no money anywhere. This was not what he told Bruce on Friday about what would happen.

I called Morgan's office, demanding to speak only to a supervisor, and explained the trouble, that Agent Morgan had broken his word to my accountant. The supervisor put me on hold then merely reiterated that I had been delinquent, that I had been told the deadline was Friday.

He claimed Agent Morgan's conversation with Bruce "never happened." This was staggering. I could, I was instructed, fax a form to protest this decision, so I left the school, form in hand, ran to the copy place at the corner to use their fax machine; it turned out I didn't even have enough cash in my wallet to do that.

This situation set off waves of self-hatred. *How could I be 57 years old and be such a failure? I was a failure. How shameful!* I decided to go to the bank to see if they could release the money that had originally been taken out of the account for the cashier's check, which the state tax bureau had not received yet. I sucked dark air, but I made it to the bank, resisting the urge to head down to the subway and throw myself in front of a train. I knew that killing myself in the most gruesome way was what I deserved; let the rats nibble my brain away. At the bank, I talked to a customer service agent, a kindly middle-aged woman with brown skin, judging from her accent perhaps a recent immigrant. I explained the whole story, she listened, but said she could do nothing for me. I sat, stilled, unable to move. I asked her if she had children; she said she did not. "Me either," I said with bitterness and I walked out. Outside, I stumbled, panicking, trying to breathe, but feeling like the deepest breath I could get was icy, suffocating. Tears and moans came from me, as I leaned against the building. *Where was the closet subway?*

I saw a cop and asked him for directions to the nearest subway station; he took a good look at me and asked if I was okay.

"No."

Did I want him to call anyone?

"No." *There is no one to call.*

In my mind, I pictured an incoming train, rushing towards me, to end this pain. I imagined the pain of impact would hurt, but it would be a few seconds and that pain was no match for my mind's pain.

"Listen," the cop said, obviously trained to be attuned to seriously distressed persons seeking a subway station. "Think of your family. They would care."

"I don't have any family," I said bitterly. And then, "Thank you, officer."

I headed toward a subway stop I knew of; it might not be the closest but the 7th Avenue 14th Street stop had some pretty fast trains. As I walked to what I imagined was my death, I plugged in my iPod, and started listening to the play list I called "Comforting Songs." At least I would not throw myself off the subway platform in a state of agitation. I could barely hear the music, but it was a subtext to those few blocks. Nearing the subway entrance, I began to feel very, very scared. I had an intense fear of rodents. I always joked that fear of rats and mice was the only area wherein I lived up to my gender role; I tended to leap on top of tables and scream if there was a mouse in the house.

Maybe I should kill myself another way. I didn't want to feel even dirtier than I already did, there in the grime of the subway. But maybe that was where I belonged, face choking in grime and garbage, with the rats. Simultaneously though, that cool, brutally honest voice surfaced, the one that had always come to the fore when I thought about doing myself in.

Does the doubt mean, Lizzie, that you don't really want to do this? That you are looking for a way out? A rescue? If so, you are not allowed to try to kill yourself. There's an alternative for that.

I found my Metro Card and swiped in, and walking through the station, I could hear the music more clearly. Playing at that moment was my father's favorite hymn, "Bringing in the Sheaves." The chorus, "We shall come rejoicing, bringing in the sheaves," swelled in my ears, and I remembered when Dad told me that he loved this hymn the most, echoing the joy of harvest for that young farm boy.

Still, I headed on to the A train platform.

The next song had often moved me away from depression, Springsteen's "Reason to Believe." The last line goes "at the end of every hard-earned day, people find some reason to believe." I came close to a chuckle. At the moment, I had no belief in anything hopeful.

The empty subway track beckoned in front of me, but no audible rumbling to signal an approaching train. I would have to wait a bit. Suddenly with an abrupt clarity I had a new thought. *There are two tracks. The subway and the music. And I hate rats.* A stench of garbage in the bottom of the subway bed made me gasp. *Maybe this isn't where I belong. After all, there are always two tracks. I could stay on the other track, the music track.*

I walked out of the subway station.

Chapter 43

Finally, Enough Help

Back on the sidewalk, the air was still chilly and damp; I was cold. But if I hustled back to work, if I walked fast, I could warm up and wouldn't even be late for the first afternoon meeting. First, I had something else to do. I left urgent messages for my psychopharmacologist, Dr. Mierlak, and for my psychologist/therapist, Dr. Grossmark. I needed help, instantly. Now. Right away, and I asked for that clearly. They were my team. Then I went into the work meeting and apparently seemed normal enough.

By the end of the day, I had talked with Dr. Grossmark, who gave me his cell number and an appointment the next day. Dr. Mierlak was willing to see me that evening. Dr. Mierlak, a tall, handsome man, likely 20 years younger than I, primarily charged with helping people get the right medicine to help with their mental distress, was a good listener. I had been seeing him for about five years, usually at his Upper East Side office (the ritzy part of town), but this time, he could only fit me in at a clinic in a high rise in a rather gritty midtown neighborhood. (Besides treating the "worried well" on the Upper East Side, he worked with addicts of all kinds, using psychopharmacological approaches to help folks get sober).

In his tiny office, I had trouble looking him in the eye. He listened carefully to my despair but did not indulge it. After outlining what had happened with the taxes and at the subway, and my sense that nothing ever got better, he intervened.

"You are in the middle of a major depressive episode. This is not the time to ask big existential questions. I know the things you speak of; I talk to my friends about the value of living in a philosophical way, but you can't ask those questions right now."

Though I did not like this limit, I nodded. I got the point: I needed to contain the feelings, not make them bigger.

He wanted me to go to the hospital, but I refused, having felt such stigma from my hospitalization 30 years before. He suggested raising my antidepressant dose, said he would see me next week, and that he wanted to call my therapist. I accepted those recommendations.

The next day I left work in the middle of the day to see Dr. Grossmark. As he opened the door, the concern and compassion on his face prompted me to talk more about the events of the day before, the shame of not being able to provide for myself, and my thoughts as I walked from the fax place to the bank to the subway. My body shook with self-loathing and despair.

He listened calmly and intently, taking these emotions in, without reacting. But he did name it. "Not having enough money brings up your deepest shame, that you are disgusting."

The recognition felt okay, almost good. I nodded.

"But we know these are old feelings, feelings that began with the boys down the alley. And to do with your brother's death."

Electricity shot through my body, revisiting the feeling of those boys next to my naked, little, brother-abandoned self. I could sense what he said was true, that yesterday I was driven more by shame than money. *Money, what was money anyway?*

"Okay, but how am I going to live?" I broke down, sobbing hard.

Dr. Grossmark handed me a tissue. "Do you have a plan about the taxes?"

Choking back the tears, I answered, "Yeah, I'm going out to Bruce's office to get the cashier's check and deposit it back. It will get sorted." Sometimes with Dr. Grossmark, I lapsed into Britishisms.

He smiled gently. "There is a way forward. You have come so far, in getting disentangled from Richard. The money situation will improve as you grow your practice. You are now a senior child clinician. Are you charging enough?"

"Of course not." I grinned, laughing at myself.

"The most important thing is how this is inside yourself, what it means to you. And how you respond to money difficulties with such shame."

Though I knew he was right, this also seemed a bit psychobabble-ish. I mean, I still had to pay the rent. Then again, I had not sent out invoices to my patients for the last couple of months. Somehow the thought of doing so was daunting. As these thoughts passed through my head, I met Dr. Grossmark's gaze. "You know I shoot myself in the foot a lot."

"Yes, and you need to put the gun down."

"No kidding." I replied. We held the gaze.

He changed topics. "We are about out of time. Let's plan to meet twice next week and do a phone call over the weekend."

I left feeling acknowledged, not better but I was engaged in a process I believed could help with the deepest levels of pain, despair, and shame. In the meantime, I would try to listen to the musical soundtrack, not the other one.

My friend Connie called one evening; she was frantic. A good friend of hers, someone also close to Mollie had killed himself. I consoled her as best I could. And I felt shaken. I wasn't sure that anyone had told Mollie that Jim had killed himself. Mollie had felt loved by Jim, who always insisted that she was as smart as her favored brother, now a brilliant San Francisco entrepreneurial tech guy. This was an important message in her early life. I wanted her to know and called her.

"Hey, Mollie Mo. I got some bad news."

"What?"

"Well, you might know from Connie that Jim was really depressed. He did kill himself."

There was silence on the other end.

Then, in an urgent, almost angry tone she said, "You better not do that."

When you are suicidal people often ask you to promise not to die, to sign a contract, to commit to staying alive. I had always laughed at these requests. *If I could promise that I wouldn't be in this situation.* For the therapists who cared and didn't want to have to hospitalize me, I did sometimes say, "I promise not to kill myself before I see you again." It was a moral imperative not to break a promise and that had gotten me through a few times.

This was different. I didn't want to lie or be glib because Mollie mattered to me. I thought about that day in the subway, and about the two tracks. I knew, suddenly, deep inside, that I could keep choosing the music.

"I promise."

Chapter 44

Bodied. Early Summer

Early on a summer day, I looked down at my feet, and took a deep breath in as I left Dr. Grossmark's office. *Put one foot in front of the other as best you can, Lizzie.* The deepest depressive fog had lifted, and I was back to "basic dysthymia," a chronic state where life just felt heavy most of the time. On 85th Street, I noticed the health food store at the end of the block was gone, the windows papered over. As always in NYC, the neighborhood was changing. A sign read "Coming soon. Upper Westside Yoga Studio."

Health food to yoga, that's my neighborhood.

I was still reeling a bit from my session. Dr. Grossmark had listened carefully to the elements of my shame—money, body, untidied home, untidy self—and had gently accepted and challenged each. Though difficult to be so close in with those feelings, I experienced a tiny bit of relief, a tiny bit of difference, percolating in my head. It was hard for shame to flourish when aired out and light bleached its odor away.

A month later, when I passed by that corner, UWS Yoga was open. I wondered, with a bit less body shame, could I try this? I had done one weekend yoga retreat at Kripalu, in western Massachusetts, with two college friends who were devotees. Other friends called yoga "life altering." I wasn't so sure. I could never deal with the New Age, faux spiritual aspect; yoga practitioners could be so humorless and sanctimonious, things that always turned off my irreverent self. Yet, that first day's workshop at Kripalu, my very sore shoulder, which had been examined medically and treated with physical therapy, was cured after just one long pose.

I do need to find a way into my body and out of body shame.

Maybe this was a little positive karma (not that I fully believed in karma)—a new yoga option right on the route from my own psychotherapy office to Dr. Grossmark's office. I took a brochure. In my next therapy session, I broached the topic of trying yoga. Dr. Grossmark smiled; he too had noticed the new studio. I reviewed all my fears—that others would look at me, that others would see how foul my body was. This brought me back to the sexual abuse, and I began to tell Dr. Grossmark something I had not thought about in years.

"When I joined that sexual abuse survivors' group in Cambridge, it was a teaching group led by Judith Herman." He leaned slightly forward, a focused look on his face, his eyes alive behind his glasses. Herman was a renowned researcher, teacher, and clinician in the field of trauma.

"There were therapists in training behind one-way mirrors, on both sides of the room. When I realized I was being watched, I freaked out. The impulse to bolt was intense and I had to call on my childhood restraint, forged in church, to just sit. But I left my body and hovered up by the ceiling. I hadn't known that being watched was such an intense part of what I had experienced with those boys," I stammered, shaking a bit at how much of a role that humiliation had played. "They all watched while each one did something to me. Especially that little boy penis up my ass." My voice tightened with rage. "And sometimes they made some animal noises." I felt so disgusting. Tears rolled down my face as I cried silently for a few minutes.

Dr. Grossmark held my gaze; I knew he was there. He wasn't just watching. Then I felt a speck of relief.

He said, "Those old feelings are so strong." He paused. "And I can see the special humiliation of them watching."

I nodded, blowing my nose.

"But you stayed in the survivors' group?"

I nodded again. "They worked it out so that the observers would only be on one side of the room and I would be told where they were. That way, if it felt bad, I could at least stare them in the eye, so to speak, and register my distress at being watched." I calmed down and grinned. "It worked and I got a lot out of the group. The different stories were all the same; I belonged there."

While it was still hard to feel my body was real, I needed to feel alive in my physical self. And, maybe, I had to risk the possibility of being visible as I did so. Though I'd lost 80 pounds after the lap band surgery, I still hadn't challenged my new body in any serious way. Maybe I could tolerate this.

I called the yoga studio and left a message. *Could I begin with a private lesson to see what class I should join?*

A few hours later, a friendly male voice, Stephan, called back and I booked a private lesson on the Saturday coming.

I had to get busy. I had to do this right. I must dress the part of an aspiring yogi. Off I went to Lululemon, the most fashionable yoga store. Mostly they fit twig-sized women there, and though I was at a good weight, I still needed their extra-large size. I came away with a calf-length pair of yoga pants, black with a tiny bit of blue trim. I planned to wear my baggiest t-shirt over the form-fitting pants.

On Saturday afternoon, terrified, I climbed up the two little steps to the yoga studio. A woman perhaps in her late 30s or early forties smiled up at me. She was beautiful—eyes glowing, dark hair pulled back from her face, her body clearly toned. But she was not a perky young blond thing. Hurrah for the first step.

"Let's come over here," Ingrid said, and we both sat on the floor on the far side of the studio. "Have you ever done yoga before?"

"Just a tiny little bit." I was getting older, I explained, and felt I needed a gentle way to get in shape.

"Yeah, yoga is really good when you are aging. I'm not getting any younger either," she laughed. I knew from the brochure that she and Stephan were married and this studio was their dream. *A yoga teacher with a sense of self-deprecating humor—just my style.* I liked her, despite her body being close to perfect.

Ingrid led me through some basic breath exercises and poses. I got left and right wrong a few times, had to think hard about putting my body in precise positions, and sometimes failed to attain the pose, wobbling more than a little.

"Here. You need a hand to balance," she said as I swayed, putting her hand gently on my arm. "You are really flexible in some of your joints."

Like my father, who used to give his lectures on American history to the undergraduates from the lotus position. "Yeah, that runs in the family. But sometimes I think I might be too flexible. I fall over a lot."

"You do? Hmm. Let me see you stand up."

I got to my feet and as always when I tried to stand still, rocked a bit. Ingrid looked at my legs, knees, ankles, and feet. *This is scary; she is looking at me.*

"You are extra flexible in your ankles. That could be partly why. You know, yoga will really help with balance."

"That would be amazing," I said, and made eye contact, and smiled my more real smile, where my whole face lit up, the smile from my first date with Richard. Ingrid suggested what classes might work for me, recommending Level 1 or chair yoga, because balance is an issue, or any restorative class. Then she said, "Your energy is like mine: out there, a little intense."

Now this was the sort of remark I thought I wouldn't like from a yoga teacher, new agey and all, but with Ingrid, it did not feel intrusive or voyeuristic, but honest and accurate, a recognition of something real in me. I left with a class schedule, still a little terrified but determined.

Two weeks later, in a Level I class, taught by Stephan, a slim young man, with a bald shaved head and an open face, eyes shining, I took a place at the back of the room. *Would I turn into one of those ladies that carried their yoga mats around with them? Such a New York statement!*

Stephan began with an "Om," seated cross legged in the front of the room. Next was some breathing work, and then some gentle movement of the head, side to side. The workout intensified, and to my surprise, Stephan occasionally called out corrections to folks as they held a pose. "Susan, move your left foot to center." I prayed he would not call me out. I was really sweating and often had to think concentrate intensely about where and how to position myself; I had no idea where my arms and feet were in relation to the rest of me. When I nearly fell switching my feet from side to side, I had to laugh. Stephan noticed and smiled. At another time in my life, this would have caused me to feel so bad about my klutzy self, that I would have shut down but now, it was okay. I just kept going.

Later, Stephan circled the room, paying attention to each person as they held a standing pose. When he came to me, he didn't say a word, just put two fingers on my shoulder, and gave a gentle downward push. He meant for me to relax them. My shoulders and neck were usually so tight and frozen. With the gentlest of contact, Stephan helped me find a bodily easing.

I kept coming back over that summer, two or three times a week. I felt better than ever physically. I knew where I was. My body and body shame kept easing. *Life altering.*

Chapter 45

Resolution and Divorce

By fall of 2013, more than two years after I left Richard, he was well enough to meet with the mediators again. This time we met in Abby's office, sitting side by side, while she sat behind her desk. Richard was now drawing Social Security Disability benefits and living in supported housing in the South Bronx. He had let our apartment go into foreclosure, and it appeared he was planning his future life as a disabled, mentally ill person.

"So, the conclusion is that your debts are equal and there are no other assets," Abby told us. Then she turned to me. "You are now the moneyed spouse."

"Moneyed, hardly. But what does that mean?" I asked.

"Well, you have more money than he does. And, in New York State, that means Richard is entitled to spousal support."

I was surprised, and yet not surprised. *How else could this end?* Though enraged that I still owed, I wanted this over. Choking back emotion, I said, "Okay. How much and for how long?"

Abby looked at her notes. "For five years, given the length of your marriage. What seems a fair amount?"

Nothing. Financially, I was still far from secure. Richard did not look at me. "How much do you suggest?" I asked.

"I think the minimum that the guidelines support is five hundred a month."

Calculating quickly in my head, this meant I had to give this guy $30,000. Terror swept over me, but I wasn't flinching. Time to be tough.

"I will write this separation agreement up, and after you review it with your attorneys you can file it. And then you are divorced 12 months later."

"Thank you." I fled the office, leaving Richard behind without a word.

The price of my freedom was steep but the horizon was clearing.

Two months later, after some haggling points, the agreement was set. Laurieanne, my attorney, said after dealing with Danny, who was acting as Richard's unofficial counsel, "I would hate to go to Thanksgiving at these people's house. He is so long winded. Seems like Danny doesn't have enough to do."

"No kidding. But also think of it this way, he doesn't know you are doing this as a favor to a friend and we are on a flat rate here. I am sure he thinks he is running up my bill."

Laurieanne chuckled.

"So, don't listen for too long. Don't waste your time," I said.

"You sign here. And we will get Richard to sign and then I will file it in Bronx County."

"There may be some ridiculousness about another lawyer because I don't think it's ethical for Danny to actually be Richard's attorney. There may be another hoop."

"No, no. That step is done."

"So, we just gotta get Richard to sign?"

Laurieanne nodded.

A month later, Richard had still not signed; neither he nor Danny were returning her calls.

On the phone with Laurieanne, I yelled, "That motherfucker. What is he waiting for?"

"How aggressive do you want to be on this?" Laurieanne asked.

"As aggressive as you can be without kicking him in the balls."

"Okay, let me get a guy to serve him with these papers. Do you have a picture of Richard you could email me?"

This stumped me. I said I would try. "You can't miss him. He is over six feet, slightly chubby, bearded, and the only white guy for miles around in the South Bronx."

Over the next two evenings, the process server missed Richard. On the third night, the served called, asking for a better description.

Instead, I dialed Richard's cell phone, which was still on my plan. He didn't pick up. Another opportunity lost. When Richard did call back, I didn't hold back, screaming before he could say a word. "You asshole, trying to avoid getting served? If you don't go sign tomorrow, I am cancelling your phone."

"What? What? Lizzie? Please don't yell at me." He sounded oblivious.

"There has been a process server at your door trying to give you the divorce agreement to sign."

"I wasn't expecting anybody. In this neighborhood you don't answer the door if you don't know who it is."

"Well, you motherfucker, this is overdue. You were supposed to sign a month ago."

"I was? Dan didn't tell me that."

"Of course, he didn't." My voice was still loud and nasty. "If it's not done by noon tomorrow, your phone is cancelled."

"Tomorrow is the weekend. And please don't do that to the phone. Please, give me a few days."

"Tomorrow noon, asshole." I hung up, knowing I was being irrational, but his lethargy, failure to act, his utter passivity was what drove me mad about my not-yet-ex-husband.

I cancelled Richard's phone the next day. He claimed he would go into Laurieanne's office at the first of the week to sign. I would believe it when it happened.

Yet he did do this. And Laurieanne filed it in the Bronx; we would or should be divorced by the end of 2014. Now I just had to pay that god-damned alimony. And of course, I couldn't send a check or anything to Richard directly. Danny now ran Richard's life. I had to play by his rules, and this meant I had to make a deposit directly into Richard's account on the agreed day. This was before I knew anything about PayPal, Venmo or internet banking apps. Every month I had to take out $500 cash from my bank, walk it down a block and deposit it into Richard's account. I was enraged on that day, every month, for five years.

Chapter 46

A Hot Day's Reckoning

It was an almost too hot summer day as I sat on the terrace, iced coffee in hand. Charley was under the picnic table, away from the sun. I was thinking about Richard. Most of the time now, I was just grateful to feel free but I had loved him so much. As I thought, I realized I didn't fully understand why he ended in such a collapse. I had just been fleeing it. I took another sip of iced coffee. I didn't want a heart-to-heart with Richard. But what had really happened? It was related I knew to the loss of Michael, and Carrie and the life we had supposed we were going to have, as favored aunts and uncles to their offspring. It had something to do with how unloved he had felt as a child, the undiagnosed Asperger. It still didn't fit.

It hit me I should ask Leslie, his friend from childhood who was now my friend. She knew him before and after, though now she was truly my friend too. Richard had proposed to me in her apartment, when she still lived, pre-child, in the city. She had kept me close during the early stages of leaving Richard.

I went inside to get the phone. Charley stayed put in the shade. Leslie picked up on the first ring. I put her on speaker and we chatted about the heat. Then she said, "You seem good."

"I am," I replied. "It's been a long road." Faltering just a bit, I went on. "I want to ask you a very big question."

"Sure." Leslie laughed. In the background her dogs, Charley's cousins Crash and Biscuit howled. Charley poked his nose out from under the table, looking for his friends.

"I have been thinking about what all went down. I still don't know how much Michael killing Carrie affected Richard's collapse." I was now sweating in the heat, wondering what she would answer.

Leslie was quiet, seemingly lost in thought, reviewing her knowledge of us both. "I think back to the toast at your wedding, 'To absent friends.' Do you think that was about Michael or Carrie?"

"Michael. Both, Carrie. I don't fucking know." I pondered that day. There was a long dark shadow over the wedding, a day that was supposed to be only happy. Such a peculiar start the marriage. "But you knew Richard before I did. What do you think about the effects of Michael killing Carrie on him?"

"He was the most confident and happy when he fell in love with you than I had ever seen him. But he was still Richard, on the depressive side."

"Well that worked, So was I. But I don't think Richard ever really dealt with what it meant to lose Michael. His asshole psychoanalyst didn't ask him about it for like 8 years."

"Really?" Leslie sounded astonished.

"Yeah."

"You told me a long time ago that Richard didn't remember that he was supposed to go over to Michael and Carrie's in the morning the day he killed her."

"No, I don't think he does remember that. He got in a fight with his mother and didn't want to be ordered over there. It's never been in his narrative of that day."

"He's fallen so far. He is at the bottom, getting by on nothing, not working—and he was a workaholic, living with a very paranoid psychotic roommate in his crappy supported housing apartment in the South Bronx. He's given up on what he used to be." She paused. "I think, without knowing it, he is punishing himself for failing to save Michael and Carrie."

I felt struck by a bolt of lightning.

Whoa. I had never considered this. Richard, like Michael, was paying for the crime? His own mind destroying and destroyed by what happened? No wonder, Richard, the man I had loved, and now kind of hated, was all gone, even though some shell survived in the South Bronx. Richard and Michael might never come back. But I was back. And I would always love the Richard I knew before all this. His love and help were so vital to bringing out from behind the glass wall. But his guilt had done him in.

Chapter 47

Redemption

After seeing my last patient out the door, the sun in the back-of-office windows faded into twilight, darkly illuminating the autumn leaves. I began to feel weekend-ish, looking forward to a long, relaxed walk with Charley in the park and the single gin and tonic with two limes, which I allowed myself on Friday evenings. As I put the day's session notes on the desk, I saw the light blinking on the answering machine. One of my grad school colleagues and friend, Ben, sounded mildly upset.

"Hey Liz, I don't know if you could see someone over the weekend, but a friend of mine just lost a baby to what they think is SIDS. They have a three-year-old son. They're in shock and want to talk to someone about how to handle it with the kid. I thought of you immediately. It's kind of urgent. Call me back."

I sat quietly, letting this request wash over me. *Was this a little too close to home, me aged three with the dead brother?* But this felt urgent to *me*, as it was my story. Then with certainty and a whole-body-resolve, I thought, *I could be of help.* I dialed my colleague back.

"Liz? Hey, thanks for calling back."

"Sure. Give me some details."

"Upper middle-class family. Lives on the west side. Dad seriously Type A. Mom too but she has an arty vibe. The dad, Mark, left early for work this morning and when mom got up later, she thought it was strange her one-year-old daughter Bonny hadn't woken her up. Claire, the mom, found the baby blue and not breathing in the crib and called 911. Claire tried not to panic, because Angus, the three-year-old, was up. Angus saw the cops and the medics and watched as the baby was taken out of the apartment. I think Claire was really freaking out too. Mark called me—he is a friend of my brother's—after the baby was pronounced dead at the hospital. He is worried about his wife, and his son."

"I can see them tomorrow morning before yoga. Nine?"

"Sure."

"Did the father describe the three-year-old's reaction at all?"

"I think he is usually pretty rambunctious but after it all went down, apparently the kid has refused to talk, and is very subdued."

"Got it. Why don't you just call them back with the time and give them my name, the office address, and my cell number in case by morning they change their minds. I assume they can afford a full fee?"

"Definitely," Ben responded. "Great, I knew you were the person for this."

"Thanks." I hesitated and then said, "I think I am too."

Ben was a good guy. We had bonded over leukemia; Ben got sick with it in adolescence and had been able to tell me about that experience. This helped me to know what it may have been like for my brother. *Sometimes the universe is a sticky web. We get stuck in with those we need to know.*

As I hung up, I realized I was somewhat daunted by the intensity of this referral, but felt it was necessary I take it on. *What will I learn by touching the rawest parental grief over a lost child? Would I learn something about what my parents really went through when Jim died, or what I went through then too?*

The weekend feeling vanished but I was still up to mixing my gin and tonic.

The next morning, I knew I needed to be centered and calm. Before my shower, I breathed in the roses on the terrace and then gave Charley's belly some extra rubbing. As Charley and I walked to the office, I kept my awareness on what I could take in through my senses, the silver-grey concrete, the smell of traffic, the feeling of my foot hitting the pavement and the cool morning air. I would have to steady my own feelings so my own ancient grief did not disrupt what the family needed to bring to me. I had been known to get tears in my eyes when my patients were in pain.

At the office, Charley snoozed under my desk and I settled into my buttery soft leather shrink chair. I kept working to find the right emotional space to work from—calm, steady, receptive. I didn't get to stay put long when the outer doorbell rang. Game on.

I tried to softly smile as I greeted them. "Hi, I'm Liz Tingley. Please do come in."

The father shoved out his hand and said, "Mark McNitt. This is my wife, Claire Holm." They were in their late twenties, both tall, the woman quite thin. She was blond and the man's hair had a reddish tint. They wore jeans, he with a jacket and button-down shirt. She had on a light-colored linen sweater, her long blond hair held back from her face in a ponytail. Their expressions were somber. Neither looked like they had slept.

I studied her face, pressed lips, red, swollen dull eyes. This plummeted me back to my own mother's dark hole eyes the morning after my brother died, the look that made me back away so as to not get sucked all the way into her blackness. I felt a muscle in my neck tighten.

Stay in the present, Lizzie.

"Please come in," I repeated, gesturing toward the adult patient chairs on one side of the room. Mark took his wife by the hand, and almost deposited her in the first seat.

Type A alright, but protective too. She needs that now. That memory of my father pulling my mother to him, as we left the hospital where they learned Jim would die, reverberated in my head.

"Ben only told me a bit of what's happened to you," I said as I sat back. I made eye contact with each of them slowly, lingering a bit with Claire, her eyes tearing as she met my gaze. "Just tell me where you are."

Mark reached over to hold Claire's hand. He spoke first. "In shock, really." Claire nodded.

"Yes. And it will take a while for that to wear off," I said softly and paused. "Do you want to tell me about it?"

Claire nodded. "It was a usual morning, except that we had been out late to friends for dinner with both kids the night before. We put the two of them down for bed about an hour or so later than usual. So, in the morning, when I didn't hear Bonny stirring, I didn't think anything of it." She broke down, sobbing. Mark put his arm around her.

She must be feeling guilty, like if she had checked right away the child might have lived.

"You had no reason to think it wasn't normal for her to sleep in a little."

Claire nodded as she sobbed. She pulled herself together. "Angus was playing in his room. I could hear him. So, I put the coffee on first and then went into Bonny's room. She was lying on her side, with her head in an odd position. When I touched her, I knew something was really wrong. She was blue. I screamed, grabbed her up, and called 911. They had me try to clear her airway and do mouth to mouth. When the paramedics got there, they took over. They took her away and I called Mark to meet them at the ER." She looked down, her voice tapering off to a whisper and then she stopped.

Mark finished the story. "She was already dead," he said. "The EMTs told me that at the hospital." In a monotone, he continued, "They let me see her." He teared up too but bravely went on. "They told me it was an unexplained death and they had to investigate. They called the Agency for Children's Services and the cops. They've kind of been at the house since."

Claire continued, "They said it's a 'SIDS like' death, but she was too old for SIDS." She was trying to hold onto her tears but couldn't. "She was nearly a month premature, but she had caught up at her one-year check-up. She seemed so healthy."

"Yeah," I said, trying to match my tone to hers, this inexplicable crazy fact of her dead baby.

"And Angus," Claire again began to cry, with a panicked tone.

"That is why we are here, Dr. Tingley, to figure out what to do for him." Mark sat up straight in his chair, ready for instructions.

Inwardly I groaned. They couldn't fix this for their son, or for themselves any time soon, and I could see that at least Mark wanted a solution *now*. They were going to have to live in grief with him and themselves for a long while.

"Yes, let's do talk about Angus. But let's not go too fast to him. Before I can share what might help you with him, I want to know more about how you are experiencing today and yesterday. What has this been like for you?"

Claire sat back in her chair, with an air of defeat. "Devastated. And I feel a cascade of things. Exhaustion."

That's it, the sense of helpless defeat when you can't protect your child. Though no one's fault, it feels like a parental failure. I decided this was not the moment to elaborate this. What agency they had left they needed to carry them through the next few days.

Mark too leaned back in his chair, looked at his wife, and then made piercing eye contact with me. I held his gaze, to reflect the pain I saw on his face. Mark added slowly, "I didn't know something could feel this bad."

"Those feelings for you aren't going away for a long time. And there is a lot to get through," I replied.

"I know they just have to do their job, but I feel like both the cops and the social workers are very suspicious of us," Claire reported.

I nodded.

Mark jumped in. "We know we didn't do anything to cause this. The autopsy will show that. They just have to follow up." Claire hung her head.

"You want to know how I am?" Mark continued, his tone now angry. "I am so mad. Not at the cops, but this is so unfair. Cosmically unjust. And Angus is suffering."

Ah, he is trying to protect his son, because he "failed" to protect his daughter.

"It is," I said with emphasis, "Completely unfair."

Mark met my eyes again and a tiny sliver of real connection seemed present but he was rushing to solve the problem at hand, his son's trauma from this abrupt death of his sister. "So, what can we do to help Angus?"

I decided to work with his wish for some answers. "What has been his reaction so far?"

Claire grimaced. "I'm not sure what he was doing when I found her and I was screaming and trying to breathe life into her. He came out into the living room when the EMTs arrived. He looked spooked. And my son is usually a little bit of a tough kid." Here she smiled just a bit.

Mark added, "He is usually a little bit oblivious and is very active, in his own world."

Claire went on, "After they took Bonny away, he started to cry and asked where she was going. I feel like I came to my senses then and told him she was sick and going in the ambulance to the hospital and that

Daddy would meet her there. He seemed to take that in. I said Sandy, his babysitter, was coming while I went to the hospital too. He asked me to stay with him but then I left him with Sandy. She was reading to him when I went out. We didn't know what so say when we came back, with Bonny dead." Claire started to sob uncontrollably.

I sat, looking at them both, trying to generate warmth, allowing her strong affect to flow and for me to receive it. Mark went over to hold Claire, his eyes wet too. Finally, Claire's sobs receded and she sat up, grabbed a tissue from the table next to her.

"How does it feel to let it out?" I asked.

She smiled faintly. "It's not like regular crying. It doesn't get any better if you let it out or hold it in."

"Yes, the grief is intense and it won't go away altogether, ever. It may, with time, be less intense."

She nodded, then continued her description of Angus's reaction to the chaos. "When we got back, Angus was not himself. He clearly knew that something was terribly wrong. He won't talk now, not a word. And he is not his usual bundle of energy. He kind of just sits there." Claire paused. "What should we say?"

"It's hard to know how to explain this to him when you can't explain it to yourselves," I replied. Both parents looked so utterly sad, helpless, and young. "I don't know what you should say exactly, but we can think about it together. It has to be honest. You have to say that she is dead, that her heart and brain stopped working, and that she is never coming back. Do you have any religious views that you want to give him about death?"

They glanced at each other and then said, "No not really," simultaneously. That was a good sign; they were attuned to each other. That could go a long way to help them get through this.

"Has he ever stopped talking before?" I asked.

Mark shook his head. "He did have some pronunciation problems and he's had some speech therapy but no, he's never stopped talking before. Though he is an action kind of kid usually."

"How old is he exactly?"

"Three and a half."

That gave me an idea of how he thought. Concretely. And with probably slightly underdeveloped narrative skills given what else they were saying about his language. It might be hard for him to participate in creating a coherent story about this.

"Okay. Basically, what I said before goes to the main point, to let him know that Bonny is dead." I watched to see how they would react to this clear statement of the reality. Mark minimally flinched but I went on. "Angus will not understand death at his age. I always recommend the book *The Dead Bird* by the lady who wrote *Goodnight Moon*. It is simple and direct. You can read it to him over and over if he wants to help him understand."

Mark took out his phone and made of note of the book. "I will order it when we leave."

I continued, "And even though you tell him once, that Bonny is dead, he will likely need to hear it more than once, because he will understand it differently than you think he does. I mean, cartoons make sense to kids; when the guy gets run over and then he pops back up. Permanence doesn't mean the same thing to preschoolers as it does to us."

Both parents nodded.

"Don't force him to talk but keep talking *to* him. Empathize with his state of shock. Label his feelings, including confusion. Children often regress under stress. His language sounds a little vulnerable. It's not surprising that he might lose that. He might regress in other ways too, toileting for instance, or not being able to sleep alone."

Mark almost chuckled. "Claire had him in our bed last night, and he had been in his own room for more than a year."

"I had to be sure he would make it through the night, Mark," Claire said, distressed.

"I understand completely," I replied. "And it was wise. He needs your physical presence more than anything and to the extent that you can, your emotional presence as well. Children are most reassured by their parents. You need to help him feel safe. Mark, can you be okay with that for now?"

"Of course. Claire, I didn't mean…" She nodded at him.

"One part of this, as you try to manage what Angus needs, is to allow each other to need things that might be different. There is a lot of research suggesting men and women often grieve differently."

Claire asked, "What do you mean?"

"Let me ask Mark. When are you going back to work?"

"Oh, I'll want to get back in a couple of days. I can't imagine sitting around like this for very long." Claire looked horrified.

"That is what I mean. To feel useful and in the routine can often feel like healing to men. Often women find they just need more time, together. And that conflict, it can be misunderstood by both. I wonder, Mark, if you really will want to get back to work so soon, and if you will be able to meet your need to do that and balance what Claire and Angus might need."

Mark looked at his wife. "We can talk about it, of course." She smiled for the first time.

"When we have the funeral, should Angus be there?" Claire asked.

"Yes, unless there is some compelling reason elsewise. But you need a back-up plan, in case he is disruptive or too upset, or you feel you can't grieve as you need to with him there. Someone who could take him out and could bring him back. It has to be someone he knows and trusts. Though he won't understand all the nuances, he will be a part of saying good-bye to his sister, with you and family and friends. That's what matters," I said.

I could have cried right then. I had succeeded in pushing my past away during most of the session, but something felt very big, pressing down inside of me, my own emotional exhaustion at trying to hold them and me at the same time. They were hurting and it so hurt to see that, to feel the hurt with them, as I suggested what they do for Angus. *Why couldn't have someone said these things to my parents? Why?* But I had to push that question away for the moment. I still had work to do.

"This is, not to sound clichéd, a process," I continued. "It is going to take time. The goal with Angus is to help him have a story to tell himself about this time and about his lost sister, a story that will become part of his life story, that helps him feel that it is coherent and hangs together. To do that, you are also going to have to be willing to be with him over time and to talk about your own sadness and grief and confusion—of course in a modulated way when you can—so that he feels you all together."

Mark let out a big sigh. "That fits with so much of my gut instinct, but already I can see that Claire's mother wants to take him out to her house in Westchester so we have time to make arrangements. But I want him with us. Don't you Claire?"

"I'm not letting him out of my sight for more than five minutes," she answered forcefully.

"Is he close to his grandmother?" I asked.

"Well, yes and no. She travels a lot, but when she is around, she is super fun with him."

Grandparent as playmate. Not what this kid needs right now.

"Some of that will be fine, but more as time goes on. You will deserve breaks sometimes, but now he needs you. As best you can, give him that,"

I said softly. Both were quiet for a moment and I saw Mark disconnect and return to some state of shock.

"I think this is enough for now," Mark said. "You have given us the start of a road map. Claire?"

Claire nodded, tearing slightly, and said, "Thank you Dr. Tingley. I feel like I have some better ideas about helping Angus."

"I'm glad it feels helpful. It's going to be a tough row to hoe, but I think you have what it takes to get it done. And remember, like always with parenting, taking care of yourselves is also a way to take care of Angus." I made full-on eye contact, first with Claire and then Mark. "And remember I am here. Call if you need more."

Claire bowed her head at me as they stood. Mark shook my hand.

When I returned to my chair, I let the tension of holding myself together through the session evaporate. Silently, I still felt all the same terror, confusion, sadness, helplessness, and anger as Mark and Claire, but I knew I had done decent work with them. I also thought, as Ben had said, that I was the perfect person for this—on many levels. It wasn't just my 40-plus years in the field, working in childcare with toddlers, where I lived with children's everyday tears and frustrations, or the career in academic developmental psychology where I learned the research that supported work with young children, or even my time as clinical psychologist, where I found a theoretical frame and the tools to connect with and manage pain and growth. It was all of that combined with my own experience of early loss, that brought me here to be able to do this job this day. That felt satisfying.

There was another feeling, too. Gratitude. These two grieving people had come to me, trusted me, taken in my empathy and knowledge. I was honored they had let me in at such a time in their lives.

A circle was complete. My career began because I wanted people to take the emotional experience of young children seriously, as my parents had not. I had just done exactly this for Angus. This small child, whom I'd never even meet, allowed me to finish what I started, unconsciously, so very long ago, saving myself, and all the children I had touched in my career, from the denial of young children's grief and pain and the aftermath.

A quite different sensation took hold: *I am done. I will not be compelled to do this work anymore. My mission is complete.* I could work, but I didn't *have to*, the compulsion gone. I slumped down, exhausted, and exhilarated. Was there time to get to yoga?

Chapter 48

The Location of Joy

On warm October Saturday afternoon, I sat on my terrace with a glass of iced tea and thought back to the last child patient I saw yesterday. He had spent a year with me playing out huge battles between his two stuffed elephants, named Meal Mouth and Harold, and an unnamed evil. The battle was especially fierce yesterday and my office was in shambles from toys flung about in the melee. Just before the end of the session, the boy stopped playing. Making eye contact, he said that the war was almost over.

Why? I inquired. The child reported that his parents had stopped fighting now that they each had their own apartment. He thought Meal Mouth and Harold might be safe now.

This was a satisfying end to my work week.

I think about how I help others change, how I have changed, and how both Michael and Richard are stuck, in psychic torment. Carrie is still dead and that dream and life gone. The pain from that is still part of me, and I can feel it, but not be overtaken by it. I will be able to use it, to help others who are also hurting, because I'm not afraid to go there.

Outside, the sun moved lower in the sky. Though I was feeling physically comfortable after morning yoga, I decided to take Charley for a long walk, to get my heart pumping. As I got the leash, Charley wriggled with anticipation. Down the four flights of stairs we went, out on our usual route towards Riverside Park. Out first stop was the flirtatious doorman, Eric, a short guy with a military bearing, working at the corner of 91st and Riverside. Once I had treated his flirtations as real and offered him my phone number, but he revealed he was married. The banter cooled a bit but continued.

"Hey, Charley," Eric began, always greeting my dog first. "You gonna let me get next to your Mama?"

I laughed. "Hey," I said as we shoulder bumped. "How's by you?"

"Can't complain. It's a beautiful night. You lookin' good," he told me. I laughed again and walked on.

"You be good to her, Charley," Eric called as I crossed Riverside Drive.

We walked briskly into the park and towards the community garden, a favored spot. Except in the dead of winter, something was always in bloom; just now we were treated to the golds and oranges of marigolds and sunflowers. Some dark pink roses, next to the fence, were still in bloom, and I bent down for a sniff, a gentle, sweet smell recalled from childhood. I breathed in deeply and scanned the dark blue horizon, the sun still a few yards above the Hudson.

It's really beautiful here in my neighborhood.

There was an assortment of fellow humans about, some walking home after a sweaty day of sport in the park, others with families. Like me, some had dogs. Little kids rode tricycles and scooters, while groups of strong, serious athletic men in Spandex and bike helmets sped past. I saw the guy who always dressed to match the wrap of his standard poodle's long legs—today both were attired in garish lime green.

This was my community and strangely, newly, I felt a part of it.

When we had walked the length of Riverside Park, Charley and I headed back uptown along Broadway and came to my regular small food market, the Barzini Brothers. Their maxim was to buy stuff that was about to expire and sell it at a discount. Reviews on Yelp suggested that many people found the store dirty and the business practices shady. I didn't mind. I knew all the taciturn guys in there, especially the late-night ones. And the worker outside watching the produce would, for a buck, watch Charley while I shopped. I left Charley with him, smiled at the guys who would make eye contact with a woman—not all of them—and picked up some crackers and cheese for my dinner plan.

Just past the market was a little newsstand, where I usually bought my lottery tickets, run by Bahar. I poked my head in. "Hello hello," he said. I had known him a few years back from another stand on 86th Street when he was saving money for a trip to the World Cup. He had disappeared for a while and then resurfaced here a few months ago.

"Three quick picks, please and one with my usual numbers, 3, 15, 29, 31, 55 and 11." As Bahar typed this in, I inquired about his new wife and baby.

"They are well," he beamed. "Do you want to see a new picture of my Habiba and Laboni?" He pulled out a photo and held it up.

"They are so beautiful, Bahar. So beautiful." He seemed so happy now to have a family. "Thanks for the tickets."

Charley and I turned the corner, to walk home.

I do belong here. What a novel and hard-won idea for me, that I belong anywhere.

Climbing the stairs, I realized we were soon due at a friend's house in Westchester. After a shower and quick change, Charley and I drove to Edgemont, where Diane lived with her two little girls and her husband, Noah who had helped negotiate with Willy Ramsey. They often invited me for dinners on the weekend. They were recent émigrés from Brooklyn and still found my slightly offbeat city vibe appealing, even though they were making suburban friends. I had known Diane for nearly 16 years, her first husband a colleague from my professor days at Bennington. She had been around when I first met Richard.

As part of these weekend dinner rituals, Noah always made a new and interesting cocktail for the adults before dinner while I read a book to the kids: Sabina, five, who had just started kindergarten, and her sister, Mo, still in preschool. They were fun, lively girls, with sparkly grins who were fond of Charley, sitting at our feet for the story. It was Sabina's turn to choose the story, and she brought over a Frog and Toad book, a very gentle witty series for early readers. She had chosen *Frog and Toad Together*; the story I opened to was "The Garden."

I know this story from somewhere, I thought, and as I read, I remembered. I had received this book as a present from my goddaughter Mollie's mother Gayle back in 1984 when I moved in with their family after my hospitalization. Gayle had said the book might cheer me up. Tonight, coming to dinner was a more than adequate antidepressant, but now I also got to read a charming story to two little girls I adored, on the topic of the hopefulness of gardens, a subject near to my heart.

We settle in the couch, Sabina on one side, Mo cuddles close on the other.

I begin, "*Frog and Toad Together*, by Arnold Lobel. This story is called, 'The Garden.'" The story opens as Toad passes Frog's garden, which required a lot of work to make, and Toad admires it. Frog, the more sensible of the animal friends, gives Toad some seeds, so he can make his own garden, but that Toad too will have to work hard to get his seeds to grow. I inwardly groan at this Protestant work ethic morally imbedded in this little story but continue. Toad is quite impatient to get his seeds to grow and they of course take their sweet time. He orders them loudly to grow, which occasions Frog to explain that the seeds are too frightened to grow because of all the shouting. So, Frog tries to calm his seeds, reading them stories and poems and singing and playing music.

344

The girls are very attentive, eager to know what would happen. When the story comes to the line where Frog cries out, "These seeds must be the most frightened seeds in the whole world," I read the passage with full dramatic intonation. Sabina and Mo laughed and leaned in even closer to see the picture of Toad falling asleep after all his work. When he wakes up, Frog is there and his seeds have sprouted. Frog remarks to Toad that this was, indeed, hard work.

The kids jump up as Noah brings me the cocktail of the evening, something with lemon, thyme, basil, and vodka, which I sip as the adults discuss books—Noah reads mysteries as I do, and Diane, who has written and published her own book, reads contemporary literary fiction, like I do. We always catch up on what to read next. Charley sleeps on the floor. I am relaxed and content, with dear, old friends welcoming me in.

I don't stay long after we have eaten as Diane and Noah go to sleep shortly after they put their daughters down. Saturday over, I don't have to feel bad I don't have a date. Back in the city, I find a parking spot close to the apartment. How lucky. Upstairs, I read a bit, Charley jumps up onto the foot of the bed, and we fall asleep.

The next morning, Sunday, the sun feels hot filtering through the terrace door onto the bed. I wonder if I could make coffee before taking Charley out. He looks at me as if he is questioning my plans. I decide to be nice and we go out right away. I sweat a little on our very short walk, stop to get the paper. I am really hot by the time we climb the stairs again, so I make some iced coffee and take the *New York Times Book Review* out to read on the terrace. I sit, sipping, and admire the pot of zinnias I planted, shimmering red in the sunlight.

I feel unaccountably happy, having gotten better and better the last few months. I've held onto the two tracks, pledging tenaciously to stay alive. I'm grateful to Dr Grossmark, who stuck with me through it all, and to all the other therapists, friends, and teachers along the way. The pain of losing a marriage to someone I loved, the death and isolation of my early life, and the tragedy of Michael killing Carrie had not disappeared. But now I know they were not the only real parts of my life. Looking at the zinnias, I am fully present. The sensation that I used to struggle to feel and had been rare for so long—what I call pure joy, what Freud called the "oceanic feeling"—instantly, wholly, fills me up.

But then I realize, the joy is not coming from that pot of zinnias. It's located without, and—within. I make it with my mind, greeting the flowers. I can exult in the bold red flowers because the glass wall is gone, the black lens removed.

I make joy? Wow.

I savor this revelation. I am not alone, though I live by myself.

Just in case, next year I am going to plant two or three pots of zinnias.

Acknowledgements

Thank you to Tamar Schwartz and all the other folks at IPBooks for publishing this memoir.

So many people have helped along the way. I start by thanking my very dear friends Connie Biewald, Diane Simon, Leslie Mignault and Maggy Sears who supported me in every way through the writing of the book. They all read drafts, commented and helped me manage my complex feelings as I worked to tell this story. They were there for me when I needed them.

I had so many great writing teachers. Heather Sellers in the NYU summer program taught a beginning writer so much about the craft of writing. All the teachers at the Fine Arts Work Center helped make me a better writer, Julia Glass and Elizabeth Strout when I thought I was writing fiction, and especially the late Richard McCann who told me to write what I most didn't want to write. At the Iowa Summer Writing Festival Kelly Dwyer and Marc Neison helped me with openings and endings. I especially need to thank Charles Salzburg, writing teacher extraordinaire, who I have studied with for nearly ten years. His generous support has been so important to this book.

I would also like to thank the regulars in Charles' class who have critiqued chapters from this book multiple times: Terri Campion. Cynthia Ehrenkrantz, Coree Spence, Phyllis Melhado, Jack Eppler, Judi Rabinor and Carol Hymowitz. I want to thank Sharon O'Brien for reading an early draft. I also cannot say enough about the support I got from my mentor/ friend Arietta Slade, Ph.D. who read and edited both an early and later draft. She believed in me and the project. I also want to thank Lisa Romeo for her very thoughtful editing which helped the book along immensely. Ruth Riegel also expertly edited an early draft.

Most of my therapists are mentioned, and recognized in the text but because I might not have survived to tell the tale without them, they deserve extra appreciation: the late Larry J. Seidman, Ph.D., Laurel Bass Wagner, Ph.D., the late Richard Q. Ford, Ph.D., Joyce Steingart, Ph.D., Robert Grossmark, Ph.D. and my current mind helper, Lawrence Jeckel, MD.

Other important people in my life who have contributed love, humor and tolerance necessary to keep on going include Mollie Biewald, MD, the late Maryhelen Snyder, Lesley Koplow, Chuck Ramsey, Mark Holley and Wendy Hamand-Venet. Thanks Guys. In this group I also put my parents, who loved me with all their hearts, even when they didn't and couldn't understand.

Thank you to Richard Laudor, not enthusiastic about publicity, but who found a way to applaud my writing this book. Love to you.

Author Bio

LIZ TINGLEY grew up in a small mid-western town, publishing her first paper at age 13, in the youth journal, *Illinois History*. She has a B.A. in English from Oberlin College. She migrated East after college and lived there, with a couple of minor detours, for forty years. She has a M.S. in Infant and Parent Development from Bank Street College of Education. She worked as a teacher and director of the Harvard Law School Child Care Center early in her career. She then obtained a Ph.D. in developmental psychology from Boston University and held faculty positions at the University of Texas at Dallas, Bennington College and Bank Street College of Education. She received her second doctoral degree in clinical psychology from the City University of New York CUNY. She did her post-doctoral training in the Child and Adolescent Psychotherapy Program of the Institute for Psychoanalytic Training and Research (IPTAR .) She was in private practice as a psychologist in New York City for many years and taught and supervised at IPTAR, CUNY and Pace University. She returned to Illinois in 2017, where she practices as a clinical psychologist, directs the Child Diagnostic Clinic, acts as the chief psychologist, and supervises and teaches psychodynamic psychotherapy to the psychiatry residents at Carle Health in Champaign-Urbana, Illinois. She returned so her dog Charley could have a big yard, and to fight Trump on the ground.

www.ingramcontent.com/pod-product-compliance
Lightning Source LLC
Chambersburg PA
CBHW070903120626
46546CB00001B/117